The Revolution
Is Only A
Tea Shop Away

*A family's odyssey through Thailand and Burma
in search of justice, peace and
democracy for the people of Burma*

*'The blood and tears of the people will become a large river if
they cannot be dried.'*

Tony Stokle

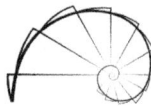

Diadem Books

Diadem Books.
Newcastle-upon-Tyne.
www.diadembooks.org.uk

ISBN: 9798594993785

Contents.

Acknowledgements.

With thanks to my parents, George and Rosemary. Without their sense of social justice and charity, this book would not have been possible.

Foreword.

Teashop.
by Maung Maung Tinn.

There is a small table with four stools.
A boiling pot and four cups are on the table and hot water is free to drink.
The main drink is called tea;
a mixture of condensed milk, fresh cow's milk, tea and warm water.

Teashops and Burma cannot be separate themselves.

It is not magnificent
but it is traditional and essential.
It can be seen on the small roads, in the small towns and big cities.
It is the place to relax, to show off, to meet the friends, to have a date.
It is the place
to share, to discuss many topics; politics, business, social, gossip.

It is a very important part of the country.

Help.
by Maung Maung Tinn.

Normally no one is allowed to commit murder.
If they do, the person should be prosecuted.
*Right now in the world, there are evil people who create
situations of violence and death.*
It is called war.

There is civil war in Burma.
There has been for almost 60 years.
Many people are being killed and raped and tortured.
Many people are dying and suffering.
*Many children are being left as orphans as their parents are
disappearing.*

*The blood and tears of the people will become a large river if
they cannot be dried.*
There is fear and weakness in their minds.
Their energy is almost gone.
It is often difficult for them to speak or move their feet.
*They now need others to extend their hands to help them stand
and voice their hopes for peace and security.*
Help Burma to become a peaceful country.
Do whatever you can.
Please...

Chapter 1.

Mae Ra Moe Refugee Camp, 2000.

A person's life can change in the briefest of moments. You can be travelling in far off places and you see something or you meet someone and your life is changed forever. Looking at the world through different eyes. I'd never been to a refugee camp before but I'll never forget it.

Every twenty-one seconds there is a new refugee created by war or famine somewhere in the world. That's not a long time to lose your home, your family, your entire way of life.

So here I was in a refugee camp. I didn't know what to expect and, of course, my imagination was in overdrive. We were invited to the camp leaders home to eat. The form in this situation was to eat enough not to offend anyone but leave enough food on the table for everyone else. As a guest you are given priority for food. The family had given up a week's ration to cook this one meal. Everyone had to eat. This would become a recurring theme as I visited so many refugee camps and displaced communities over the years. They would feed you and go hungry themselves – so selfless and welcoming.

After the meal we were shown around the camp. I met an old man who asked when I thought the British would return to help the people of Burma. He was a Second World War veteran who had fought in the British army against the Japanese. He showed me his identity card from the war. He said the problem was that no-one knew about the situation in Burma. He asked me to help by letting the world know how his family and friends were suffering. His plight hit me and I don't think I've ever recovered from the blow. My life was changed in the briefest of moments.

I went back to my bamboo hut and tried to sleep. The heat was sweltering, the darkness, darker than I've ever known, and the noises of the jungle so strange. Of course I hardly slept. Where had I come to? These people should be angry at me. I was British and I didn't know about their situation. I was to learn more in one week in a refugee camp than I'd learned in a lifetime in the UK. (As Bruce Springsteen says 'We learned more in a 3 minute record than we ever did at school'). And yet they were so friendly.

Just before dawn the crowing chickens woke me and my friends. I cursed them as I had only just dropped off to sleep. It was 5:30 am; way before I usually woke up but this refugee camp, like most in the world, had no electricity and our day depended on the sun. My back ached after 6 hours on a bamboo floor. I gingerly stepped across the flimsy floor – the huts were all made from what can be harvested from the jungle – banana leaf roof, bamboo for the main structure and bamboo sheets for the floor and walls. As I approached the door my foot went straight through the floor matting. I was 13 stone and the usual weight of a Karen refugee was around 8 stone. These floors weren't designed for the 'golowah' (white man in Karen language). With only my upper body in the hut and my legs dangling below the floor, my refugee friends came in to see what all the commotion was about. When they saw me they laughed and laughed. This was the standard reaction to accidents, I was to learn. After they had stopped laughing they helped me out and checked that I was OK. Although shocked, nothing was broken. We were at least a six hours drive from a hospital, so I was mighty relieved to be injury-free.

The thought of breakfast lifted my spirits. The sun was just starting to rise above the mountains that surrounded us. It was going to be another blisteringly hot day. I washed in the nearby stream, the water refreshingly cool coming off the high mountains. The toilet was a hole in the ground, as expected. No lock on the door so singing or grunting was essential to ensure you weren't disturbed. In any case you didn't hang around long, for obvious reasons. I headed up the dusty path for breakfast. What feast awaited us? Little did I know that last night was indeed the rations for a week all used up. Two small dried biscuits and a glass of warm water was all we were offered. No-one dared to complain or ask for more. We were sure lunch would be substantial as we had researched and knew the Karen only had two meals a day – obviously not breakfast!

So it was on to class. I had prepared well for my teaching duties and was looking forward to meeting my students. With sweat pouring from every pore, I banged my head on the bamboo door frame as I entered the classroom. I was to do this a thousand times over the years as I am over six foot tall and Burmese door openings are always less than this. The class sat silently as I entered. The eight students were a mixture of men and women, and ranged in age from about 20 to 45 years. I nervously introduced myself and started my first English as a Foreign Language (EFL) class.

Two characters stand out in my memory, Sit Blut and Gay Moo. Sit Blut was a lady, about 45 years old, with four children. She had lived in the refugee camp for almost five years. She was slim and round faced like many Karen, but there was a deep sadness in her eyes. During our week together in class she told me her story. She was a widow, her husband having been shot dead by the Burmese Army (the Tatmadaw, as they are known). Her family were fleeing an attack on their village by the Burmese, and her husband stayed to fight and delay them to allow his wife and children time to escape. She ran with the children not knowing what would happen to her husband. Days later she heard from a survivor that he had given the ultimate sacrifice for his family. He had been shot and killed along with several other men in the village, who stayed to allow their families to escape. Sit Blut and her children had hidden in the jungle for days, travelling at night and hiding by day until they reached the safety of Thailand, where they applied for refugee status and were given permission to stay in Mae Ra Moe refugee camp, sharing a home with over 30,000 refugees.

He has gone.
by Maung Maung Tinn.

I have lost my husband.
He was essential for our family.
He arranged almost everything for us.
He found food, shelter and a regular income.
I can not do that because I need to spend all my time with my three children.

Last rainy season he died after Burmese government troops attacked our village.
My oldest daughter was injured, but not as severely as her father.

Now I feel so weak.
I don't know how to find regular income and it will be difficult for my family without him.
There is nothing to see in the future but tears.
Do the people who create the war understand how many problems are left after one bullet is fired?

Gay Moo had a sparkle in his eye. A young man, about 22 years old, he lived in the camp with his brother, 'Chubby'. The Karen have an unusual custom of giving nicknames to people because of their features, and 'Chubby' was indeed. Gay Moo was probably the weakest student in English but he was the most enthusiastic, always asking questions (quite unusual in Karen schools) and always trying to improve himself. I was very taken with him. Through his questioning he found out that I was a physics teacher and this really interested him. I found out why one day when he asked me if I knew how to make a nuclear bomb. I said I knew in theory how to make one but it was very difficult to do in practice. I was intrigued as to why he was so interested. He told me he wanted to make one and drop it on the Tatmadaw in revenge for them killing his father. This opened a long discussion at the time, and over subsequent years when I met him again, about nuclear weapons and the indiscriminate nature of them, killing all in the blast zone, and thousands more dying over the years from radiation sickness.

The discussion of nuclear bombs came up years later at home in Newcastle upon Tyne when I attended a meeting of the Burma Star Association, veterans of the Second World War in Burma. One veteran was called Alan Shearer; yes, the same name as the famous footballer. He was in his nineties but still very active. Alan told me of the night they had heard about the dropping of the first nuclear bomb on Japan. They were in the jungle of Burma waiting for orders to attack the Japanese. They knew the Japanese would not surrender and that many of them would be killed in the attack. It was a terrifying period in their lives. They were so relieved to hear that the atomic bombs had forced the surrender of the Japanese and they would not have to fight hand to hand with them in the jungle. At the time they did not know the horrific consequences of such bombs, and on reflection had grave doubts, but in 1945 they were truly grateful. Many of their comrades had already died fighting or from diseases such as malaria and dysentery.

Alan also gave me an original leaflet from the Second World War. The Allies were dropping propaganda leaflets from airplanes onto the people of Burma in June 1945. Alan had kept a few of the leaflets all these years, but they were written in Burmese and he never knew what they said. He asked if I could get it translated for him. I was delighted to help out and asked my Burmese friend Maureen to translate it. She returned her translation a few weeks later and I set it out in the same format as the original leaflet.

Alan was really excited when he read it. For over 50 years he hadn't known what the Allies were asking of the Burmese.

5

The leaflet was entitled 'Victory Letter' June 1945. The sub title was 'Independence is the goal for the Union of Myanmar' with paragraph titles such as 'Japan's false independence', 'Fair policy of the British' and 'Real Independence'. One particularly important message was 'Nobody will be punished for supporting the Japanese before or during the war. The British now occupy Myanmar again but we do not seek revenge and will not copy the Japanese cruelty. British rule means we will treat everyone equally. The people of Myanmar helped the British defeat the Japanese. This is the beginning of independence for Myanmar.' I wonder if the people of Burma today feel that the British did treat 'everyone equally'?

The nights in Mae Ra Moe were long and sultry. It gets dark very quickly, at about 6:30pm, and as it was the hot season the skies were clear. For the first time I saw the Milky Way. I was amazed at the sight of so many stars. That band of millions of stars so far away, it looks like a path of spilt milk across the sky - as the ancients believed it was, hence the name. The small hut I was sitting outside seemed so tiny in comparison and I wondered at the enormity of the universe and the task that lay ahead to stop the war in Burma and bring peace and democracy to all. I had heard stories of courage and determination, of hatred and oppression, and of love and bereavement in my classes that week. What an introduction. I think it hit me sometime during that week and it has never left me. They say the Karen 'grab hold of your heart and never let it go'. I knew for certain they had hold of my heart. What I didn't know was that they would never let go.

Sunday came in the camp and, at last, a day off from teaching. I was physically and emotionally drained; combined with a diet of rice and vegetables, I was running on empty. But an invitation to play football in the afternoon was too good to resist. The temperature was approaching 35°C as I walked through the long sprawling camp to the football field, a bottle of now cooled, boiled river water in my hand. I dispatched my sandals and put on my training shoes. Teams were selected and

I went into my most comfortable position of centre-back. I had no intention of running too much in this heat and would use my passing skills and football brain. Looking around at my teammates, I hoped the ball would be in the air a lot as I would certainly win a contest for heading the ball as I was a good foot taller than most. Then I looked at their feet; most had no boots or shoes on. Some, in solidarity, had a left boot on whilst their friend shared the right boot.

The game was fast and furious, with little passing, as is the case in much of Asian football. Everyone wants to dribble. Passing doesn't seem to have reached these people yet, like so many other things. Running was difficult in the heat and on the uneven earth pitch. No grass to be seen and there were huge holes and ruts everywhere. I began to have nightmares of being carried off with a broken ankle and having to endure the long journey in the back of a truck in agony. I wondered what sort of painkillers they would give me. Probably rice whiskey and a paracetamol. I gingerly made my way around the pitch, not having a great game as fear had gripped me. With sweat pouring down my body like a river, the match finished with a victory to the opposition. The two 'golowah's' had been defeated as Peter and myself had wilted in the heat.

Next stop, the river, until from somewhere a miracle occurred. A bag of ice was produced to cool the coke that was now being offered. Coke never tasted so good. Ordinarily I would never drink Coke, but these were exceptional times. After a bath in the river and a bottle of boiled river water we made our way back through the camp. We had made lots of friends. Football for all its commercialisation unites people and nations. I slept well that night without the nightmare of a painful journey out.

The week flew past and hunger pains lessened as a vegetarian diet with no alcohol and no fatty foods started to benefit me. On our last night we were invited to Saw La Say's house for dinner. Saw La Say was head of the Karen Education department, and he wanted to thank us for our efforts. Little did I know that his son (who I had nicknamed Mr Happy) had been in my class all week, so I was glad to be able to say what a good pupil he was.

The conversation turned to the war in Burma, and this was my first introduction to war, close-up and real. I had seen landmine victims in camp trying to get about on crutches. Some had lost both legs, some one leg and an arm; others were lucky to have a crude, prosthetic limb fitted. As is required of a refugee camp, there were no soldiers, but the war was only a few miles away over the border. Saw La Say brought out a map of Karen State, Burma, and proceeded to point out where the KNLA (Karen National Liberation Army) were in control, and where the Tatmadaw controlled. He pointed out the main battle grounds and discussed war and battle tactics.

The KNLA were very few in number in comparison to the Tatmadaw, but they knew the jungle better and were fighting to save their families and land, so there was no way they could lose. I was forty years old and thought I was quite worldly, but I had never listened to a man talk battle tactics and hear the courageous stories of a people fighting for their existence. I was hit again with that feeling that my life would be changed in the briefest of moments. How could I listen to a man, about the same age as myself, with the same aspirations in life, talking about fighting for his and his family's existence, and not be changed? I thought of my family 7000 miles away. I had a wife and three young children. What would I do to protect them? Could I give the ultimate sacrifice, as I had heard many had over this last week? How could I forget Sit Blut and Gay Moo?

Remarkably, I slept well that night after a week of bamboo floor digging into my back or hip or stomach, depending on how I tried to sleep. I felt humbled by my experience and the words of Saw La Say had left me pensive and somehow changed. I think it was this conversation and knowing I was so close to war for the first time that I realised how lucky I was, and that I could not turn my back on these courageous people.

Leaving the camp was emotional but the Karen are a 'dry eye' people. They let go very easily, so no gushing goodbyes, just a thank you and 'tee law tha la key' (see you again). It is said the Karen have no word for 'goodbye'. As tribal people who have lived in close family units for thousands of years, they all stay together, so no-one ever really leaves until they die. 'Goodbye' is only for the departed.

The journey out was horrendous. The truck we were travelling in was only a two-wheel drive, but these roads needed four-wheel drive. Climbing out of the steep dirt track, with a probably fatal drop to one side, my heart was racing. There were six of us in the back of the pickup, with red road dust covering us as the wheels started to spin. At the steepest part we started to roll back and our Karen friend jumped out of the truck. I thought we were going to roll back over the edge and he was deserting us - saving himself and not caring for us. I was petrified and didn't move. Was this to be my last moment on Earth? Would I ever see my wife and children again? Why had I come to this place anyway? My thoughts ran out of control. And then suddenly we stopped rolling backwards and our Karen friend emerged from underneath the now stationary truck covered in red dust. I clamoured off the truck to see what had happened and saw the most enormous rock wedged behind the rear wheel. I suddenly realised that our friend had jumped off, grabbed a rock from the side of the road and dived beneath the truck to stop its inevitable journey backwards and down the mountain side. He had saved us from impending catastrophe, and all I had been thinking moments earlier was how could he save himself and not us. I learned a lot about the Karen and human nature in those 20 seconds or so. Another lesson remembered for life.

We all got off the truck and waited for a four-wheel drive to come up the mountainside. A tow rope was attached, and we all helped push the truck from the edge and up the mountain road to a safer section. We got back in with trepidation. It was a two day walk if we didn't fancy the drive. Everyone sat in silence and I said quite a few prayers of thanksgiving, asking for forgiveness for doubting our new friends.

Six hours later we returned to Mae Sariang, a sleepy Thai town surrounded by the most beautiful mountains and streams. We booked into an upmarket guest house, showered to rid ourselves of the red dust and headed to the bar. I enjoyed the beer and food but it was the clean white bed sheets I remember the most. Six nights with bamboo sticking into my back or side was enough for me. I slept soundly, feeling quite satisfied with myself. I had roughed it and survived. I was being selfish - congratulating myself on a job well done, when I knew people, human beings, were being slaughtered in the nearby jungle. I would deal with that later. This was to be a long journey with many high and lows, periods of hunger, times of joy and great sadness. But at that time I didn't know where my journey would lead me. At least I had been into a refugee camp and had learned a little. Bangkok awaited me tomorrow, and as I had never been there, I had more experiences to come.

Chapter 2.

How did we get involved in the Revolution?

The Bodega pub in Newcastle upon Tyne on a cold Friday night in November 1999, following a game of football and four pints of beer, is where it all started. Peter asked if I fancied going to the Thailand-Burma border with him at Easter to teach in a refugee camp. I'd never been to Thailand, and being the adventurous type I said 'of course I'll go.' Twenty years later I'd travelled the length of Thailand, stayed in over six refugee camps, and explored more of Burma than almost any other Westerner.

How would I tell my wife, Anne, that I was going to Thailand in six months' time? All she knew about Thailand was that men visit to experience the 'sex industry'. I would have to take care how and when I introduced the topic. I needed to find out more. I knew where Thailand and Burma were, and that Burma was an ex-British colony, but that was about all. Don't tell her when I'm drunk, was all I thought as I went home dreaming of a 'holiday' with a few friends. We had three children, Sarah age fifteen, Patrick age ten and Declan age seven, at the time. How could I afford to spend so much on myself? How would I sell this one?

A miracle happened that very next week at work. I was a teacher in a secondary school and the government announced that teachers would receive individual bursaries for in-service training, and the teacher would choose how to spend the money, not the school. I had £500 to spend on my own teacher development. I was quick to check if it could be used overseas, and yes it could. I could spend my £500 on an airfare to find out how teachers taught science in refugee camps. I applied and it was accepted.

Now I only had to convince Anne.

I knew I had to wait for the right time to 'ask' Anne. No good getting flowers and candles- she would definitely think I was going for the 'sex industry'. There was a Thai café/restaurant in town, and we often went for a meal on a Saturday night, so I thought we should go there. The meal was great and the service was fantastic. We had the 'Land of Smiles' here in Newcastle. Anne was so happy, I thought this was my chance. Plucking up all my courage – it was like proposing all over again, but this time I wasn't sure of the answer.

'How would you like to go to Thailand?' I asked.

'I'd love to' replied Anne.

'Well…' I explained everything, giving her the background that I would be travelling with a group from Amnesty International, and that we would not be staying in Bangkok, but in a refugee camp, and this was the chance of a lifetime. Little did I know it would also change my life, and that of my family, forever.

After months of preparation about how to teach English as a foreign language – the past participle of the verb 'to be' and all that – I was ready to go in Easter of the year 2001. Travel arrangements were sorted by Bob, the group leader. I had received my bursary – the head teacher even remarking he thought it was the best use of the money in the whole school, as others had 'frittered' theirs away on textbooks and visits to museums.

I had done lots of research on the situation in Burma; it was 'governed' by a military dictatorship and there had been civil war since 1948. It was a closed country with few foreign visitors. There were 9 refugee camps along the Thailand-Burma border and they had over 100,000 residents. We would be working in Mae Ra Moe refugee camp, somewhere in the mountains separating the two countries. I had tried to locate the camp on a map but I could only get a vague idea of where I was going. I put my faith in Bob, said my goodbyes to Anne and the children, and wondered if I would ever see them again? This was my first flight to Bangkok. We flew from Newcastle to Heathrow and then onto Bangkok. A quick change and up to Chiang Mai in northern Thailand. We transferred to the Orchid, a luxury hotel. I was so tired but the pace was relentless. No time to acclimatise to the heat, smells and sounds of a new country. Most of us were teachers and only had a two week Easter break so we had to make the most of our time. After sleeping so well in an air-conditioned room we were up early for a journey to Mae Sariang, a small town close to the Thailand-Burma border. It was so hot we were thankful for an air-conditioned mini-bus. I remember running across the road in Mae Sariang to dash from one shaded sidewalk to another. The accommodation was not so good in Mae Sariang. A cheap Thai hotel with no air conditioning and insects everywhere.

We ate Thai food at a local restaurant and tried to sleep, but it was too hot. At 4am Bob woke us saying the trucks had arrived for the next leg of our journey. We piled into the back of the pickup trucks with eyes hardly open but thankful it was still the cool of the night. Off we went, witnessing the most beautiful sunrise I have ever seen as it came up over one of the many Buddhist temples we passed. Stopping for a breakfast of three-in-one coffee and a sweet bread bun at a roadside stall, we all marvelled at the scenery. We were in an unspoiled jungle area heading along a dirt track deeper into the jungle. The temperature was climbing towards 35°C but the open truck gave us all the air conditioning we needed.

A barrier across the road stopped our trucks. Thai soldiers appeared, with guns and rifles at the ready. I was starting to get frightened now. They asked us to get out and searched the truck. This was 'bandit' country, with many people trading in drugs and guns. We all stood silently, wondering what would happen. Our driver chatted with the soldiers, a 'tax' was paid, and we travelled on deeper into the mountains.

The roads became narrower and more difficult to navigate. The drops over the sides of the mountains were spectacular. About ten years later, a Karen friend of mine crashed off the same mountain side, several people being killed. She survived with serious back and leg injuries. I wondered what would happen if we crashed. We were many miles from a hospital and there would be no helicopter rescue. I know now you just wait for another passing truck. Throw the injured in and get down the mountain back to the small hospital in Mae Sariang. The chances of survival are slim if a patient is seriously injured and there is no way of rescuing from down the steep mountain side. I prayed again for the driver to slow down. Years later I learned how to say 'slow down' and 'drive slowly' in Karen, Burmese and Thai.

After what seemed like an eternity, we pulled up at a barrier across the road and a sign read 'Welcome to Mae Ra Moe Refugee Camp'. The journey had only just begun but at least I had reached the camp. If I never came out, at least I had arrived and had achieved what I had been preparing for over the past six months. I was tired, hot and hungry, but I felt a peace I had never felt before. I was among 30,000 or more displaced people, many who had lost loved ones in a horrific and never-ending war, but I felt so welcome. I thought of it as Heaven and Hell in the same place. We were shown our accommodation. Six of us sharing a bamboo hut, sleeping on the floor, with one toilet to share down some rickety steps, and no electricity. A far cry from the luxurious Orchid but for some reason I felt more at home, safer, more secure and at peace. Welcome indeed to the life of a refugee.

Arriving back in Bangkok and staying at a four-star hotel was so comfortable. I was never to stay at such a hotel again on my travels in South East Asia, but someone else had organised this trip and the price was easily within my budget for a two night stay, so why not? Thailand is the 'Land of Smiles' and everyone who has visited will know this is true. But if you look beyond the smiles you see a country at odds with itself. The people are very conservative, and genuinely helpful and welcoming, but Bangkok has dreadful poverty and prostitution. There is no social security net like in many countries in the West, so everyone has to work. The most notorious area of Bangkok is Pat Pon, where young girls (and boys) and older women (and men) work the bars and clubs. This area is no place for the faint hearted after 9pm. Many of the workers are from the poorer northern areas of Thailand and the nearby countries of Burma, Laos and Cambodia, where poverty is rife and job opportunities are limited. Clearly drugged, young people parade themselves to suspecting and unsuspecting foreigners. It is a dangerous mixture in the heat and with alcohol flowing freely.

Tuk-tuk drivers offer to take you to these places as soon as you jump in their vehicles. The unsuspecting are drawn into the street market which sells the usual fake football shirts and all things Thai. Tourists who are tired and requiring refreshment find the many bars surrounding the night market welcoming. Most tourists don't see beyond the façade of a bar and a few girls dancing to entertain. For the inexperienced traveller this is a dangerous place where you can lose more than your wallet. My first experience was shocking and unforgettable. Tired and hot, I was naive and saw first-hand street prostitution. This is not a pretty sight. Thankfully I was not too tired to see beyond the façade, but it opened my mind and I wondered what was really going on in this part of the world. It was clearly linked to poverty, the Vietnam war, Pol Pot in Cambodia and the military regime in Burma.

For fifty years people had fled from war and destitution to this city, but only found a different kind of war and destitution. I think for the first time I was starting to think about real people, and how war and government destroy lives and hopes and dreams. And how the dream of making your fortune in the big city is often a nightmare from which there is little chance of escape. I thought about the refugee camp I had just left. Many workers in Bangkok were refugees or illegal migrants from Burma. They had escaped in the hope of a better life. Unless the situation changed in Burma, these workers would never fulfil their dreams; never see their families again, never really live.

Next day I flew home to England with so many new experiences and tales to tell, and I'd only been away for two weeks. After telling my wife and children about the adventure I went back to work, but I couldn't let go of the thoughts in my head of refugee camps. The health issues were huge for these people, and as Anne was a nurse, it was a topic I discussed with her, hoping she would be interested so that I could continue to be alive to this issue that was now burning in my heart. Without a change of government in Burma nothing would change and my new found friends would be in refugee camps forever. I'm sure Anne thought I was crazy, but I persisted and persuaded her to go to the Thailand-Burma border and witness for herself the conditions and issues. She is a nurse who works with people with learning difficulties, and in the refugee community these were often the least supported, often hidden-away and forgotten about. I knew she would want to help them. It was her life's work, even as a child caring for her younger brother who was severely disabled, so I knew she could not resist the opportunity to make a difference to so many.

Next year she flew to Thailand whilst I stayed at home with our three young children. It was an experience for me to be a single parent, but Anne's world was blasted apart, like mine, by what she witnessed on the Thailand-Burma border.

Chapter 3.

A family to Mae La Refugee camp, 2002.

It took a lot of organising and persuading, but we did it. Anne and I arrived in Bangkok in July 2002 with three children, Sarah age sixteen, Patrick age twelve, and Declan age nine. I stood on the balcony of the hotel looking out over Bangkok. It was a beautiful sight and I was so relieved that we had arrived safely after so much planning.

Anne had travelled to the refugee camps on the Thailand-Burma border in the spring of 2001. She has been so taken aback that she wanted to bring the whole family, so here we were. Flights, injections, suitable bags and clothing, transport, hotels, insurance, etc. I was ready for a beer, so hurried the children and Anne along and headed downstairs for our free welcome drink. I was going to enjoy this after all the planning. We had at least arrived, anything else would be a bonus. I ordered my beer thinking this will go down in one. The lady looked at me and, in broken English, explained that it was a Muslim hotel, and that they did not have any alcoholic drinks! I laughed and laughed. All I wanted was a beer, and I had booked probably the only hotel in Bangkok that didn't serve it.

A fruit juice was almost as enjoyable; the children had a coke, and off we went on our adventure to Khao San Road, the famous backpack area of Bangkok. I had chosen this hotel near Khao San Road to appease Sarah, who didn't want a holiday in a refugee camp. The exchange rate was good so I felt wealthy. 'As many cokes as you want', I told the children; at 20p a bottle compared to five times that in the UK, I was convinced they would not be able to drink more than five bottles.

The children loved Khao San Road. I was happy. We had to balance their needs with Anne's and mine if this was going to be a successful holiday and refugee experience. We had five weeks to fill in Thailand, and three young British children needed some home comforts. The food was delicious (only later learning about MSG), and the beer thirst-quenching. Our 'Geordie' voices must have been raised, as a young man approached us and introduced himself. He had been travelling for nearly a year and we were the first 'Geordies' he'd come across. As the children and I are all football mad, the talk was of Newcastle United (Anne isn't a football supporter but has learned to live with it). By midnight we were quite excited and enjoying singing football songs (we hadn't learnt about Thai culture yet). The MSG had woke us all up and jet lag was nowhere to be seen. Dancing a 'Conga' around the bar to the tune of the 'Shola Ameobi' (a Newcastle United player), we thought we were having fun even if no-one else did. The bar staff just laughed and let us get on with it.

Our first night in Bangkok as a family was a hit. The children loved it and wanted more. Next day, the children experienced their first ride in a tuk-tuk. These amazing taxis are Bangkok's replacement for Disney World. Who needs rollercoasters, when you can have a tuk-tuk ride weaving in and out of traffic and taking risks at every junction? The children loved it. Thailand was winning their hearts. The Thai people were being so friendly to us. They loved that we were a family as they usually only met couples. The children adapted well to the heat and food. It was also the rainy season, so they needed to adapt to the humidity and the slippery footpaths. Bangkok was a success. Now onto Mae Sot, a small town in Northern Thailand close to the biggest refugee camp, Mae La. I had arranged a mini van to take us north so the six hour drive was comfortable. The children slept most of the way, jet lag finally catching up on them.

Arriving in Mae Sot was quite different to Bangkok. It was dark and there were few streetlights. The DK hotel is safe, clean and comfortable, but not four-star. The rooms are large with air conditioning. As it has no restaurant, we headed out into the dark looking for somewhere to eat. It was only eight o'clock but everywhere seemed closed. We wandered aimlessly until we found a Chinese restaurant open (or was it Vietnamese – I couldn't tell). The food was awful and the children were looking disappointed to say the least. Maybe it was a mistake to bring the children here. I had a contact to get Anne and I into Mae La refugee camp, but what would the children do? We headed back to the DK hotel stopping off at the 7-11 shop to buy some coke, beer and crisps.

I slept uneasily, wondering if it would be better tomorrow. I reassured myself that arriving in a new place in the dark was always a bad experience. The daylight would reveal a much more interesting place and one the children could enjoy.

Mae Sot is a border town, but there was little trade at that time between itself and Myawaddy, the town on the other side of the Moei river that separates Thailand from Burma. As Burma was a mostly closed country, little was known about what was going on except that there was a war and the border was closed. Mae Sot had been a sleepy little place until the war in Burma between the Karen National Union and the Burmese army spilled over into Thailand in 1985. In the rugged, teak-forested hills of Eastern Burma, across the river from Mae Sot, the Burmese Army was closing in on one of the world's longest-running and least-known separatist struggle - the Karen rebellion. Thousands of civilians from Karen State in Burma fled across the Moei River in the last few months of 1985 to seek refuge in Thailand. They were running from the shelling and burning of their villages, and from a forced-labour portage system that the advancing Burmese were using to move arms and equipment across difficult, roadless terrain. Between 15,000 and 20,000 Karens were living in a string of refugee camps stretching north from Mae Sot to the confluence of the Moei and Salween rivers, where the rebellion and its leader, General Bo Mya, had headquarters. By 2002, thirty miles up the road from Mae Sot, Mae La Refugee Camp had been established, home to more than 30,000 refugees, mostly ethnic Karen. A further 8 refugee camps were strung out along the border, all run by the United Nations High Commissioner for Refugees.

Waking up in Mae Sot, we needed breakfast. Last night's Vietnamese or Chinese had not gone down well with the children. Thankfully, over the road from the DK was a small café which sold 'English style' food. Bo, the lady who owned it, cooked ham omelettes with toast for them.

'This is more like it,' the children said.

We enquired about a swimming pool and were told about several, but the only clean one was at the Mae Sot Hills Hotel on the outskirts of town. This was a four-star hotel built on the main highway to the border, aimed at business people and tourists for Burma. But as a war raged, this hotel was hardly used. The Thai tuk-tuk was godsend. Anand, the driver, sat all day at the DK hoping to pick up a fare. There are no buses or taxis in Mae Sot, so tuk-tuk was the only option.

Anne and I had arranged to meet our contact, Htoo Khu, so the children would have to go on their own to the swimming pool. They could all swim and Sarah was sixteen, so we felt they would be safe. After all, the pool would have a lifeguard, wouldn't it? Anyway, off the three of them went in the tuk-tuk, while Anne and I met with Htoo Khu, who would hopefully take us to Mae La camp.

Mae La is an incredible place, stretching along the main border road for over three miles. It is really a small shanty town built between the road and the mountains. Bamboo huts were cramped in side by side. Even today when I go past it, I am still amazed such a place exists. The official population is 30,000, but many more than that live there. To be a resident of a refugee camp you have to prove you have been displaced by war. The optimum word is 'prove'. How do you 'prove' you have been displaced by war, when you live in a small village in the jungle?

As we approached the camp in our friend's truck, we were stopped by the Thai army at the roadblock. War was only miles away, and this was bandit country with drug runners and people traffickers plying their trade. It needed a strong presence to police it, so I was reassured by the presence of soldiers. We had documents to say we could visit the camp as Anne and I were going to teach. I was to work in the Teacher Training College and Anne was to help train nurses about children with disabilities. Passes checked, we proceeded into the camp. I headed to the college and Anne went off to do some home visits.

It was hot and humid as usual in the rainy season. I was sweating and uncomfortable as I entered my classroom, but I had prepared well and would show how I deliver science lessons in the UK. Burmese teaching is very didactic, completely teacher led and reliant on rote learning. I did my best to show pupil-centred and active learning.

By lunchtime I was shattered and needed time on my own, so after a lunch of rice I had a walk around the nearby camp buildings. However, within minutes of stepping foot outside the classroom, I was confronted by a Thai soldier with an automatic machine gun strapped across him. Where was my camp pass? Oh dear, I had left it in the classroom. He couldn't speak English but I knew he was not happy with me. He marched me back to the classroom to see my pass, explaining I should keep it on me at all times. This taught me two lessons: one, to carry my pass with me at all times and two, (and more importantly) how the Thai soldiers treat people without the correct documentation. They have a job to do, 'policing' thousands of refugees and many more illegal migrants. As with all soldiers, some do it within the law and some don't. I certainly wouldn't want to be an illegal Burmese migrant caught by the Thai authorities. I had heard many stories of what happens to them, and had experienced it in a small way myself and was very shaken.

After a day's teaching I met up with Anne who had been all over the camp, walking in the oppressive heat, so she was very tired but enthused about how she could make a difference with the most vulnerable children. 'What about our children?', I thought. I hoped they were safe in Mae Sot. We had left them all day on their own. As we travelled back, I thought about how very young children all over the world were left on their own every day so that their parents could go out to work in the field or the factory. No crèche for them, no nanny, just survival.

Back at the DK hotel the children were waiting for us – thankfully safe and well. They had had a great day. The pool was super, and they had found some better places to eat. Patrick and Declan hadn't even fought! They had been together in a strange place and so bonded for safety. Relieved, we all went out to find these better places to eat. Bai Fern restaurant, Crocodile Tear bar and the Steak restaurant were perfect, all serving a choice of Western and Thai food, and it was much cheaper than Bangkok.

We spent many evenings at these bars, which the children enjoyed immensely. Crocodile Tear has a singer on every night (the same singer) playing John Denver 'Take me Home, Country Roads', and other country / easy-going tunes. For me, I was thankful that the children were safe. Leaving a sixteen year old in charge of her two brothers was a little risky, but they seemed to grow closer each day. After food we usually went to Kung's bar, a dark and seedy place I thought at first, but soon grew to like the ambiance. The reason for us going: a pool table for Patrick and Declan. Today they are both cracking pool players. A misspent youth? I don't think so. This place was an education in itself, with people from all over the world relaxing and chatting.

Our children experienced cultures and characters they could never hope to meet anywhere else. And Kung, the owner, became the boys' best friend. He was a local Thai man who was a fantastic pool player. I do believe they never beat him unless he allowed them to, but what a coach he was. Declan won money a few years later playing 'killer pool' with lads several years his senior. Kung deserves the credit but I always take it, saying what a great teacher of pool I was to them. Kung loved tennis and the boys soon persuaded him to take them to the tennis court during the day, so their days became filled with adventures. You'll have to read their stories to find out, but it gave Anne and I the opportunity to travel to the refugee camp each day.

Ten days passed quickly. We were all learning so much. Language lessons, cultural lessons, security lessons, history lessons... lessons in life. If it stopped here we had learned so much, but mostly we were learning about ourselves and how to 'live life to the fullest'.

On leaving Mae Sot we headed on 'holiday' to Kanchanaburi and the bridge over the River Kwai. It was another six hour drive, but as we were all so tired we fell asleep in the minivan. I had arranged all the transport whilst in the UK and was pleasantly surprised that it was all going to plan. The hotel at Kanchanaburi was beautiful. I had never stayed in one so opulent. The river flowing quietly by the side of the hotel, our rooms luxurious, and an infinity pool by the bar area. Immediately we all felt we had left the 'Hell' of a refugee camp and landed in 'Heaven'.

Relaxing at the pool, we all wondered what we were getting into. Would our world ever be the same again? This was my second experience of working with the Karen, and I was totally absorbed by a need to do more than just teach these people. What they needed was change. They needed to go home to their villages, but what was stopping them? I vowed to find out more and campaign more. What use is treating symptoms if the cause still exists?

The bridge over the River Kwai was another great history lesson for us all. The museum at Kanchanaburi is fascinating, and to see and walk along the railway bridge (Death Railway) was like walking in history. I could almost feel and smell the thousands of men who had died during the Second World War while building this supply-line for the Japanese. It was such an education for the children to witness it, and to be present at such a historical place. Travel does broaden the mind, and to see them asking questions and finding out about the Second World War made the trip truly worthwhile.

After two days we headed for Hua Hin and the beach. Hua Hin is a seaside resort where the King of Thailand has a home. It is also the home of a wonderful hotel called 'The Railway Hotel' which featured as 'Hotel Phnom Penh' in the film 'The Killing Fields'. It is the hotel where foreign journalists stayed and where they were evacuated from as the Khmer Rouge invaded the city-another history lesson for me and the children as we wandered around this magnificent hotel. A few years later we would go to Cambodia on holiday to witness for ourselves 'The Killing Fields'.

I had my first Thai massage on the beach at Hua Hin. I was terrified by the reputation of Thai massage parlours in Bangkok, but I did want to try one. There was a very old lady on the beach offering a massage. She would come by each day, smiling and asking tourists if they wanted a traditional massage. She had no teeth and was clearly very poor. Anne encouraged me to give it a go. Well what a laugh. I couldn't stop giggling as she touched my legs, arms and body. This was not what I thought a massage would be, but it was great. The massage industry does have a reputation for all the wrong things but this was innocent fun. The children did bareback horse riding on the beach and we swam in the warmest sea I have ever experienced. A far cry from Seaton Carew beach and the North Sea of my childhood.

Five weeks had passed and we had to go back to the UK. All five of us would be changed forever. Some more than others, but all changed for the better. We all had to go back to school and work, but it had been the most amazing holiday I have ever been on. Life changing indeed. What would we do now? Could we just slip back into life in the UK? Life is a journey and this one was destined to continue.

Chapter 4.

Refugee camps, Dr Cynthia's clinic and Australia, 2003.

Another year had passed and we couldn't forget our friends. We had told everyone of our experiences. For Anne and I, our hearts had been grabbed. We needed a plan to continue our journey. Sarah was seventeen and didn't want to come on a family holiday. She was dreaming of a holiday with her friends out of reach of her parents. But who would look after Patrick and Declan if we went into a refugee camp? Patrick was only thirteen and Declan just ten. A dilemma solved by tempting her with a trip to Australia. I had always wanted to go, so why not? We would be already most of the way there, so a ticket to Perth, Australia with a stop off in Bangkok wouldn't cost much more. Sarah was easily persuaded, and for Patrick, it gave him the opportunity to see his friend Josh, who had emigrated a few years earlier. We were killing lots of birds with one stone, so off we went again.

Mae La and Nupo Refugee camps.

Back in Mae La at teacher training college, after one year away. Nothing much had changed. The war was still going on. The camp was full to overflowing with many more than the 30,000 capacity. People were coming from all over Karen State to escape the war. Anne and I got the chance to go to Nupo Refugee Camp, a smaller camp about 100 miles south of Mae La. So the whole family headed south.

We stayed in Umphang village close to the camp in a large teak house. We had one room in the house and two mosquito nets. It had taken us most of the day to travel the wet and muddy road, and darkness was already imminent. Umphang is a very remote village and is the starting point for trekking to the nearby jungle and waterfall. We quickly scouted the village for a restaurant, as everyone was tired and hungry. Rice, vegetables and a small amount of chicken were available in a small cafe. The children were disappointed but it was good for them to do without, or so I thought. It was pitch black in the village, as there was no street lighting, as we cautiously walked back to the house.

It was just 8pm, and the children were still wide awake but without TV or computers or other entertainment, we wondered what to do. A great time for a family to bond? Our driver and guide were already turning in, so by candlelight we chatted and played 'I spy' and other great games. By 9pm everyone was ready for bed. This was the children's first experience of mosquito nets. Anne explained that they needed to keep them tucked into the mats on the floor so as not to allow mosquitoes in. This was the rainy season and it was a malaria region.

Sleeping on the hardwood floor was fine for me but the children missed their comfortable mattresses. They were up and down for the toilet in the dark and readjusting the net all night, it seemed. Just before dawn the chicken chorus from the village woke us all. It seemed like I had had only ten minutes of sleep but thankfully I felt quite refreshed.

Breakfast of eggs and rice was fine for me, but our three Western children didn't care for it, and even less for three-in-one coffee. Showering with the pan and water from the tub was also new to the children, so they gave it a miss. Actually, it's very refreshing when you get used to it, as I have done over the years.

With no time to waste, we jumped into the truck and set off for camp. It was only 20 miles away but the mud road was wet and slippy, so it took us over two hours. Some more Karen friends had joined us in the back of the truck and they frequently jumped off to be sick. Getting the children through security at the camp was interesting. Only people who could genuinely assist refugees would be allowed in. Anne was a nurse, I was a teacher, but how could they help? We explained that children conversed much better with people their own age, and it was a great opportunity for the camp children. This must have worked as we passed smoothly; either that or the guards were given a 'present'! Now, I think it was the latter, but at the time I was so naive.

The children were gobsmacked at the sight of the camp. How did people live so close together in bamboo huts? And it was pouring down with rain, making it a miserable place to visit. All our children had their first experience of 'teaching'. They chatted and played with the camp children, being amazed that they were all so smartly dressed in full school uniform even though they had had to walk to school in the rain and mud. The most important lesson for me was that children all over the world are the same. They all want to go to school, to play with their friends and have fun. Sarah, Patrick and Declan all had fun talking and playing with children their own age. I wondered what they thought of it all.

The day passed quickly as it always did in camp. We had rice and vegetables for lunch, and more three-in-one coffee. The children were very quiet on the journey back to Umphang; they fell asleep even though it was very bumpy. Had we done the right thing, exposing them to refugees and poverty? They would need protecting as the shock could be counterproductive.

They all slept well that night, no complaints about rice and vegetables, or about no TV. The mosquito net was now no problem and they all had a bucket shower. It is easy to adjust when you have to. I'm sure they all had questions to ask, but now, at least, they knew what their mother and father had been doing. Declan, only ten, was the quietest, perhaps the most moved by what he saw.

Dr Cynthia's clinic.

Back in Mae Sot, we wanted to visit the famous Dr Cynthia's clinic but we didn't know where it was. Dr Cynthia is a Karen doctor who fled Burma after the 1988 uprising. She has built a clinic in the border town which delivers healthcare to Burmese migrants working in Thailand and those who have no healthcare in nearby Burma. Burma spends so little on healthcare it is almost non-existent, so many people travel for days to the clinic. I didn't believe this at the time, but ten years later when visiting inside Burma, I saw so-called hospitals in Pathein and other remote regions and then I believed the stories about non-existent healthcare.

Many victims of the war die of dysentery, malaria and other preventable diseases, but the most disturbing are landmine victims. Landmines are planted by all sides and aim to maim, not kill. A group of soldiers in the jungle will not leave a comrade who has stood on a landmine. They will try to carry him to safety. This takes up lots of soldiers and prevents them from fighting. The victims are sickeningly disabled if they survive the journey to clinic. Not to mention the pain and trauma they suffer.

Wandering around Mae Sot, we had been given some general directions of how to find the clinic, but we were lost. A police van stopped and asked where we were going. We explained about Dr Cynthia's clinic and they offered to take us there. We were uncomfortable, as we knew lots of illegal migrants used the clinic and wondered, would the police arrest us? Anyway, we felt we had no option as the police were quite insistent. The van had a motorcycle in the back, so we had to climb in around it – all five of us.

A short drive and we turned left into a small compound of buildings. It was getting dark as we jumped out. People were very curious as to why a group of Farang (foreigners) were in the back of a police van with a motorcycle. We saw people disappearing out of sight of the police – obviously fearful of them. One brave man approached and asked, in good English, if we needed hospital treatment. We were surprised at this question, but quickly realised that he thought we must have crashed the motorcycle and needed treatment. He laughed when we explained we just asked for directions to the clinic and the police had brought us along. He breathed a sigh of relief when the police bid us goodbye and left the compound. Our first visit to MTC (Mae Tao Clinic, as it is officially called), would not be our last. Anne would go back many times.

Since 1989, MTC has grown from one small house to a large complex of simple buildings that provide a wide variety of health services to different groups of people. Today it serves a target population of approximately 150,000 on the Thailand-Burma border and provides consultations to over 100,000 patients annually. About 50% of those who come to MTC for medical attention are migrant workers in the Mae Sot area; the other 50% travel across the border from Burma for care.

Australia.

The end of another trip to Thailand came too soon. We had introduced the children to the reason we had come to such a remote place. They seemed to understand now, and talked about their experiences to each other. It was great to hear they were as enthusiastic and interested in what was going on as Anne and I. We knew we needed their backing if we were to continue our journey.

On board the flight to Perth, Australia, Sarah asked for an alcoholic drink with her meal. The air stewardess was very polite when asking Sarah her age. Sarah, being honest as always, told her seventeen. I didn't know but air regulations prevent anyone under the age of eighteen consuming alcohol on board. So Sarah couldn't have her glass of wine. The flight stopped at Singapore, so I said she could have a drink there as a reward for looking after the boys in Thailand. It was so hot at the outside bar at Singapore airport, I was desperate for a drink.

However, Sarah was denied a drink again, along with myself. Anyone who knows me and knows Singapore airport will know why – the price of a beer is ridiculous, bordering outrageous. I certainly couldn't afford £12 a beer and £5 a coke. That sort of money would last me a week in Mae Sot!

Meeting old friends in Perth was great. They had booked a caravan near to their home for us, and Patrick was renewing his friendship with Josh. I had so wanted to go to Australia for many years and here I was.

Although it was winter, the sun was shining and it was warm enough for us Brits to go swimming in the sea. It was a lot warmer than the North Sea on the North East coast of England. We had a great time. I loved the outdoor life and the 50 metre swimming pools in Perth were amazing. I love sport and was all for emigrating. I could speak the language; well, only just, as I'm not sure there are too many common words in the Geordie and Aussie languages. Anyway, what decided it was the price of beer. I played football with my friend and loved it, then we went for a few pints afterwards. I wondered why my friend stopped me as we were going into the bar and explained we would just buy drinks for each other, instead of going in a round. Being the guest, I went straight to the bar and ordered two pints of beer. I didn't realise I needed to consult my bank manager for an overdraft! I thought the price of beer in Singapore was expensive, but it was even more here. Well, if I couldn't afford a round of beer in my local pub, then Australia might not be for me.

Chapter 5.

Gregory and India, 2004.

It was now 2004, and Sarah was eighteen years old. She decided she didn't want to go back to Mae Sot so the boys would have to look after themselves during the day if they couldn't go into the refugee camps. Patrick was now fourteen and Declan eleven, and they had a few friends in Mae Sot, so they would be safe on their own during the day. This year we tempted the boys, if they needed tempting, with a trip to India on the way home. We would fly home via Delhi, where Anne's friend Emma lived, and hopefully experience some of the sights, sounds, smells and tastes of Indian culture.

Back in Mae Sot, Anne and I spent time working in Mae La Refugee Camp, delivering training in our specialist fields. Our friend, Ywa Hay (more about him later) wanted to take us to visit some of the many refugee schools that were springing up in and around Mae Sot. These schools were providing basic education for the thousands of migrant children who, at that time, couldn't access the Thai schools as their parents were working in Thailand illegally, doing the three d jobs – dirty, dangerous and difficult.

One day Ywa Hay didn't have any transport, so he rang a friend to see if he was available. Half an hour later, a man about my age turned up with a pickup truck. He was wearing a camouflage jacket and trousers. We thought he might be one of Ywa Hay's soldier friends from the Karen National Liberation Army (KNLA). He stayed with us all afternoon, taking us to a few schools. At the end of the day, he asked if we wanted to visit his school. We were very tired and hot but as he had been

31

so kind, we felt obliged to go. So off we went to his compound on the outskirts of Mae Sot. It had a beautiful driveway with neatly tended flowers, very different to any other school we had seen over the past few days.

We saw the name of the school at the entrance, Two Hearts in One. A little strange, I thought, but not unusual. Then we were greeted by some of the children from the school. They were lined up on either side of the pathway in full traditional Karen clothing. As we got out of the truck we were given a traditional Karen shirt to put on, and then one of the youngest children pinned a rose to each of our tops. I can still picture Declan receiving his top and flower from a young girl who was so polite and beautiful.

Then our driver introduced himself as Father Gregory Doh Soe, a Catholic priest from the Irrawaddy region of Burma and, as he told us on many occasions, he had a 'Karen heart'. The school was so different to the others we had seen that day. Many of the children had a decent grasp of basic English. The grounds were clean and they had flowers and vegetable patches and even a fish pond. The children had come from various refugee camps along the border. Not all were Catholic but many were.

Father Gregory was to become a good friend, and we had many exciting adventures and journeys with him. Ywa Hay had told him we were also Catholic, so Father Gregory invited us to Sunday Mass with the children the next day. As his school was a few miles from our hotel, he said he could pick us up. We thought it would be great and even the boys were keen as he said that they could play football after Mass and stay for breakfast. Then came the stumbling block, as was to happen many times in Burma when trying to attend Mass. He said Mass was at 6am and that his driver would pick us up at 5:30am. The boys' faces contorted as I agreed that it was a little early, but I was delighted by the invitation.

For Anne and I, our Saturday night out was curtailed a little. We limited the Chang beer intake and got to bed before midnight. As the alarm went off at 5am I thought, I'll never be able to wake Declan. Patrick was usually a good riser, but not Declan. After many knocks on their door I had to go to reception and ask the night manager to open their door so I could wake them. Ensuring I had Declan's room key when he went to bed became a common occurrence over the years, as it was almost impossible to wake him from outside the room.

It was still dark as we drove to the school. All the school children were up and waiting for us. Father Gregory was now in his priest vestments. It was only now that I believed he was a priest, as yesterday in his camouflage outfit I had had my doubts. Mass was in Burmese, with sections in English for our benefit. Some priests' sermons can be boring, but Father Gregory is not boring, so when Declan fell sound asleep during the service he was forgiven because of the unusually early hour for him. Father Gregory often reminded us of Declan sleeping through his sermon on future occasions when we met him. Pope Patrick, as Gregory called him, had no such problem, always an early riser, and still is today.

After Mass we had breakfast of, you guessed it, rice and vegetables, and then we met some of the older students. Notably, we were introduced to Saw Albert and Geoffrey. They spoke excellent English, and both in their late teens we guessed. We were to come across both of them many years later and Saw Albert go on to become Field Director for Karen Human Rights Group (KHRG); he put himself in great danger to report on the abuse perpetrated by the Burmese military. The KHRG is a grassroots, Karen-led human rights organisation, established in 1992 and now operating across rural southeast Burma. With over twenty-five years of experience, and twice nominated for the Nobel Peace Prize (2000 and 2001), KHRG is recognised internationally as a leading authority on human rights issues, such as forced labour, landmines, internal displacement and conflict in southeast Burma.

Geoffrey helped us when we visited Mae Khon Ka Refugee Camp many years later, where he was living with his wife and child, hoping to be repatriated to a third country by the UNHCR.

We had brought with us second-hand football shirts donated by children in our community, and gave them to the children of Two Hearts in One school. Most of the shirts were Newcastle United, but some were Sunderland tops. The children were delighted at our small gift and show of solidarity with them. Future 'Toon Army' fans in the making, we hoped, instead of the usual Liverpool, Chelsea and Manchester United fans. We stayed for most of the day as the boys enjoyed playing football and making new friends. Gregory told us he was a soldier of Christ now, having been a soldier in the Karen army in his youth.

Also staying with him at the time was Father Justin, another priest from the Irrawaddy region; he was a jovial character who became a close friend when we lived in Mae Sot a few years later. Gregory's role was to support the Catholic community in and around Mae Sot. He was a formidable character who could get things done. Later, Father Justin took over his role and was equally formidable. It was amazing how these four people came into our lives and inspired and helped us. We offered very little to them, and yet they remained close and trusted friends for many years, our paths crossing in the most obscure places. Visiting the Buddhist countries of Thailand and Burma, where people openly pray and offer thanks at their temples, and meeting the small but energised Catholic community, certainly opened my mind to a greater spirituality. Back in the UK it's so hard to explain and talk about, but it is certainly one of the most important aspects of life in South East Asia.

This year we had spent less time in the refugee camps and more in Mae Sot. Although there were over 120,000 refugees, we now knew that there were up to 2 million migrants working in Thailand, many illegally. Estimates of those working in and around Mae Sot were 100,000 or more. They planted the paddy fields, cut the sugar cane, knitted the clothes in the sweatshop factories and scavenged the streets collecting plastic bottles and cardboard for recycling. I knew little about this, but would find out more when I chose to live in Mae Sot for nine months a few years later. Ywa Hay had given me a little introduction. This problem was enormous and growing, as the atrocities continued in Burma. With no jobs, no education system and little healthcare millions were making the decision to leave their country and seek out a better life in Thailand. I knew little about any of this as I had not been to Burma. The Burma Campaign UK and other organisations, and even Aung San Suu Kyi, had told foreign tourists not to come to Burma, as any spending would only support the military. I supported this stance and so only knew what I had read or been told. I wanted to see for myself and would be persuaded to do so next year.

So it was off to India as we left Thailand and our new friends, knowing we would have to come back. Father Gregory had changed our hearts forever. We arrived at night at the airport in New Delhi. We had flown Air India and the plane had rattled and shook the entire journey. I was relieved to land safely and looking forward to a new experience. Our friend, Emma said she would send a car to meet us so no need for a taxi. We waited patiently but no-one came with a sign for Mr Tony, so I decided to venture outside, leaving Anne with the boys. It was about 4am so I expected the streets to be deserted. I was in for a shock. It was pandemonium outside. People going to and fro everywhere. The streets were packed and the noise was incredible. I couldn't find our lift, so went back inside to warn Anne and the boys. I said they needed to prepare themselves. This place was going to be different and more difficult than Thailand. The heat was stifling and the boys were falling back to sleep. At last we got in touch with Emma. She said there had been a mix up with the arrival time but Samson, her driver, was on his way. Soon afterwards we were on our way to Emma's. Thankfully she had lots of spare rooms in her house, and was looking forward to some company.

India is a wonderful place to visit but it's not for the faint-hearted. The boys loved Emma's air conditioned house and watched DVDs and TV. We had some marvellous experiences, visiting the Taj Mahal (quite frankly, a little disappointing with all the street hawkers harassing us) and seeing Old Delhi by rickshaw. The highlight of the trip was our visit to the Golden Temple at Amritsar, and learning about the massacre at Jallianwala Bagh, Amritsar, Punjab. The Sikh people were so welcoming and much more relaxed, unlike in Delhi, which was quite stressful. The Golden Temple was so special in August 2004, because over four million Sikhs were expected to arrive in the holy city to celebrate the 400th anniversary of the installation of Sikhism's scriptures in the Golden Temple. We washed our feet and donned suitable headwear before being shown around at no cost, and then fed with naan bread and chickpeas. They were such a wonderful example of how to treat visitors. I was even interviewed on Indian TV news, who were covering the celebrations.

I shall always remember India for a sad reason as well. While there, I heard my father was quite ill at home and had been admitted to hospital. I went to the cathedral in New Delhi and prayed I would see him again. I left my father there with my prayers. We flew home a few days later and he was very poorly in hospital. I managed to visit and say my goodbyes. I was thankful for this opportunity. I just arrived back home in Newcastle from the hospital in Hartlepool when I got the phone call that he had passed away a few minutes ago. I shall always remember the prayers I said in Sacred Heart Cathedral, New Dehli, for my father. It was the place I let him go to heaven.

Chapter 6.

Federation of Trade Unions, Kawthoolei and Maung Maung Tinn, 2005.

Ywa Hay.

I don't remember the first time I ever met Ywa Hay but I will never forget the last time I saw him in Thailand. It was in Mae Sariang, and we had just left Mae Kon Ka Refugee Camp. Anne and I were heading north for Mae Hong Son. Ywa Hay was going back into camp where his wife and children lived. I shook his hand, and promised I would see him one day in a free country where we would be able to talk and travel freely together. Years later I was able to fulfil that promise, when I travelled to Australia to visit him in Perth after he and his family had been relocated under the UNHCR repatriation scheme. I had only half-believed my promise, but dreams sometimes do come true.

Ywa Hay was General Secretary of the Federation of Trade Unions Kawthoolei (FTUK), and married with five children. He lived in Mae Sot, but his family lived in Mae Kon Ka Refugee Camp. Ywa Hay had fled Burma many years ago, like thousands of others, when his village was attacked by the Burmese Army. His escape from persecution was typical, hiding in the jungle, scavenging for food, hoping for survival for his family - willing to sacrifice himself. Fortunately, he managed to find his way to a refugee camp and was given food and shelter. Ywa Hay was a religious man, even his name means 'God be with you, but most importantly, he was fired by the desire to stand up for his own and his fellow workers' rights. Along with Dot Lay Moo, he formed the FTUK while in a refugee camp. With 'solidarity, rights and responsibilities' as their mantra, he set up trade unions for teachers, health workers and farmers. They had thousands of members, both in refugee camps and in Karen State.

Ywa Hay did most to open our eyes to the plight of refugees and the poorest in society. He showed us around the 'real' Mae Sot. We knew the restaurants and bars, and we had visited the refugee camps, but what about all the migrant workers and their families? Like in so many places, they are hidden from view, in secure factories and shanty houses on the edge of town. What we found out from Ywa Hay changed our perception of what was going on inside Burma and on the borderlands. There were far more migrants in Mae Sot than refugees in the camps. At least two million in Thailand, mostly unregistered and illegal; all in dirty, dangerous and difficult jobs. We had heard stories of human rights violations among these workers. He took us to visit the people who were suffering such abuse.

There are two stories in particular which I would like to share about Ywa Hay. The first one was when he took me to visit the Assistance Association for Political Prisoners (AAPP) in Mae Sot. The AAPP office is concealed up a side road. There is no sign on the gate, to prevent unwanted visitors. A short alleyway leads to the house which also doubles as a museum. Ex-political prisoners work in the office and show visitors around the small museum. AAPP keeps accurate records of all political prisoners in Burmese jails, and has pictures of many of them on its walls. It has a scaled version of the infamous Insein Prison in Rangoon, built by the British in colonial times. It also has a mockup of the notorious dog cell, which visitors can go in. These are the solitary confinement punishment cells, originally built by the British to house the prison guard dogs; they are tiny, with hardly any room for a person to turn around. Shackles are bolted to the floor and locked to the prisoner's feet to further make life unbearable. You truly get a feel for what it must have been like for a political prisoner.

Sitting outside the museum while I was chatting to an ex-political prisoner, Ywa Hay was reading one of the many books that AAPP have written. I heard a thud and looked up to see the book on the floor. Colour had drained from his face, and I asked if he was ok. He picked up the book and looked at it again. I asked what was wrong. He could barely speak, but then slowly told me. He knew his father had been killed by the Tatmadaw when he was a young child, but he hadn't known when or how. The AAPP book detailed the murder of civilians by the Tatmadaw, through eyewitness accounts. Ywa Hay had just read a story about a man who had been taken as a porter by the Tatmadaw, and as he had become sick was thrown down a ravine in the jungle and left to die. The man describing the terrible event was known to Ywa Hay, a man from his village. What he had just read was the story of how his father had died. The name of the victim was his father's name. Ywa Hay started to cry as he explained that this was the first time he had known the real truth about his father. He was so thankful to AAPP for documenting his death. He said that it would help him now he had the truth, and that maybe one day he would get justice.

The second story is linked to his father's death. In 2007, Ywa Hay was invited to Europe with Maung Maung, leader of the Federation of Trade Unions Burma (FTUB), to speak in Geneva at the International Labour Organisation (ILO). The FTUB were providing evidence to the ILO of crimes of genocide committed by the Burmese dictatorship. Ywa Hay bravely told the story of his father on behalf of his family and thousands of others whose brothers, sisters, fathers and mothers had been murdered by this brutal regime. He was so proud to be able to do this, but it was not without risks. On returning to Thailand, at Bangkok Airport, immigration officials intercepted him. Ywa Hay had to take the risk of travelling on a false passport. He could not obtain an official one from Burma, as return to Burma to obtain a passport as a known trade unionist would have meant arrest, imprisonment, torture or worse. Thai immigration suspected his passport was forged, and took him to a side room. Extensive questioning took place. Immigration knew that he had come from Geneva, and knew that he was unlikely to be a Burmese government official on business to the UN, as Burma was a piraha state, and had limited contact with them. Ywa Hay was frightened. They threatened to deport him to Burma. After hours of interrogation, he was allowed to make a phone call. He telephoned the FTUB office in Bangkok. They knew what to do, but it would cost. FTUB collected £1000 and headed to Thai immigration; that was a lot of money, but the only way to release Ywa Hay. The 'administration fine' for incorrect paperwork was duly paid and Ywa Hay released.

The life of a trade unionist on the Thailand-Burma border is dangerous and precarious. Shocked and frightened he arrived back in Mae Sot saying he would never travel outside of the Mae Sot area again. He had a wife and five children who needed him - and he wanted to stay alive! I told him his father would be proud of him, and that it took great courage to do what he had done. How many of us would do the same?

Naw Paw Gay Khoo.

One of Ywa Hay's colleagues in FTUK was Paw Gay Khoo, General Secretary of Karen Health Workers Union, born in the late 1960's in Karen State. As with Ywa Hay, I can't remember the first time I met her, but I think it was in 2004. She is an exceptional lady who has a great love for her community. She lives in Mae Pa with her mother, where she has an open house - there are always visitors from near and far living with them. She fled Burma when she was a young girl, and it had a great effect on her. She told me her story a few years after I met her. The Tatmadaw attacked her village, like so many other villages.

Her father, along with the other men, stayed behind to fight and give the women and children a chance to escape. She recalled running away up a hill with her mother and her siblings, hearing the sound of guns behind her. The family hid in the jungle and waited for the men to join them. They waited all night, listening for the fighting to stop. Next day, some of the men came up the hill and joined the hiding families. It was then she was told her father had died. He had been shot defending his village and protecting his family. The Tatmadaw had been driven back, but at the cost of many lives. Paw Gay and her family went back down the hill and recovered the body of their father to bury him.

The area was too dangerous to stay in, as the Tatmadaw were nearby, so the family fled to Thailand and Kwakalo Refugee Camp. This camp was very close to the border, and was subsequently attacked by the Burmese Army who came over the border. They then moved to Mae La Refugee Camp under the control of the Thai authorities and the UNHCR. After she finished her education in Mae La, she found a job in the Karen community as a health worker.

Run!
by Maung Maung Tinn.

Run! Run! Villagers scream.
Run!
Dad's loud voice.
Run!
I know the only right now is running.
My mind is ordered to run.
My body is ordered to run.
I don't know which direction.
Where am I heading?
To the hills? To the trees? To the big rocks?
I'm not sure.
I just follow the people who are running in front of me.
The soil is different.
It is more rough.
Yes, of course, I am running without slippers.
Some pieces of stone are very sharp and their edges are like nails. But I ignore how painful it is.

The most important thing right now,
is to reach a safe place away from the danger of gunfire.
The noise from the gunfire has stopped.
People are still running.
Oh my god! Look!
There are so many people.
Behind me.
Beside me.
In front of me.
Some are old.
Some are so young, and they are the same age as my younger
sister.
I remember my family, now.
Father, mother, sister!
How about my grandmother?
Constant noise from the gunfire is still on the border.
Many incidents have happened here before,
and landmines are still active in some areas.
I worry for my family, my friends, my relatives.
Can they avoid landmines?
Can they escape from the constant bullets?

I had heard all about Paw Gay from her sister, Mu Lay Khoo, who I met while she was studying at Newcastle University in 2002. Mu Lay Khoo was part of a group of six students who were given scholarships to study Education at the university. Our family used to visit her and her friends, and offer them support: to adapt to our culture, and in their studies. Two of the group, Hla Htay and Hla Min, did their research-based work at Ashington High School, where I was working at the time. Mu Lay Khoo was very sociable, and asked us to visit her when she went back to Mae Sot. A few years later, Mu Lay Khoo left Mae Sot with her husband for Canada, under the UN repatriation programme. Paw Gay has had many opportunities to apply to be repatriated over the years, but has never had the desire to leave her community and often tells me she wants to go back to live in Karen State.

Paw Gay is always our first point of contact when we arrive in Mae Sot. She is always there, or somewhere along the border, or inside Karen State working for her community. She was General Secretary of the Health Workers Union when we first met her, and was promoted to General Secretary of FTUK when Ywa Hay left for Australia in 2009. Her mother is quite old now, born around 1945, but still active in the community. She gives an excellent traditional Burmese massage, to relieve tension or aches and pains. A very slight lady, she is sprightly on her feet and always busy in the community.

Paw Gay is like a sister to Anne and I, and an auntie to Declan. Whenever Declan is in Mae Sot on his own, he stays at the FTUK house and Paw Gay makes sure he is well looked after. Declan doesn't need the comforts of a hotel when he has his 'Karen family' to look after him. Paw Gay organises many things for us at the border. She arranges our transport whenever we are travelling on the border or inside Karen State. She ensures we have a safe driver, and that all permissions are in place. Without her we would not have been able to fulfill many of our activities and adventures over the last twenty years. Like many Karen in Mae Pa, she is very unassuming - but never to be underestimated. She speaks Karen, Burmese and English perfectly and can get by in Thai. She is the glue that holds the community together, and continues to inspire me every day.

Saw Lay Say

Is Saw Lay Say the strongest, bravest man I have ever met? As Father Justin is a man of the people, Lay Say is a man of the jungle; a worker in Karen Agricultural Department and the 'field worker' for Karen Agricultural Workers Union (KAWU). His day job is to travel on foot inside Karen State, co-ordinating and training workers in agricultural methods, storing seeds, distributing supplies and generally trying to improve the amount of food grown in rural Burma, so people don't die of starvation and malnutrition. His work during the conflict was incredibly dangerous, often having to avoid patrols of the Tatmadaw as he passed through Burmese military areas. The first time I met him he had malaria from living in the jungle without adequate netting to sleep under. He looked so frail and vulnerable, and yet when I really got to know him and travelled with him after the peace agreement had been signed, I realised just how durable, strong and courageous he is.

Lay Say was born in 1970, is married with two children and comes from a remote village called Lay Bu Der. The village was formed by clearing the jungle after his family fled the Burmese Army. It is by a small stream and has about 40 houses. There is no running water and no toilet. The first time I travelled inside Karen State, shortly after the peace agreement, he wouldn't take me to his village as it had no toilets. He thought I wouldn't be able to use the jungle toilet. A few years later I did visit, and was pleased to stay overnight and share the jungle toilet with the village pigs. His father is the head of the village. It has a small school and a chapel. It is extremely poor, a hand-to-mouth existence, but they survive. No priest visits, but they say prayers in the chapel and use it when a villager dies.

Lay Say is a massively keen trade unionist and one of the main reasons for the success of FTUK. I recall one training session he was leading with the KAWU, and he asked me to interview one of the members.

I asked the member, 'What are the benefits of being in the trade union?' The worker replied, 'When you get shot and killed by the SPDC, the union makes sure your name goes on the International Labour Organisation list of victims.' I was stunned, and asked Lay Say to confirm his answer. He asked him again, and the same answer was repeated: this was the environment agricultural workers were working in, along with land confiscation and slave labour.

44

On another occasion Lay Say was with a group of young workers explaining the benefits of a trade union. He gave the simplest but most memorable demonstration of worker solidarity. He stopped his session and asked all of the delegates to go outside, find a stick and bring it back into the room. We were in the FTUK office compound, so there were plenty of sticks and twigs within the grounds. A few minutes later they were all back in the room holding their sticks. Lay Say asked one of the delegates to come forward with his stick. He handed it to Lay Say, who snapped it in half. He then asked the delegate to collect all the sticks and bring them to him. After a few moments Lay Say had about twenty sticks in his hands. He then tried to snap the sticks all together. Of course, he couldn't, and so demonstrated the principle of strength in unity. So simple, yet so effective, and never forgotten. I guess that sums up Lay Say as well.

Burmese High School for Orphans and Homeless - BHSOH and Headteacher Kai Oo Maung.

Ywa Hay knows many of the 100 or so migrant schools in and around Mae Sot providing education for the illegal migrant workers who cannot access Thai education. Perhaps the most intriguing is Burmese High School for Orphans and Homeless (BHSOH). The school is in the village of Mae Pa, where many Burmese migrants live. It is rundown and in disrepair after the storms of the monsoon season. The headteacher is very glad to see us - he relies on foreign donations of money and time to run his school. He invites us to sit down and brings coffee (three-in-one coffee- awful stuff, but the sugar keeps you going).

He begins with his story. I get the impression he has done this many times before, but I can tell he is genuine. His name is Kai Oo Maung; he is about 60 years old, but looks much older. He has a thin face with strands of long hair coming out of his chin, and jet black hair now starting to go grey. He had been a teacher in Rangoon when the uprisings started in 1988. He was an activist who wanted change after suffering so much since General Ne Win came to power in 1962, after overthrowing the democratic government. Like many activists, when the crackdown came in 1988 he had a choice: stay and be thrown into prison, or run and join the student revolution in the jungle with the Karen rebels who were already fighting the military. He chose to run. After years of fighting with the KNLA and the All Burma Student Democratic Front (ABSDF) against the Tatmadaw, he was eventually forced over the border into Thailand. An experienced teacher, he put his skills to good use by opening BHSOH. The school had about 100 students, and catered for pupils over the age of 12 - quite unusual, as most schools in the area were primary. When pupils reach the age of 12 or so, they were useful in the factories and fields, earning a small wage so vital for their family.

As the school had many older children, some of the boys played football at the end of the day. Declan and I would often join them for a little exercise. When my brother Geoff came to visit, he was keen to play and went to the school to join in. Typical of Geoff, he was very competitive, keeping the score and tackling some of the younger students a little too aggressively. Declan would come away laughing at his must-win attitude. But that was Geoff; he really loves playing football, but he loves it more when he wins!

As with all these people, the life of Kai Oo Maung was full of tragedy, and one was unfolding right in front of us. When he heard Anne was a nurse, he told her his daughter was sick and being cared for in his house. He lived on the school premises, as most of the teachers did, for safety and affordability. Anne enquired about her and was told she had tuberculosis. Anne knew it was very contagious, so suggested she visit on her own. She found his daughter, a lady about 35 years of age, seriously ill, and being tended to by a few of the older girls at the school. They would wash her and feed her, but they had no masks or gloves to protect themselves. Anne enquired about taking her to hospital. They couldn't afford it, and she didn't want to go anyway. If she was dying, she wanted to die at home. A shocked Anne advised the young girls on protecting themselves and we agreed to buy personal protective equipment for them.

Again, we felt traumatised that we could do so little, but Kai Oo Maung was so pleased a Western nurse was tending to his daughter. Anne visited regularly during our stay, but we had to go home not knowing the outcome. A few months later, Ywa Hay emailed, informing us she had died. A sad tale, but one being repeated all over Burma and the borderlands.

Maung Maung Tinn and the Garbage Tip.

Ywa Hay introduced us to Maung Maung Tinn (MMT) in 2003, an artist and philosopher who lives in Mae Sot, and we meet up with him every year. A refugee and migrant worker at Mae Tao clinic, MMT's artwork is provocative, and shares with the world the plight of the Burmese in and around Mae Sot. It is remarkable and has been shown in the USA, Italy and Japan. But MMT is not just an artist; he is a tour guide for those who want to see the real Mae Sot.

I quote from the back page of his incredible, not to be missed book, *On the Border*.

'Maung Maung Tinn has enjoyed drawing since he was a child.
Before paper and pencil were available to him, he used a stick and the clean surface of the ground as art materials.
Maung Maung Tinn was born in the countryside.
He grew up in the countryside.
He loves the countryside.
His parents wanted him to be educated.
So Muang Muang Tinn had to move to a small town when he was 11 years old for his education.
He worked after he finished high school.
Like many other people from Burma, Maung Maung Tinn's life was not easy.

In 1994, he left home and of course, his countryside as well.
He arrived in another country.
Here he sees many Burmese people.
Some work in factories, some live on the town's garbage dump,
some are in brothels, some are in prison, some are in hiding in
the forest.
He is unhappy about this.
Their tears, their voices, and their lives motivated him to start
painting again.'

Ywa Hay had never been to the garbage tip on the edge of Mae
Sot, so MMT invited us all to visit together. MMT has been
many times, and has used the workers on the tip to illustrate the
life of a refugee, working at the very bottom of the food chain.
A friend of Patrick and Declan is travelling with us this year.
Michael is 19 years old, and a keen photographer hoping to get
some pictures. We hired bicycles to get to the garbage tip on the
edge of town.

As we approached the tip the smell hit us! It was
overwhelming- difficult to keep cycling, as I needed to cover
my mouth and nose. Then the flies increased in number and I
had to start swatting them off. I couldn't ride the wobbly
bicycle any further, so I jumped off. Garbage for as far as you
could see.

We pushed our bicycles to the primary school, Sky Blue
School, the migrant school for the tip workers. A huge sign
greets us: No Photographs. MMT indicates we should come
back to the school after going to meet the workers on the tip. As
we approach the edge of the dump, the smell is even more
horrific, making us cover our mouths and noses. It's the rainy
season and the dump is a quagmire.

'This is too dangerous,' I say. 'Broken bottles, needles and
sharp tin cans could be under the piles of stinking garbage.'

In the distance, on the top of the tip, I can see a group of
people scavenging through the rubbish. MMT heads straight
across the tip in his flip flops. The tip is infested with rats, and I

can now see broken glass is scattered all around. We have two young children with us. MMT encourages us to keep moving, he wants us to meet the families - he will translate.

'They will be pleased to meet you,' he says. 'They don't get many visitors.'

I didn't have to ask why. This was crazy, but we decided, as we had come this far, we might as well continue. Patrick went first; his foot sank deep into the rubbish. He pulled his foot out without a flip flop. I shouted at him to stay still as I cautiously retrieved it. I had sandals with straps, so mine stayed on. Anne was desperately trying to weigh up the risk – it was far too risky! Just hoping not to slip and fall into the quagmire, we inched our way across the garbage. Anne is close to vomiting but the boys seem to be taking it in their stride.

Eventually we reached some bamboo huts. MMT beckons us inside one of the huts and we realise these are the homes of the garbage tip workers. Safely in a hut, I surveyed the family's possessions. Nothing more than a pan, a few blankets and a bag of rice. We sat down and MMT introduced us to the family; a man, his wife and their two young children.

MMT translated their story for us. They were migrants from Burma who earned enough to survive by collecting glass, plastic and metal from the rubbish. Sometimes, if they were lucky, they found food. We were offered a cup of tea, which we accepted for fear of offending. We were so humbled. How could they survive, never mind live in such conditions? It was so hot and humid, with flies everywhere. My heart was broken once again. They say the Burmese grab your heart and never let go - they have grabbed mine so tight this time, I can hardly breathe. MMT indicated we should leave.

I am too embarrassed to offer the family money directly, but leave 500 baht under a cup on the table while they are not looking. This would be more than the weekly income for the entire family. I feel ashamed that a fellow human being lives like this. MMT senses my anguish, and reassures me that these families are fine. They have jobs and feel safe on the tip, as no one will attack them there, for obvious reasons. They are incredibly resilient and have built up immunity to the germs on the tip. I'm not convinced, but we need to get the boys off this tip before they get hurt (physically or emotionally).

It takes us about ten minutes to carefully slide and slip through the mud back to the school on the edge of the tip. One of the teachers comes out and provides a hosepipe to wash our hands and feet with, but we can't wash away the smell. We are given a quick tour of the school, which has about 100 children, and MMT explains that an NGO is willing to relocate the school away from the tip, but the families don't want that. They feel more secure with the children nearby. Feeling embarrassed at their poverty and our wealth, we ask MMT how we can help. He suggests buying some sacks of rice and bringing them back. Giving them money might cause arguments, he advises.

'Each morning we wake up to the foul smell of garbage' by Maung Maung Tinn.

We wake up to a foul smell, every morning.
The morning garbage truck brings more valuable items than the one at noon.
We collect plastic, glass and aluminium, whatever we can sell at the market.
We also collect fish, meat and vegetables that don't look perished, to feed our families.
We buy drinking water because then we know it is safe to drink, but use the water from the well near the dump to cook and to wash.
We know that no person should live in these conditions, breathing toxic fumes, walking and living on polluted soil, eating in the company of flies.
But living at the local dump, far from the nearest town, has its benefits.
We don't need to worry about being arrested by the police.

Living at the city's dump is easier than living in our native land...Burma.

Next day, we returned with two sacks of rice. On arrival we were greeted by the head of the community, who brought out a list of families living on the tip. He told us how many families there were, and that we should divide the rice up equally between them. We bought plastic bags from a nearby shop and divided the rice as requested. Then he called for a member of each family to come and collect their rice. The rice was a small bag, worth about 50p, but each family came in turn and thanked us. We were giving so little, really, but it meant a lot to them. It would last a family for a few days. I felt ashamed that I had so much and they had so little. But what they lacked in material possessions, they made up for in community, friendship and solidarity. I was now starting to understand the role of MMT in his community. He was trying to open our eyes and ears to the suffering of his people by allowing us to meet them in their own environment. We were learning and slowly understanding the meaning of charity: it is not to give spare change and old clothes, but to walk with the poor and oppressed and receive from them the gift of friendship.

We returned to MMT's house as we wanted to buy some of his calendars, which depict the life of refugees and migrants. At his one bedroomed home, the room is bare apart from a mattress in the corner. He provides us with pizza; hospitality is so important, and he thinks we will like pizza. After buying his calendars, he says he will donate the money to his friends: the backpack medics, who take medical supplies to those who have fled their villages in Karen State, but refuse to leave their country. They live in the jungle and eke out an existence. This is the only medical help they get. Although so poor, MMT still shares what he has with his fellow countrymen.

To misquote the band James from the song *Sit Down*: If I hadn't seen such poverty, I could live with being rich. Oh sit down, sit down next to me.

Chapter 7.

Karen National Union (KNU).

The Karen National Union (KNU) is the Karen government in exile waiting to return to its capital, Hpa An. Most of the government is based in Mae Sot, but some are resident in Chiang Mai, and some live inside the KNU controlled areas of Karen State, Burma. The KNU is the political wing of the Karen government. The Karen National Liberation Army (KNLA) is the military wing. The KNLA are based in the liberated areas of Karen State, and are a well-organised but small army, with few modern weapons. Many of their soldiers carry weapons left over from World War Two, but for over 60 years they have defended parts of Karen State against a massively superior, in terms of arms and soldiers, Tatmadaw. Many have spent their entire life in the jungle fighting a guerrilla war to defend and protect their family and culture. At the time of writing, it is the longest running civil war in the world and thankfully surviving the longest ceasefire arrangement, allowing political discussions to take place for a lasting peace.

Dot Lay Mu.

My closest friend involved with the KNU at a senior level is Dot Lay Mu (DLM). Born around 1960, a charming, intelligent and dignified man. Over the years I have had many conversations with him, as he sought my advice on particular situations or events involving the Karen people and the KNU. DLM served for several years as Second Secretary in the KNU.

A most memorable conversation with him was about family days in Karen State. He described how people would show off their vegetables and get prizes for the largest ones, and the great fun of racing pigs and showing off the goats and chickens. He wouldn't believe me when I said that in England, we do exactly the same thing. He told me of great picnics with political speeches. I told him of the Durham and Northumberland miners' picnics, where thousands still attend to hear political leaders and trade unionists. As a trade unionist, DLM was so interested in this and couldn't believe we shared such similar events.

I first met DLM in 2004 when I was introduced to FTUK. About the same age as me, we had lots in common even though we lived worlds apart. It is surprising how much in common we have, and as murdered MP Jo Cox says: We should celebrate what we have in common, rather than be concerned with what divides us. He was general secretary of FTUK, having formed it several years earlier. He was also head of the Agricultural Department in the KNU (effectively, Minister for Agriculture) - a large responsibility, as Karen State was, and is, effectively an agricultural nation, with little or no other industries. He was also a deeply religious man, being a minister in the Baptist Church. One year he told me he was not going to church on Sundays at the moment because of an incident.

A few weeks earlier, he had been in church when a stranger came in asking for Dot Lay Mu. The congregation were suspicious (everyone is suspicious of strangers after 60 years of war), so they directed him to another area of the church grounds, whilst quickly informing DLM to hide. Eventually the man realised he had been misdirected and came back, this time waving a gun in his hand. He told them that DLM needed to watch his back and stay out of politics. It was not uncommon for Burmese military spies to infiltrate the Karen community and kill or threaten people in order to undermine the government in exile. It was clear DLM had been very shaken up. For weeks he wouldn't leave the compound where his house was, unless in a car with a guard. It made me consider my involvement with FTUK: not so much worried for myself at the time, but for Anne and my children. Patrick and Declan had many Karen friends and often played football with them. They were very vulnerable and could easily be kidnapped, or worse. Anne and I discussed it at length, and made the boys aware of the real dangers of Mae Sot, and the situation we were up to our necks in.

Prior to this event, DLM was a very gregarious man. He was married to Naw Kwi, with one daughter who had left for Canada under the UNHCR repatriation programme. He also had one granddaughter.

Naw Kwi missed her daughter and granddaughter so much. The pain was in her voice, and she took solace by going fishing. She would reflect and meditate, and plan to see her loved ones again. Many years later she would leave for Canada herself, her broken heart finally fixed.

Living with refugees, I learned how painful enforced separation is, and how broken hearts are hard to mend. Every family had a story to tell. DLM would often play his guitar and sing songs, a great voice and big personality. In his youth, like most young Karen men, he had served in the KNLA, telling me stories of his near misses in the jungle, putting my life into perspective.

He told me his story of leaving Burma so many years ago. Like many, he had lived in Manerplaw, the capital of the resistance movement during the height of the fighting in the civil war. The Tatmadaw attacked it many times. The brave resistance of the KNLA was finally broken and the town had to be evacuated. DLM and his family fled into the jungle and eventually into refugee camps in Thailand. He fled with all he could carry, just like the others. Now he served his country in the government, but his brother still lived inside Karen State and was still a member of the KNLA. Years later, I was lucky enough to meet him on one journey along the Salween river when returning from Karen State.

Padoh Mahn Sha.

In Karen, Padoh is the salutation given to a respected man. All members of the KNU leadership are referred to as Padoh. I only met Padoh Mahn Sha once, shortly before he was assassinated in 2008.

I first met Zoya Phan, his daughter, in 2002, when she was visiting Newcastle upon Tyne with her friend, Nightingale. I think she was about 20 years old at the time, but looked much younger. She was studying at university, and a friend asked if I had a spare room where she and Nightingale could stay. We all had dinner together and shared our cultures by singing traditional songs. We had a great time. Zoya Phan's book, *Little Daughter*, is well worth a read.

Next year I was sitting in a cafe in Mae Sot when this pretty girl kept smiling at me. Although I was flattered, I knew very well why pretty Thai girls smile at middle-aged foreigners, so I politely acknowledged her and continued with my snack. Then she came over.

Now, I was getting anxious, until she said, 'You don't recognise me, do you? I'm Zoya, who stayed at your house last year.' I was so relieved. She sat down and asked what I was doing in Mae Sot. I told her all the family were here. We were on holiday, and Anne and the boys would be along shortly. Zoya had now graduated from university in England and was working for Burma Campaign UK. She was in Mae Sot visiting her father, Mahn Sha. She said he would love to meet us, as we had shown such kindness and friendship to her. Unfortunately, we couldn't arrange it that year, but in 2007 we did eventually get to meet him when we returned to Mae Sot.

We were on our regular trip to Mae Sot and had promised Zoya we would call and visit her father. We asked Paw Gay to take us there, but she said it was not so easy and would have to be arranged.

'Padoh Mahn Sha is the leader of the KNU, a very busy man and we need security clearance,' Paw Gay told us. But Paw Gay knew how to arrange these things, and a few days later all was set up for us to go and see him. A truck picked us up outside the DK hotel. The driver, we found out later, was his adopted son, Say Say.

Padoh Mahn Sha Lah Phan was born on 5th July 1943. He graduated from Rangoon University in 1966 with a degree in History. He joined the Karen National Union (KNU) in 1963. In 1964 he became a member of the KNU Central Committee, and was elected Joint General Secretary in 1995. He was elected General Secretary in 2000.

Mahn Sha lived in a house on the outskirts of Mae Sot. As we approached, the gates slid open and the truck drove into the compound. I was surprised there was so little security for a man who was the leader of a revolution and at war with the Burmese. He came out to greet us and was delighted to meet some of Zoya's English friends. We were offered coffee and snacks, while Mahn Sha told us about his life and the struggle. He had maps of Karen State with the locations of all the Karen army brigades and also where the Burmese military brigades were. He told how his wife, Nant Kyin Shwe, had died a few years earlier, and that now he lived with his adopted children Say Say and Slone Phan. His two daughters, Zoya and Bwa Bwa, were both living in England. He seemed quite lonely, but was fully occupied leading the Karen State against the Burmese. After a few hours we left, with Say Say taking us back to our hotel. What an experience it was, to hear all the stories of the revolution from its present-day leader.

Several months later, on 14th February 2008, we heard the tragic news of his assassination. He was shot at point-blank range by two men who had arrived at his house on a motorcycle. They entered the compound and greeted him in a friendly manner, before one of them pulled out a gun and shot him. They fled on the motorcycle before anything could be done. Mahn Sha died on the veranda of his house with Say Say by his side. The assailants were never caught, but many suspect they were Burmese military spies, paid to assassinate him. Mahn Sha was an Animist in a largely Christian KNU. He was a threat to the Burmese, as he was a leader of all Karen people. It is suspected that the Burmese were trying to drive a wedge between sections if the KNU, a classic divide and rule policy that so many dictatorships use. A tragic end to a good man and, once again, a family devastated by murder.

'Rocky'.

I still don't know Rocky's real name. Everyone knows him as Rocky. Married to Lisa, a Scottish lady, they have two children, and Rocky is very much in the mould of Lay Say: strong, resilient and determined - another jungle man. Rocky was head of Karen Youth Organisation (KYO) when he was younger, but when I got to know him he was in charge of Karen National Sports Association (KNSA). As a keen sportsman myself, I knew the physical and psychological benefits of sport and exercise. Over many years our family collected football shirts from our friends in the North East of England to make them aware of the situation. We took them with us, or shipped them out to Rocky, to show solidarity with the Karen and encourage them to live healthy lifestyles.

I am a very keen footballer and a qualified referee. When Rocky heard I was a referee, he asked me to run training courses for referees in the league he organised. I was very pleased to do this and ran several courses over the years. One year, Rocky asked me to referee a big game that was coming up. It was a Saturday evening top of the table clash, and he said they needed an independent referee. I was only too happy to oblige. I cycled through the heavy rain to get to the game, and had Patrick and Declan as my linesmen. Although wet, I felt confident I wouldn't let Rocky down.

As we cycled into the school grounds we could see hundreds of people waiting to watch the game. Rocky came over and checked we had a whistle and flags. I asked about the large crowd.

'Top of the table clash,' he said. 'Lots of interest.' The pitch was heavy and waterlogged in places, but Rocky wanted the game played, so off we went. The players were respectful of my decisions but very competitive, so the game went reasonably smoothly, and even a large downpour didn't dampen their spirits. When a team scored, wild celebrations came from pockets of the crowd. As the game was nearing the end I could feel the tension, more in the crowd than the players. One team narrowly won 2-1, and I felt I had done a good job. I left with Patrick and Declan after picking up my fee - a can of Chang beer!

As I cycled home I kept thinking that something was amiss. The crowd had behaved very differently to a British crowd, but I put it down to cultural differences. A week or so later, Canadian Dave came over as I was having coffee in his cafe. He said I was the talk of the Karen community. I asked why, and he explained how a lot of money had been gambled on the result of the football game I had refereed. Many people had lost money as the favourite had lost. It was then that I realised why I had been asked to referee. I had heard that referees were often bribed. Rocky had not told anyone I would be refereeing and had let the appointed Karen referee know at the last minute that he wouldn't be needed. Nothing could be done to change the bets.

The crowd discovered I was the referee when I went onto the pitch. I had been part of an elaborate reversal of match fixing - Rocky had turned the tables on all the gamblers. Dave said they were all talking about the 'golowah' who had turned up unexpectedly. He reassured me that I was safe. No-one was blaming me, but some people were very upset, while others were very happy. Next time I saw Rocky he just laughed and laughed. He thought it was a great plan of his that had worked really well. I think many of his friends had profited from me, as they bet on the winning team.

Chapter 8.

Burma: The first time, 2006

Mandalay.

After five visits to the border we had never been into Burma, except over the Friendship Bridge at Myawaddy to renew our visas. ASSK and the NLD had advised tourists for years not to visit Burma. The money spent would go into supporting the military government and subsequently into the persecution of the Burmese people. One friend put it like this: you are buying bullets for the regime's guns.

ASSK said there would be plenty of time to visit when democracy was won. So for five years, until 2006, we adhered to this policy. So why did we go against the advice of ASSK? Our Burmese friends persuaded us. They said that we would not be tourists. Our family knew the situation from outside Burma-now it was time to witness, with our own eyes, the real situation in Burma. We would be given guest houses to stay in, which were not government run, and that many of our exiled friends' families would welcome us. We should go and enjoy Burmese culture and hospitality. So in 2006, Anne, Patrick, Declan and I decided to apply for visas to enter Burma for the first time.

At first I thought we might be turned down, as we had been active in criticizing the Burmese government and supporting the exiled democracy movement. I decided to apply at the Burmese embassy in Bangkok, via a travel agent in Chiang Mai. The travel agent was confident we would get visas, saying they would send our passports with an agent to Bangkok on the overnight bus. The agent would visit the Embassy and return the next day. I was a little reluctant to hand over our passports, thinking the agent might sell them. The travel agent reassured us and then duly booked our flight from Chiang Mai to Mandalay, promising we would get a refund if the visa was refused. We had an anxious two day wait, with the visas due to return on the day of our flight. A tight schedule, but something you get used to in Asia.

Anxious about going to Burma for the first time, we set off for the travel agents on the morning of our flight.

'The visas are on their way and will be here soon,' the travel agent said. We only had an hour to spare.

'No problem,' said the travel agent. 'Go to the airport and we'll deliver your passports to you there!' Now I was really worried. Would this really happen? We had no choice. So, bags packed and a friend of a friend meeting us at Mandalay International Airport, we set off without our passports.

At the airport we waited and waited; time was running short, and we needed to check-in, but couldn't without passports and appropriate visas. Finally, a man came running up to us with a big smile holding a handful of passports.

'Mr Antony and Ms Anne?' he enquired. We opened the passports and frantically looked for the visas. There they were.

I turned to Anne, saying 'What was all the fuss about? I told you it would be OK.'

Checked in and ready to board, we wondered what we were doing, taking two young children to Burma with little or no plan, relying on contacts of friends. We knew that healthcare was almost non-existent. What would we do if we had an accident? But it was too late, as we climbed up the steps to the Mandalay Airways aircraft. The air stewards were impeccably dressed, in traditional Burmese longyis - Burmese men do not wear trousers, but a kind of sarong which is known as a longyis. The stewardesses were in beautiful, traditional long-dresses. And they all spoke perfect English.

As we approached Mandalay we could see Burma for the first time. The difference, even from the air, was staggering. All we could see were green rice paddies, with only the occasional golden pagoda (a Buddhist temple) breaking the greenery. As the plane approached for landing we seemed to be in the middle of nowhere. There were no buildings at all in the surrounding area. We wondered what strange place we were landing in. The pilot announced the local temperature and time, and advised us to adjust our watches. Burma is one of the few countries in the world which adjusts it's time by half an hour.

Declan turned to me and said, 'Dad, we have to turn our watches back by half an hour. But from what I can see outside, I think we might have to turn them back half a century!' Never was a truer word said.

The airport was brand new, but almost deserted. It looked like there had been few, if any, other flights that day, and this was Burma's second biggest city. Our friend, Thein Lwin, had arranged for us to be collected and taken to our hotel, so we declined the advances of the local taxi drivers. I laughed with Anne when we saw the taxis. The cars were at least 50 years old, some classic cars indeed, and I said I wasn't getting in any of them as they looked like death traps. As we looked around for our lift, I spotted a man with the smallest volvo car I have ever seen. He was tightening the wheel nuts. I had never seen a volvo like it, so I went for a closer look.

As I approached he smiled and asked if I was 'Mr Tony, friend of Dr Lwin?'

'Oh dear' I thought, 'this was our transport.'

'Minglabar', I said, meaning 'hello' in Burmese. He shook my hand warmly, different from the 'wye' culture in Thailand, and introduced himself as Win Nyunt, from Phaung Daw Oo Monastic School.

'I will take you to Mandalay,' he said happily. I called Anne and the boys over. The 1950's Volvo car had two seats in the front, and covered pickup space in the back. I looked and wondered how we would all fit in. Anne and the boys climbed in the back on top of our bags, and I tried to get in the front seat. I say 'tried' because it was almost impossible. My knees were at my chin and my neck was bent at a right angle. This was the smallest car I had ever seen and there were five of us squeezing into it.

We were the last to leave the airport, which was now deserted. As it was getting dark, he switched on the car headlamps- well, one headlamp, as the other didn't work. There was little traffic, apart from a few oxen and carts. We trundled along for a short while and then the tarmac disappeared into a dirt track. There were no streetlights, so now it was completely black. I shouted into the back of the van to see if Anne and the boys were still alive. They replied saying it was very hot and squashed, and they could still breathe, but only just. As we drove along, cars without any lights suddenly appeared out of the darkness, our driver swerving to avoid them. This was getting very scary.

At last, buildings began to appear by the side of the road. Then it became more built-up, but still with very little traffic. I didn't want to distract our driver, but we needed to exchange some money. We had no local currency and I had been told that we needed to exchange clean American dollars. So Win Nyunt, our driver, a small balding man, turned the car up a side street and stopped. It was a good opportunity for all of us to stretch our legs as we had been cramped in for over an hour. Anne and the boys clambered out, all sweaty and irritated. I explained I wanted to get some Burmese kyat, the local currency. The driver showed me up a back lane and into a house. It was dark, a small lamp in the corner barely lit the room.

After a few minutes a lady appeared. She sat down and asked how much I wanted to change. I wasn't sure how much anything cost, or what the exchange rate was, so I said $200. She opened a draw and asked me for my dollars. She turned on a table lamp and inspected each of the $10 notes. Putting two of the notes to one side, she indicated they were not good enough. I picked them up; they looked fine. She pointed to a crease on one and an ink mark on the other. I took out two more of my $10 notes and handed them over after checking them myself.

These were OK, so she began counting the chat. A huge pile of money was counted out onto the table. There was no way I could fit it into my pocket, so I had to put it in my bag. The official exchange rate at the time was 8 kyats to the dollar; I was given 1200 kyats for each dollar, and the largest denomination note was a 1000 kyat note.

The Burmese were used to such large numbers of notes. She had counted them out very carefully and asked me to check. Taking my stash of money, I returned to the car. I showed Anne the money- she was amazed.

The driver noted our amazement and told us, 'People in Burma hire a van when they move house, not for the furniture, but to carry the bank notes!' There were no credit or debit cards here, and all transactions were done in cash. All foreign exchange was done on the black market, including huge business deals.

Back in the car, we headed for the Golden Duck Hotel. As we pulled up a young boy, aged about 12, ran to greet us with a shout of 'Mingalabar'. I learned quickly that 'Mingalabar' is never spoken quietly, but always with enthusiastic gusto, especially to foreigners. Following the boy was a large, rotund Burmese man in a pressed white shirt and longyi. He spoke excellent English and after introducing himself, showed us to our rooms. The hotel was a collection of bungalows set near a small lake. All the bungalows were up on small stilts to protect them from flooding. This was the rainy season, and the lake was inviting lots of mosquitos to feast on the new blood. It was very dark but the young boy had a torch and opened the first bungalow. The pungent smell of some sort of cleaning fluid overwhelmed us all. We wanted to open the windows and doors to let some fresh air in, but that would invite the mosquitos in. This was to be the boys room. We were then shown our bungalow, which was a little larger and slightly less smelling of cleaning fluid. The large Burmese man left us to unpack, saying we could have anything we want for breakfast, but the kitchen was closed in the evening. We should head into town for some food if we were hungry.

Going back to see the boys, we were almost overcome with the fumes in their room. This was dangerous. We decided they couldn't sleep in there, and that we would all sleep in our bungalow. It only had one double bed but we would get the mattresses from their bungalow and move them into ours. The young boy saw us doing this and ran for the owner. The owner came back, a little annoyed, but eventually agreed to our plan. All cosy in one place, we decided we should eat. There were no street lights as we carefully made our way to the main highway. We were told to follow it for about a mile, and we would find a restaurant or two. We could barely see, but made our way by the candlelight coming from the homes by the side of the road.

There was little traffic other than bicycles. After a short while, a boy on a bicycle came from behind and stopped in front of us, taking us by surprise. In the gloom he held out his hand with a torch in it. He gave it to us, indicating we might need it. Switching on the torch, we could now see it was the boy from the hotel. He'd obviously spotted we didn't have one. How kind of him, we thought, and began to relax in this alien place; it was very different to Thailand and we thought that was strange. At a busy street corner we saw a communal street bathing area. Men, women and children were washing clothes, and themselves, in a concrete tub by the side of the road. I had seen these places in refugee camps but didn't expect them in a city. But it was common all over Mandalay, as people didn't have running water in their homes. They were very discreet and washed without embarrassment.

Eventually, we spotted a restaurant – well, a bar (or 'beer station' as they are known) which seemed to sell food. We sat down outside on filthy plastic chairs and picked up the menu from the table. It was all in Burmese, so we decided to order a few beers and cokes to get started and try the money out. I asked what beer they had, but the lady didn't speak English. She very kindly showed me into the beer station and pointed to the fridge. Inside there were two types of bottled beer: Myanmar beer or Mandalay beer. Well, when in Rome. I chose Mandalay beer, and coke for the boys - not Coca Cola, but a Burmese version. Anne joined me with a beer - no Chardonnay or fizz here. The drinks were cold but still came with a glass of ice. I wondered how the ice was made, thinking about the damage it could do to our insides, but decided to go for it. After all, we would be eating here and the place was filthy!

We managed to order some chicken, fried vegetables and rice, hoping the cooking temperature would kill all the germs. We ordered more drinks as it was stiflingly hot. The food arrived and we were pleasantly surprised to get what we had ordered. We were hungry, so finished it all off. Although it was still quite early, around 9pm, the streets were starting to empty. People had finished washing and there was no traffic on the roads at all. We decided to head back to the hotel. The torch was invaluable to avoid slipping in the cow dung or falling down a pothole. Safely back home, the young boy showed us to our bungalow and sat on the steps as we went in. A while later I decided to see where the boy was; now he was lying asleep on the steps, but jumped up when I opened the door. The boy would sleep on our steps every night, our own personal security guard. I learned later from the owner, that he was a new employee, having only just left school. He told me he was sixteen, but that was obviously untrue. Education, although valued in Burma, came second to earning an income for the family.

Next morning we woke early with the chickens crowing. Outside we were greeted with a loud 'Mingalabar' by the boy who worked night shift security. He showed us to the restaurant. It was a table on a floating pontoon in the middle of the small lake, which was covered in lilies. The sun was already high in the sky and the temperature was rising. The owner came over and, again, told us we could have anything we wanted. Asking for the menu, he said he didn't have one written in

English but repeated we could have anything. We asked him to suggest something.

he then said 'Fried eggs, scrambled eggs, boiled eggs or poached eggs...' It was obviously anything, as long as it was eggs! Waiting for the eggs, we watched buses crowded with workers going past the hotel, with black acrid fumes belching out the back, and people hanging on for dear life on the top, sides and rear. Vastly overcrowded, these 1940's buses were the high speed link into town, where workers would clean, sell at the markets, or merely drink tea at the notorious tea shops.

After breakfast we waited, hoping our friend from the airport would reappear. Dr Lwin had told us he would be able to show us around a Buddhist school nearby. Waiting in the shade, we watched bus after bus heading into Mandalay. After half an hour or so, a young lady appeared at the hotel, introducing herself as Julie. As we were the only foreigners, she assumed we were Mr Tony and Miss Anne, and asked if we were ready to go to the school. We were, and off we went with her, getting very close when we had to cross the main road. Anne and the boys held hands as we risked our lives trying to cross.

Julie told us, 'The secret is to just walk out at an appropriate gap and maintain a constant pace. The cars and buses will see you and avoid you. Under no circumstances should you run. The drivers expect you to continue to walk, and anything else could be fatal.' Following in the exact footsteps of Julie, as if the road was a minefield, we made it across the road. Entering the school, we were astonished by the number of classrooms, each one crammed full of students.

In Burma, students only move up a year if they pass the end of year exam, so classes include students of all ages. The school was run by Buddhist monks. It had over 7000 pupils and 148 teachers, and ran on two shifts - with half the pupils coming in in the morning, and the rest in the afternoon- as they didn't have enough classrooms or teachers for them all to be there together. Average class size was over 70, but I did count one class with over 100 students in it!

The school was typical of most urban schools in Burma. Classrooms were concrete cells with a chalkboard. Rote learning was the only teaching method, and children could be heard chanting what was to be remembered. The head monk came to see us as they rarely got visitors, and certainly not foreign ones, although he did say that last month, someone from the British Embassy had visited to open the new library funded by British aid. As we toured the school, we noticed three young men hovering in the background. We wondered who they were - perhaps secret police? We found out soon enough, as one of them came over when our guide left us for a moment. As he approached we feared arrest. Should we be visiting this school?

He asked in perfect English, 'Are you friends of Maureen?' We had contacted our friend Maureen, a Burmese lady who lived in Newcastle, when we said we were planning to go to Mandalay. We knew she had cousins who lived there. The man was Father Alphonse, a local Catholic priest. He had been asked to come with Maureen's cousins, the two men he was with, because they spoke little English. He explained it was a little risky to be visiting this school. It was not on the official sightseeing itinerary for tourists. It seemed every day we would be confronted by restrictions, and our every move would be watched. He would wait for us outside.

The teacher returned to show us the medical centre of the school. We followed, thinking, 'What should we do? Was the priest right, were we in danger?' We decided to continue our visit, and asked questions about health and education. The clinic was run by volunteer doctors and medics, with over 100 children each day having an appointment. All education and basic healthcare was free at this school, hence it's popularity. A few foreign donors provided the funding. Having contemplated Father Alphone's information, we decided to leave; we feigned hunger and said we would like to go for lunch.

Outside Father Alphonse was waiting with Maureen's cousins. Father Alphonse took us to his workplace - a school/youth centre, where he invited young people from the area to learn English. Over the gate it read 'Dom Bosco Youth Education Service' (DBYES). Over tea we heard he had students of all religions (most people in Burma identify with one of the main world religions, only a few would say they don't have a religion), between ages sixteen and thirty. Tertiary education was non-existent in Burma. The government had closed down univerisites in 1988 following the uprising of that year, and the famous 8.8.88 demonstrations; on 8th August 1988, hundreds of thousands of people joined a massive, countrywide general strike.

Father Alphonse was a breath of fresh air. He was about 30 years old, and willing to discuss politics, Aung San Suu Kyi, the military - anything we wanted. This was very unusual. He was confident and articulate. He asked us to come to his school in the evening. His students would be there, and he would be delighted if we would talk with them. They were learning English but had never heard it spoken by a native. We agreed, and then ask him about changing money, and he told us to be careful.

'There are many government spies in Mandalay, and they watch the money changers so they can keep tabs on foreigners,' he said, 'I will change your money, if you want. It is safer.'

After going back to our hotel for a wash, we return to DBYES to meet the students. A group of about 20 turn up for the class, and of course Anne and I are expected to teach. This was no surprise to us, as all visitors are given this privilege. Their English is not so good but we are used to communicating through translators, so Father Alphonse helps out. The students are so reluctant to talk about the government or anything political. Spies are everywhere, they fear, even in this class. But it was a great way to meet some real young people. They knew so little about the outside world, Burma being very isolated at this time. And with government propaganda billboards on every street corner, along with an armed soldier, they have very closed minds for obvious reasons. Patrick and Declan are much better teachers with these guys. The students see Anne and I as elders and show too much respect, but with Patrick and Declan they are happy to talk and discuss the issues in Burma.

Next day, Father Alphonse asks if we would like to visit Pyin Oo Lwin, a military garrison town about 50 miles outside of Mandalay. It is in the hills, so much cooler, which is an offer we couldn't refuse. A few hours later two Burmese jeeps are hired, with the cousins as our drivers. Patrick and Declan jump in one jeep and Anne and I jump in the other. The open-top jeep is great fun as we start to climb out of Mandalay and leave the polluted city behind. Lush green vegetation surrounds us as we travel the winding road up, overtaking numerous motorbikes. The clouds look ominous, full of monsoon rain. It is the height of the rainy season and we are in an open-top jeep! Halfway up the hill we pull into a transport cafe. After a cup of three-in-one coffee and some local bananas, we're off again. Patrick and Declan are loving it, looking back at Anne and I and shouting comments that are blown away on the wind. At least the rains have held off so far.

Entering Pyin Oo Lwin, we go past a huge military base. Alphonse tells us it's a training academy for officers. We are not allowed to stop outside and please, no photographs. This town used to be where the British colonists would come at the height of the hot season to live, leaving behind the intolerable heat of Mandalay. The tradition is continued today, as the summer residence of General Than Shwe, the feared Burmese military dictator, is reportedly in Pyin Oo Lwin. Alphonse says nobody will talk about it in town. It's one of Burma's unspoken secrets!

We head through town, which has beautiful flowers on roundabouts, and by the side of the roads. We stop at the National Botanical Gardens to admire the flora and fauna, which is in full bloom and so well-kept; a stark contrast to the rest of the place. Alphonse whispers in my ear, that the residence we can see at the end of the gardens is reportedly Than Shwe's summer residence, but no-one will confirm this. It would be very dangerous for us to ask about it, regardless.

Leaving the gardens, we head up the road and into the grounds of what looks like a university/college. We soon find out the reason for our trip here, when Alphonse introduces us to the head of the Catholic Seminary College. This is a Salesian seminary, where Alphonse did part of his training as a priest. Great news for Patrick, Declan and I: the priests are having a game of football this afternoon. We expect just a kick around, but are greeted with two teams of 11 players, all priests or trainees. We are invited to play for one team, and take up our positions. I expect it to be leisurely, but no - this is very competitive. Challenges slam in but, as you would expect, they apologise for anything too physical, pull you back to your feet, and then hit you again at the next opportunity. One hour later, and thoroughly exhausted, we finished the game. Both Patrick and Declan had a great time. They took it a little easier on them than me, as they are so young. After refreshments, we return down the hill to Mandalay before it gets dark.

The next day we decided to take the bus into the centre of Mandalay. Getting on and off the bus is the most dangerous part; the buses are all right-hand drive, but Burma changed to driving on the right-hand side of the road in the 1960's, as a rebuff to the ex-colonial rulers. So you have to get on and off the bus in the middle of the road, a highly dangerous manoeuvre, given the height of the step and the pot holed roads! After a squashed and uncomfortable journey, we alight and head for the street markets. Rubbish is strewn everywhere, the whole place is filthy. The meat market is situated underground, where it is cooler, and there is no ice or refrigeration here. Meat, or rather fat, as little meat can be seen, is displayed on filthy tables, with the sellers wafting away the flies. With pungent smells surrounding us, almost overcoming us, it makes me consider becoming a vegetarian- except the vegetables look equally filthy and rotten.

Feeling faint in the heat and the foul smells, we spot a bank and take refuge in it. The cooling ceiling fans offer us respite from the high temperature and humidity, but once more we are transported back in time. I look around to see if I can see Jesse James, as this place is taken straight from a wild west cowboy film. A central cashier area has metal bars from desktop to ceiling; all the cashiers are locked inside with money piled from floor to ceiling. We plonk ourselves on some seats and look on incredulously. People come in with suitcases and rice sacks full of money, all paper 1000 kyat notes (worth about 40p). Some bags are so heavy it takes two people to carry them. Armed guards escort sacks going to and from small vans waiting outside. All business is done in cash. It is hard to contemplate what else we will encounter in this strange, forgotten place.

Outside once again, braving the incessant heat, we head for Mandalay Hill, the most famous place in Mandalay. With panoramic views over the city, the hill is home to a Buddhist monastery. It is a long, slow, winding road that takes you up the hill. Most people jump in a taxi, but we, being the 'fit family', decide to walk. A young monk soon catches up with us on our journey and is keen to talk. His English is good, as it is taught in school, and monks are quite well-educated. He tells us he will pray and meditate at the top of the hill, but is very keen to practice his English with us, so we enjoy a conversation which makes the climb pass much more quickly.

At the top of the hill, overlooking the city, we see the beautiful, meandering Irrawaddy river in the distance. From here the city disguises it's poverty and looks majestic, with its glistening stupas and temples. A tourist group is enjoying the view and I move closer to hear what the Burmese guide has to say. One of the group asks about the array of buildings in the extensive grounds below. The guide explains that they belong to a luxury hotel, set in it's own beautiful, walled grounds. The visitors are pleased to hear it and perhaps wonder why they are not staying there. I get even closer as their guide moves the group on, and quietly explain to a few of them that their guide is mistaken. The buildings they are looking at are not a luxury hotel, but the infamous Mandalay prison, where thousands of prisoners are incarcerated, most without trial or hope of release. The tourists look at me in disbelief - as if their guide would tell them lies! I can see they doubt my version, but hopefully I have sown a few seeds of doubt in their minds.

In the evening we have dinner at a local bar/restaurant with Alphonse and the cousins. This time we are taken on the back of motorbikes. With no crash helmets and very dangerous roads, I fear for my life. I choose to go on the back with Alphonse as I trust he will drive the slowest and safest. Not so- he accelerates the bike, so I have to hang on for dear life or risk falling off the back. The boys love it on the back of the cousins' bikes. We go round and round Mandalay Fort, avoiding the dogs, cattle and potholes. It's after dark, so there is little traffic on the road. After a few laps of the approximately one mile circuit, we stop, and the cousins ask Patrick and Declan if they would like to have a go. Having had a little practice in Thailand, they are very keen. I wasn't so sure but before I could stop them, they were both off up the road.

The next time I see them is after they have completed their first lap. They are going crazily fast. Next time they come round I shout for them to stop. They call back - 'just once more around - we're going for fastest foreigner around Mandalay Fort.' Next time round they pull over, as a police car has appeared on the road. I am so relieved they are safe. We quickly get off the streets to avoid the police and head for a beer station. Patrick was the quickest around the fort, and says he must hold the British record. I guess he has, as few would have attempted it! Declan chirps in that he must be the second quickest then, and probably the youngest. Another record!

Rangoon.

Our time in Mandalay passes so quickly with our new friends, but we have a flight booked and have to move on to Rangoon. We arrive at the international airport in torrential rain. Embarking from the plane, we rush across the tarmac to limit the soaking we are getting. The airport building is a 1930's, single-storey concrete structure. As we are drying off we see our bags being offloaded. Within minutes, our bags are dumped on the ground and we search for ours with the other passengers - no circular conveyor belt here. I think we are the only flight today as there is no-one else around.

We jump in a taxi, whose windows are all stuck in the down mode, and the monsoon rain floods in. Rangoon is the capital city, and so much more developed than Mandalay. The roads have some white lines to divide the traffic and it even has a set of traffic lights. We have no booking at a hotel, as there is no internet or even a reliable telephone system. We ask to be taken to one recommended by friends. A large, soviet-style hotel, we enter the foyer and go to the desk to negotiate a price. Everything is done in dollars. They want $50 a night per room-much more than we can afford. They will go as low as $40, but no lower, even though they have lots of empty rooms. Our top price is $20, so we have to depart. The Burmese don't barter very well.

Back in the taxi, we have another recommendation for a smaller guest house. As we only have a certain number of dollars with us, and there is no way of getting any more, I'm beginning to get worried that we can't afford a hotel in this city! It's warm enough to sleep rough but this is the rainy season, and we have two children with us. Trying not to panic, we pull into a hotel between the railway station and Aung San Stadium. It's a little rough, but they have a few rooms and yes, we can have them for $25 a night. I try negotiating again, and he's willing to drop down to $20 a night after a call to his manager. It looks clean and safe inside, even if the streets outside look questionable. Two rooms, so the boys can have some privacy, and breakfast included.

I was beginning to feel better, and Anne cracked a smile - the one which meant, 'what on earth are we doing here?' We take the lift to our rooms, stopping at the wrong floor by mistake. Strangely, this floor is not in use and the ceiling has fallen in. Not thinking anything of it we get back in the lift and go to our floor, and settle into our rooms which are surprisingly spacious and comfortable.

We can't wait to explore, and head out towards Shwedagon Pagoda, the most sacred Buddhist pagoda in Burma. It is believed to contain the relics of four previous incarnations of Buddha. It is a huge temple surrounded by markets, tea shops and beer stations. This beautiful golden temple has four entrances, each guarded by huge lion statues. Truly impressive, and certaining on a par with the Sikh Holy Temple at Amritsar. After about 30 minutes we are approached by a man asking to see our entrance tickets. We had no entrance ticket as we saw no-one else paying. We had entered, taking our shoes off and leaving them at the entrance, as advised by some locals. The official explained that foreigners must pay to come in, locals do not. Being short of dollars, we couldn't afford the $10 each he demanded. So we were asked to leave. As darkness arrived, the temple was bathed in floodlights and looked even more spectacular. It could be seen from all over the city.

I had read that Rangoon had a planetarium - a gift from the Japanese government in the 70's - and as a physicist, I wanted to visit. I thought it would be great for Patrick and Declan, but knew Anne wouldn't be interested. We asked at the hotel and found out it was within walking distance, so off we went. Set in the middle of some parklands, we wandered into a deserted planetarium foyer. A few moments later a receptionist showed up, obviously surprised that a foreign family was wanting to look around. Tickets purchased, we were asked to sign the visitors book. My initial decline caused her to issue a sterner request. I duly entered that Mickey and Minnie Mouse and family had visited on Thursday 24th August 2006. This seemed to satisfy the lady, as a smile greeted me as she closed the book.

Inside the cinema the lights went out, a signal for the rats and other vermin to come out. The commentary was in English, albeit quite broken, as the ceiling filled with stars and planets. A twenty minute Japanese version of the night sky with 1970's technology impressed Anne enormously- she was disappointed it was so short! Leaving with our feet intact, and no nibble marks, Anne remarks, 'such an interesting museum!'

The evening turned out to be even more wet inside the hotel than the torrential monsoon rain outside. Resting on my bed back at the hotel, I hear a loud bang and then gushing water. I don't think it's thunder or monsoon rain from outside. I realised it's coming from inside the building, so I jumped off my bed and opened the hotel door. Clouds of steam are filling the corridor and boiling water is pouring from the ceiling, which suddenly collapses under the weight of it all. The water, like a small river, flows down the corridor past our rooms, heading for the staircase. I can't get to the boys' room next door as the water is too hot for my bare feet, so I scream at them through the adjoining wall.

'Jump onto your beds and switch the TV off. And don't open the door. Put towels at the bottom of the door to stop the water getting in.'

'Too late', they call back, 'the room is already flooding.'

I put my shoes on and run down the stairs to let the hotel reception know. The water seems to be cooling now, and I can see the six inch pipe in the ceiling that has ruptured. The receptionist can't understand what I'm saying until Anne arrives, screaming at him to get up the stairs and sort it out. Suddenly the sleepy receptionist realises something is amiss, and heads for the lift. We try to tell him not to use the lift but .... as the lift door opens, flood water pours out. The river is now in the foyer. The receptionist decides the stairs are the best option and we join him, heading up the waterfall that the staircase has become.

Thankfully the water is cooler now and the steam is clearing. We arrive at our floor, shouting for Patrick and

Declan. I push open the door to their room and they are happily lying on their beds, water three inches deep on the floor, still watching the TV. At least they had put their backpacks on the beds. As the water receded, we all laughed about it. I thought we were in the middle of a terrorist attack, only to discover maintenance was a problem in Burma. Spare parts were almost impossible to get due to sanctions, and pipe seals were obviously on the list. Another floor of the hotel was now out of action. Sanctions were certainly hurting this hotel but at least no-one was hurt.

I saw the Rangoon Circle Train advertised in the airline brochure when flying from Mandalay. It looked like a 'not to be missed' activity for any tourist. So first thing the next morning, we head over to the railway station. We buy tickets at the booking office and then jump on the bare wooden carriage, thinking: maybe we are on the wrong train, as it's not as I remember from the airline brochure. We sit opposite a woman with a basket of chickens, either going to or from a market. The train fills to overflowing before setting off. It goes so slow there is no need to wait for it to stop. Children jump on and off at will. Traders sell everything from shampoo to pencils to condoms! We get off at Insein, a suburb of Rangoon.

Insein is infamous for it's prison, built by the British during colonial times. It's a huge, circular prison holding thousands of criminals and political prisoners. One section contains the notorious 'dog cells'. These are punishment cells for political prisoners. They were originally used as kennels for guard dogs, so one can imagine how small and cramped they are. We have no idea where the prison is, so hail a taxi. The driver speaks no English so we indicate our wrists being handcuffed. His face distorts but we continue with our mime. I'm not sure he understands but he's keen to get the fare.

We squeeze into his tiny taxi. A few minutes later he stops, jumps out and points to a building down the road. He doesn't want to take us too close, for fear the secret police will see him. We thank him and start walking. After a few minutes we stop at what we think is the entrance gate, but with no signs, we are unsure. Locals are going in and out freely, carrying food parcels for the inmates. Most prisoners rely on family and friends for food and medicine. With armed guards at the gate, we decide this is as close as we will go.

Picking up another taxi, we ask to go to University Avenue, the home of Aung San Suu Kyi, where she is under house arrest. After a short drive, the taxi driver turns around and tells us we are at University Avenue. He doesn't want to drive along the avenue, so he drops us at one end. In the distance we can see the road block - the red and white painted wooden barriers covered in barbed wire. Walking in the intense heat and high humidity, we slowly approach the barriers. A few locals are walking past so we assume we can follow. Stopping outside the residence of ASSK, we can see nothing of the house as a high gate blocks our view. I can remember this gate from pictures I've seen of ASSK giving speeches standing on a platform behind it, with large crowds gathered outside to listen to her. We smile at the soldiers and innocently ask who lives there. Patrick and Declan are staring at their guns. The first one smiles and says nothing. On asking a second soldier, he eventually simply states, 'Daw Suu Kyi.'

I ask, 'Why so much security for one lady?' He returns a smile - a smile that indicates we shouldn't be there. I show him my camera, asking if I can take a photograph, knowing the answer but wanting him to tell me. Another smile and a gesture to keep walking told us everything we wanted to know. ASSK was in there and she wasn't coming out for a long time!

Tired and looking for somewhere to eat, we found the only western looking restaurant in town. Ham and cheese sandwiches are on the menu which pleases the boys. After eating we try to engage the young waiter in conversation, but he is very reluctant.

Eventually he says, 'Our hearts want to speak, but we are afraid to talk.' He is brave to tell us this. Every cafe has a spy in it. Every street corner has an armed soldier on it. Large areas of the city are out of bounds. Brick walls, with a brick missing at regular intervals, surround government buildings. I never saw the guns pointing out through these ominous gaps, but the damage they would do if crowds ever tried to attack was obvious.

My first two weeks inside Burma came to an end. I really understood the words of ASSK: 'please use your liberty to promote ours' (words she would eventually need to consider herself) and 'the only real freedom is the freedom from fear.' How powerful those words were, ringing in my ears as we flew from Rangoon back to Bangkok. Fear prevents human beings from living fulfilling lives. The regime was a machine, pumping out fear day and night. Touching down in Bangkok, I felt released from fear. I had only been there for two weeks but I could feel the oppression in the air. I now knew what a totalitarian military dictatorship did to the minds of its people.

Chapter 9.

The Saffron Revolution, 2007.

After visiting Rangoon for the first time in 2006, seeing the hundreds of Buddhist monks on the streets around Shwedagon and understanding what a deeply Buddhist country Burma was, it was no surprise to me when the first news reports came through that monks were demonstrating on the streets of Burma. The protest movement was dubbed the Saffron Revolution, after the saffron coloured robes worn by Buddhist monks in Burma. Protests spread across Burma, eventually drawing tens of thousands into the streets of Rangoon.

It all started on 19th August after the regime raised fuel prices without warning. The demonstrations that followed were led by prominent leaders of the '88 Generation Students, a group of pro-democracy activists. The regime began a brutal crackdown on the peaceful demonstrators, arresting hundreds of people, including many of the protest leaders.

Monks first joined the protests on 28th August when they took part in a demonstration in Sittwe, North West Burma. On 5th September, tensions escalated during a demonstration led by monks in the town of Pakokku, near Mandalay, as regime soldiers fired warning shots and used tear gas to break up the peaceful protest. The monks demanded an apology for the violence, the release of all detained demonstrators and political prisoners, and action to ease the economic hardship exacerbated by the fuel price rises. They gave the regime until 17th September to respond.

The junta's failure to meet these demands triggered a new wave of nationwide protests. Initially wary of taking part in the demonstrations, bystanders cheered and showed solidarity with the monks. However, as the protests grew in size and spread throughout most of Burma, tens of thousands of ordinary Burmese from all walks of life joined the monks in the protests.

On 22nd September a crowd of 2,000 monks and civilians walked past a roadblock and gathered outside Aung San Suu Kyi's house on University Avenue. Aung San Suu Kyi left her house to greet and pray with Buddhist monks outside her gate. This was the first time she had been seen in public since 2003. The rally was a strong and clear display of unity between the monks and the pro-democracy movement. By 24th September, over 100,000 monks and ordinary citizens were marching in Rangoon and demonstrations were taking place in every state and division in Burma. Despite some of the strictest media censorship in the world, activists were able to post pictures and videos of the demonstrations on websites and blogs, ensuring that images of the protests were seen, worldwide. The regime resorted to shutting off the country's internet in an attempt to stop the release of news and pictures.

As the demonstrations grew larger, the regime stepped up security in Burma's main cities and prepared to quash the protests. The regime delayed a crackdown, while hardened troops from conflict areas in Eastern Burma were redeployed to Rangoon. On 26th September, the crackdown began. Soldiers carried out dawn raids on monasteries. Monks were forcibly disrobed, severely beaten and taken away by the security forces. During a raid of monasteries in Myitkyina, Kachin State, SPDC security forces reportedly beat four monks to death. The AAPP reported that a total of 52 monasteries were raided during the crackdown.

Army troops and riot police clubbed and tear-gassed protesters, fired shots on protesting monks and demonstrators, and arrested hundreds. Around 20,000 troops were deployed in Rangoon. The regime arrested over 6000 people, including approximately 1400 monks. Detainees were subject to physical torture, deprived of food and water, and often kept in dirty, crowded facilities.

The regime's official figures put the death toll at 10 people, but up to 200 are believed to have been killed during the crackdown. Perhaps the most notable event, in the eyes of Western media, was on 27th September, when Japanese video journalist Kenji Nagai was shot dead at close-range, after security forces used automatic weapons on protesters in Rangoon.

I watched the news each day on TV. I recall students from my Human Rights group at St Robert of Newminster School coming to my classroom each lunchtime for those weeks in September to watch the news with me and discuss the situation. At one point we were really hopeful that this was the start of something big. It captivated us in school but, more importantly, it was on every news channel across the world, and we saw the possibility of real change. The students, eternal optimists, thought this would set the people of Burma free. Like so many revolutions, it was crushed. Hope turned to despair for the people of Burma. We all learned how brutal the regime was over this short period. We had read the history of the 1988 Revolution and how it had been brutally suppressed. History was repeating itself, and my students were getting their first real-life history lesson.

I arrived in Mae Sot in July 2007 with Patrick and Declan, hoping to find out the real news about the Saffron Revolution. The boys say hello to their friends who work as porters for the DK hotel. They are a similar age to my boys yet have spent little time in school, but at least they have a safe and relatively secure job. They all play chinlo in the car park together, while I sort the bags out. The boys break down lots of barriers for me. Few Western families are seen in this remote Thai town. Anne is already in Mae Sot, and we go off to see Maung Maung Tinn at the Borderline Cafe. Burmese tea leaf salad is my favourite first meal every time I come to Mae Sot. MMT wants to show us this year's artwork. He gives me permission to take photographs so that I can create some prints when I get home. I ask to buy some of the originals but he doesn't want to sell. He'd rather keep them and show them in art galleries to promote the plight of his people. I buy some more copies of his excellent book, *On the Border*. He calls his friend to say he has some money to give to the Backpack Health Workers. He regularly supports this group of medics who go into the jungle to help the sick and elderly who can't travel to health clinics.

Next day, we visit the AAPP offices. Khun Saing, a former medical student and political prisoner, is there. He is hoping to come to the UK soon and so is very interested in the work of Peter Mulligan, a human rights activist who works in Sunderland and is visiting the border with me. The students at Peter's college have built the Sunderland Burma Wall, with each brick representing each of the 2000+ political prisoners languishing in Burmese jails. All at the AAPP are pleased with the project and accept Peter as an 'honorary political prisoner'.

Cycling from the AAPP, I pass the sweatshops of Mae Sot. The doors of the factories are closed and, of course, the walls have no windows, but I can hear the noise of their knitting machines producing low-cost (well, at least for us in the West!) garments. The children of the workers play outside, near the accommodation block - concrete cells with only a ceiling light for furniture. Basic cooking and washing facilities are outside. Huge wagons wait to collect the garments, which are often shipped to more regulated factories, to stitch in the logo tags of the famous brands. I stopped to reflect, and wondered if the shop stewards are meeting with the management to improve working conditions.

Paw Gay has asked us to do a few days of training with FTUK. Ywa Hay has just returned from the ILO in Geneva, and is recovering from his interrogation at the hands of Thai immigration, so he takes a back seat this week. Delegates travel from Umpiem and Mae La refugee camps to join others who work in Mae Sot. A total of 22 take part in the trade union and health training. The benefits and development of trade unions in society is a new concept for many of the delegates, who know nothing but dictatorship, so I slowly deal with the simplest of idea,s such as length of a working day and the need for adequate breaks in the workplace. Many of these ideas are slow to tease out of the participants, who generally just do as they are told, so as to keep their jobs.

Anne has the more delicate task of doing mental health training in a society that has seen such trauma. Star of the training is an education worker, formerly having served 30 years as a soldier, making the rank of Lieutenant General. He was certainly not used to the idea of discussing issues and listening to other people's opinions. However, he did want a new society ,and clearly wanted to be re-educated, as 30 years on the frontline had taken its toll. Many of these people have deep and severe mental health histories, having seen family members killed by Burmese soldiers or witnessed mass rape. With the added complication of physical disfigurement and disability caused by war, it was, metaphorically, a minefield. Anne successfully opens the discussion but knows this is only the start, and is concerned about opening a Pandora's box of problems.

For me, the day finishes with a phone call from my old friend, Gay Moo, who I met in 2000, in Mae Ra Mo Refugee Camp. He is working as a dentist in Dr Cynthia's clinic and wants to speak to me. I haven't seen him since, but his friend has told him a 'golowah' called Tony is in Mae Sot, and he realises it's me. I cycle to the clinic through monsoon rain to meet him, and sit outside his room while he finishes with his last patient. As I sit and collect my thoughts, a young girl, about 10 years old, walks out of a nearby room, followed by two adults. She is a typical sweet and beautiful Karen girl, but is wobbling around with the adults ready to catch her. This moment changes my life, and is an image I can still see vividly. I look down to her feet and see she is walking on two prosthetic legs - or rather, learning to walk on them. Her parents are with her, ready to catch her if she falls. A landmine victim, for sure.

I had seen many in the past, but this girl was so young, beautiful and innocent. I tried not to stare, but was transfixed in the moment. What crime had she committed other than been born in Karen State? She would have a difficult future ahead but at least there was some help for her. Shocked, I went into the room she had come out of. Lying on a bed/table was another victim. This time a young man, with his leg amputated above the knee. He stares blankly at the wall in a state of shock and in obvious pain. The question, why, is unanswerable. The young girl wobbles back into the room in her bright red Karen dress, smiling and so pleased she has legs to walk on again, albeit wooden ones without knee joints. Her parents encourage her. I leave as the tears start to roll down my cheeks.

Gay Moo comes out of the nearby room and I wipe the tears away. He has put on a little weight, but it is still the same man who wants to know how to build a nuclear bomb so he can end the war in his country. He thanks me for visiting, and for the medicine I gave him 7 years ago. I had forgotten all about it, but he reminded me that he had had stomach pain, and I had bought some medicine for him and the pain had gone away. How thoughtful of him to remember a small act of kindness. We exchange the events in our lives over the last seven years, and head off to a tea shop to sample some real Burmese tea and cakes. An unforgettable day. I pray for the future of that young girl and all victims of this war.

I reflected on this experience with my friend Alo later in the day. Alo is a very experienced Columbian missionary priest who has worked for more than ten years in Chile, the Philippines and Burma. He says that, by far, the worst regime is the Burmese dictatorship. Alo was expelled from Burma some years ago, and is blacklisted by the regime, so now teaches philosophy to trainee priests in Thailand. As he can't go back to Burma, he does the next best thing, and in his spare time he travels to Mae Sot and works in the migrant schools as a teacher. Alo listens carefully to me, and understands the pain I am going through after so many years of seeing such suffering with his own eyes. He tells me to never forget the great work the people in the clinic are doing, rebuilding the lives of the victims of landmines and helping to alleviate their pain.

The Killing Fields of Cambodia.

As if we haven't seen enough suffering, Anne, Patrick, Declan and I book flights to Cambodia; we always like to have a 'holiday' after our trip to Burma/Thailand.

After the end of the Cambodian Civil War (1970-1975), the Khmer Rouge came to power under the leadership of dictator Pol Pot. From 1975 -1979, during his brutal regime, more than a million people were killed by the Khmer Rouge. Their bodies were buried in mass graves that became known as the Killing Fields. The Khmer Rouge tried to take Cambodia back to the Middle Ages, forcing millions of people from the cities to work on communal farms in the countryside. They arrested, and eventually executed, almost everyone suspected of connections with the former government, or with foreign governments, as well as professionals and intellectuals. The regime only came to an end when Vietnam invaded in late December 1978, to remove Pol Pot.

Our flight took us directly to Siem Reap to visit the ruins of Angkor, the seat of the Khmer Empire from the 9th - 15th centuries. We had a hotel booked in Siem Reap, which is only a short drive from the airport. The next day we booked a trip to the Angkor temples. Angkor Wat is the central feature of the Angkor UNESCO World Heritage Site, containing the magnificent remains of the Khmer civilisation. The site is so large we hired bicycles to get around. It is truly a must visit for anyone who gets the chance.

Getting the bus to Phnom Penh, the capital city of Cambodia, was an experience not to be forgotten. They travel much faster than in Burma because the roads are a little better. They sound their horns continuously and it is a case of whoever is the biggest gets right of way. It is truly horrifying to sit in a bus and look at the road ahead, seeing motorcycles and pedestrians scatter out of the way. Eventually, we reach Phnom Penh bus station and I think I can relax, until I see the crowds of people all wanting to get you into their taxi to take you to a hotel/guest house. I grab Patrick and Declan and tell them to go and sit well away from this scrum with our bags. We waited until most people had left, and then I organised a taxi. It was clear that these people were desperate and needed to make a living at any cost.

The taxi took us to the north of the city, to an area of guest houses built on a lake - a very polluted lake! This was the only area in our budget as city centre hotels were very expensive. After viewing several damp and squalid places, Anne settled for one with a friendly owner. It was no better than Burma - rats scurried around and rubbish filled the lake. Clearly there was little sanitation or rubbish collection - it all went in the lake. I decided local fish would be off my menu.

We wanted to visit some of the sites of the Killing Fields, so, after an uncomfortable night, we set off for Choeung Ek, a former orchard about 12 miles south of Phnom Phen. Choeung Ek is a memorial, marked by a Buddhist stupa. The stupa has acrylic glass sides and is filled with more than 5000 human skulls. Many have been shattered or smashed-in. Mass graves containing 8895 bodies were discovered at Choeung Ek after the fall of the Khmer Rouge regime. Many of the dead were former political prisoners who were kept at the Tuol Sleng detention centre. I can recall Patrick and Declan, age 18 and 15, sitting at the foot of the stupa in the hot sunshine, asking lots of questions about the Khmer Rouge and Pol Pot; questions I had no answer to. But I felt I was experiencing history, and I hoped that such memorials would not be required in Burma - that the regime was not covering up mass murders like this.

Back at the guest house, Anne and I found our room flooded and with rats in the ceiling void. It had rained heavily during the day and clearly the roof over our room was not waterproof. As the guest house was full, we had to share Patrick and

Declan's room. They moved our bed in and we had an intimate evening together. It was just like Mandalay, where we had to share a room because of the petrol-smelling disinfectant.

Wondering whether the boys could take any more, we suggested going to the Tuol Sleng Genocide Museum, which chronicles the Cambodian genocide. The site is a former secondary school which was used as Security Prison 21 (S-21). An estimated 20,000 people were imprisoned at Tuol Sleng, the name meaning 'hill of poisonous trees'. It was just one of at least 150 torture and execution centres established by the Khmer Rouge. The boys were very resilient, and we might never get the opportunity again, so off we went the next day.

A very run-down place, with little investment from the government, we paid the small entrance fee and went in. No flash videos or cinema rooms, just a former secondary school converted to inflict torture and murder. The school grounds had been enclosed with an electrified barbed fence to prevent escape. The regime kept extensive records, including thousands of photographs. Several rooms of the museum were lined, floor to ceiling, with black and white photographs of the prisoners. Upon arrival, prisoners were photographed and required to give detailed autobiographies, beginning with their childhood and ending with their arrest. Those taken to the smaller cells were shackled to the walls or the concrete floor. Those who were held in the large mass cells were collectively shackled to long pieces of iron bar.

We didn't stay long as it was too brutal a museum for us all. I thought of Insein prison in Rangoon, and wondered if that would ever be a museum like this one. I hoped it would be, in some ways, so that I knew it was closed and all the prisoners free. Only time will tell.

Cambodia was taking its toll on me and I needed some rest and recuperation, as did Anne and the boys, so we set off on the bus to Sihanoukville - a beach resort in southern Cambodia. The bus journey was anything but relaxing. Survival of the biggest on the road. The same squabble took place as the bus pulled into the bus station, with bags being grabbed from the hold of the bus and put into taxis. After the scum had subsided, an Australian guy was still there. He ran a guest house nearby and it had a pool table. It was sold to the boys before we could ask a price. So, off we went in his truck and booked in. It had a bar and was close to the beach, so a good choice by Patrick and Declan.

Next day, we decided to relax on the beach, which had only a few tourists on it. Street children had bothered us all the way to the beach, asking for money. I thought we had left all that behind in Siem Reap. The sea was inviting so we all went in for a swim. Big mistake. Looking back towards the beach from the water, we could see some children heading for our pile of clothes. We had to rush out of the water and chase them away. After that we had to take turns looking after our clothes while the others were in the sea.

Boat trips were advertised at the guest house, so we decided to book one. A seven o'clock start was a little early, but we all got up and walked down to the meeting point at the beach. No quay or wharf, we had to wade waist-deep into the water and climb aboard. We joined a family from China and three British medical students, and off we went, heading to the coral reef and an uninhabited island. Sunbathing on the deck, we enjoyed a smooth journey to the coral. The boat dropped anchor, we put snorkel masks on and couldn't wait to see the wonderful coral. Patrick and Declan were first in and Anne and I followed. I had just started swimming when I heard Declan shout that he'd hurt himself. I swam to where he was and could see the water turning red. He was starting to panic as I swam with him to the side of the boat. A rope ladder was lowered for us to climb back in. I managed to help Declan up the ladder and lay him down in the boat.

Anne climbed in after me and we could see blood pouring from a huge open wound on the top of his foot. While swimming, he had caught his foot on the coral, which we now know is razor sharp. The captain of the boat came over, looked at the blood and immediately started pouring petrol over the wound. If you ask Declan, apparently that's very painful. Declan screamed and I grabbed the petrol can and stopped the captain. I took my towel and pressed hard on the wound to try to stem the bleeding. Declan was in shock and started shaking in the bottom of the boat. The three medical students introduced themselves, took one look and turned away - I think they were first years. Thankfully the Chinese man had a medical kit, explained he was a doctor, and said he would like to help. He took some yellow powder out of his medical bag and sprinkled it on the wound. It quickly had the desired effect - the wound was sealed and it stopped bleeding. I could now see Declan had a six inch slash to his foot, which needed urgent treatment. Patrick didn't want to come to the hospital so he stayed on the boat. The medical students said they would keep an eye on him. The boat quickly headed the three or so miles to shore, with Declan now a little more comfortable. About a hundred yards from the beach, the boat stopped. I had to jump out into chest deep water. Anne handed Declan to me and I carried him through the water to the beach, where a taxi was waiting for us. Anne jumped in and swam after us.

We put Declan in the taxi and asked to go to the hospital. The driver asked, 'Private or State hospital?'

An ethical dilemma. As we had insurance, I decided the private one might be the best, knowing what healthcare was like in this part of the world. A few minutes later we pulled up outside a detached building with a red cross above the door and a man, who looked more like a butcher with his bloodstained apron, was waiting for us. He was the doctor and surgeon and was very experienced, he told us. He was from Taiwan and would be very happy to help us. As I carried Declan into his consultancy room, one of the nurses was wheeling out a young lady. The Taiwanese doctor cleared bloodstained newspaper from the bed and asked me to put Declan on it. I could see the fear in Anne's face and I felt a little wobbly on my feet.

The doctor changed his bloodstained apron and came back in a clean white one. He took our bandage off and could see the wound covered in the yellow powder. He took a bottle of alcohol off his shelf and started to clean the wound. Declan yelped. I could see the wound now. It was very deep and would need a good deal of stitching. The doctor took a needle out and what looked like a fishing line and started to stitch Declan's foot. Declan nearly hit the ceiling as the needle went in. I had to use all my strength to hold him down on the table. If I'd had a belt, I'd have let him bite on it. Then it struck me. I asked, 'Have you given him enough anaesthetic?'

The doctor looked at me and with a straight face said 'Oh, you want anaesthetic? Usually the locals don't ask for it as it's expensive!'

I said that I'd pay. He went out and came back with a syringe and needle. He injected it all around the wound and waited a minute or so. I could see Declan start to relax and I could stop holding him down. The doctor then started again, at which point I'd had enough. My legs were wobbling now and I needed some fresh air, so I went outside and waited. Anne stayed with Declan and wheeled him out about ten minutes later, white as a sheet. The doctor gave Declan some painkillers and then me the bill. I thought, at least I have insurance and opened it to see the damage. $40 was all it was - I gave him the money and thanked him. The foot looked fine and Anne was happy with it. Delirious with painkillers, Declan went straight to sleep when we arrived back at the guest house. An hour or so later, Patrick walked in looking like a prawn on the barbeque. He had sunbathed all day without any sunblock and now he was bright pink and very sore - so now we had two sick children.

A few days later and the boys are feeling much better. Patrick persuades me to hire two motorbikes.
'We can then all go for a tour of the area,' he says.

As the boys both want to ride them, I have to give them some instructions. On a quiet stretch of road, Declan practises. A few minutes later they return and Declan is injured again. He has put his leg up against the exhaust pipe and now has a very sore leg, as well as a stitched-up foot. Declan persuades us he is fine and that he is competent, so Anne gets on the back of his bike and I jump on the back of Patrick's.

'Don't forget. I'm the fastest around Mandalay fort,' says Patrick, referring to his exploits last year. Everything is going fine, and we have an interesting day trying to keep the speed down on the bikes. Heading back to our guest house, a motorbike with two young men on it comes past Patrick and I at speed, and very close.

'That was a close call,' I say to Patrick. Then they whizz up to Declan and Anne, slow down, and the pillion grabs a bag out of the front basket of their bike.

Patrick notices and says, 'They've stolen my bag.' He turns the throttle and off we go, chasing them. Declan and Anne quickly follow. Thankfully, the young men are more proficient than Patrick and Declan and are soon way out of sight. I didn't want us to confront them. They probably had knives or some other weapon.

The bag only contained a camera and our swimming costumes and towels, so nothing too precious. However, I did think we should report it to the police, so the next day we hired a tuk-tuk and asked to go to the police station. Tuk-tuks in Cambodia are motorbikes with a carriage bolted to the back, and are even more unstable than tuk-tuks in Thailand. As we approach the police station, we can see it is up a short but steep incline. The tuk-tuk takes the left turn into it with Anne and I in the back. About a quarter of the way up the hill, the tuk-tuk stalls and grinds to a halt. We say we'll get out and walk but before we can, the driver has started it again and goes back down the hill. He crosses the dual carriageway and takes a run up at the hill.

'This is not looking good,' I think. Hanging on to the side of the carriage, we accelerate up the hill but soon slow to a stop again. The tuk-tuk then starts to slowly roll backwards down the hill and then veers to the left, and all I can remember after that is the smell of petrol. Upside down in the carriage of the tuk-tuk, with the motorbike now on top, and petrol pouring out of the tank. Anne and I climb out through the side of the carriage and roll away from the tuk-tuk which we thought was about to go up in flames! The driver was hurt and stuck underneath his motorbike. I managed to lift the motorbike and he crawled out. All the time, two policemen in the sentry box guarding the station just watched and laughed.

Shaken and bruised, Anne and I walked up the hill to the police station and asked to report the crime of the previous day. We were shown into a room and a policeman came in a few moments later. After explaining the incident with the 'motor bike bandits', he asked what was stolen. On telling him the camera and clothes, he just shook his head and said that unless our passports had been stolen there was nothing he would/could do. He shrugged this small crime off and sent us on our way.

Waiting outside was our tuk-tuk. The driver had managed to get his machine upright and wanted to drive us home. Anne and I looked at each other and decided we would prefer to walk. Licking our wounds, we arrived back at the guest house and ordered a cold beer. Tomorrow we would leave Cambodia - a country with many challenges ahead of it; with widespread poverty and corruption, it was in for a turbulent future.

Chapter 10.

Cyclone Nargis, May 2008.

'Heavy rain expected' was all the regime's state-owned media reported on 2nd May 2008, as Cyclone Nargis sped towards Burma. With wind speeds of 190km an hour and a three metre tidal surge, it would bring death and devastation to the Irrawaddy Delta. But the regime did know what was coming, the cyclone had formed offshore days before, monitored by weather agencies. The Indian government was so concerned at the regime's lack of preparation that they directly informed them about the cyclone.

To ignore warnings and fail to warn the population of the coming cyclone, or to give any advice on how to prepare for when it hit, is bad enough. What followed was even more shocking, though sadly not surprising. As news began to trickle out about the scale of the disaster, the United Nations and aid agencies began to mobilise to help, only to be told by the regime that they were not welcome.

In the days after the cyclone, the regime was blocking news from getting out of the country. The Irrawaddy Delta is low lying, so very vulnerable to flooding, and many people live by the sea or rivers which would have been badly hit by the tidal surge. UN satellite imagery showed the scale of the flooding, and estimated that 2,000 villages had been flooded.

As the regime continued to refuse shipments of aid, Burmese people in Rangoon packed cars and vans with supplies and drove to the Delta to help. They returned with horrific stories of death and devastation, of whole villages empty, or where all the children were gone, having been swept from their parents' arms by the force of the wind. Bodies were everywhere, rotting in fields and villages. People had little or no food or clean water. No shelter, and no medicine. Their regime's response was to send the army to the Delta, not to help people, but to set up roadblocks to stop people going in to deliver aid, and to stop survivors escaping.

The Delta region is one of the most fertile parts of Burma, and the regime was no doubt delighted that it has been 'cleansed' of many ethnic Karen who lived there. The land could now be turned over to their business friends.

A month after the devastating cyclone in Burma, an estimated 2.4 million people remained in urgent need of aid. While we will probably never know how many people were killed, estimates are as high as 200,000 dead or missing, and more than one million people are believed to be homeless.

Helpless,
by Maung Maung Tinn.

The sky is not clear.
The clouds are running.
The surface of the water is shaking.
Will there be rain?
It should not rain in the Delta anymore.
In our hearts, we have not accepted the rain.
A few days ago,
rain came to our village with strong winds
and brought a lot of water all over the village.
People, houses, animals, fields disappeared under the water.
People's crying, animal's screaming were drowned by the water.

The village has gone.
Families are
separated.
villages are lost.

Where are they?
Are they floating in the water?
Have they been swept away out to sea?
Often, I hear someone screaming for help ... but I am sure if it is
real or not.
The storm has left the Delta, but so many bad things remain.
We are all starving.
We have no idea where to find food, how to find clean water.
There is much water surrounding us, but it is useless.
We cannot drink it.
We cannot cook with it.
We cannot bath in it.
It has become a foul liquid.
After the storm,
people and animals died in the water and the bodies are
rotting.
The village is like hell now.
Someone may come to us to give food or clothes or clean water.
But we are not sure who will come, when they will come, what
they will bring.
Often I think that if I had died in the storm it was better than to
be left alive.
I know this idea is wrong.
I know that I should not give up so easily, but ... Where is a hand
to help us?

It was in the aftermath of the cyclone that we arrived in Thailand, in July 2008. The Burmese community in Mae Sot had mobilized, and drove cars and vans hundreds of miles from northern Thailand, through Rangoon and onto the Irrawaddy Delta. Stories of devastation and death were retold to us by many in the community. We were all deeply shocked and saddened, but what was worse was that the Burmese community were dehumanized to the atrocities of their government. They didn't expect anything else from the generals.

Anne had travelled a few weeks ahead of me, keen to do some health education in the refugee camps along the border. The DK Hotel is not a luxury hotel but after 25 hours of travelling, the welcome couldn't be warmer. The Karen boys who work as porters and cleaners greet us with a big smile, grab our bags and head off up the stairs with them. Patrick and Declan will come back down and play chin-lo. Their supervisor, Mya, a Karen lady about 50 years old, has her arm in a sling. Without being able to speak each other's language, she explains how she had broken her arm. No time off work for her. In the migrant community there are few workers rights and certainly no sick pay.

First stop the next day is the Borderline Shop, where clothes and craftwork made by refugees are sold. Maung Maung Tinn is there to meet us. We order some Burmese tea leaf salad and mango juice at the cafe/tea shop. Anne has bought over a thousand pounds worth of goods. We will ship it back to the UK and sell them to our friends and at fundraising events. This is a great way to give the community a 'hand up', rather than a a 'hand out'. MMT tells us that a group of Nobel Prize winners are in the shop, and he would like his famous friends (the Stokles) to meet them. We look in the shop but don't recognise anyone, just a group of women admiring the artwork. I found out later that the ladies were: Professor Jody Williams, an anti-landmines campaigner, Mai Farrow, UNICEF goodwill ambassador and famous American actor, Qing Zhang, Chinese labour activist, and Dr Sima Samar, former Vice-President of Afghanistan. They were promoting women's rights in Burma and Thailand. Such a shame they missed us, insisted MMT, when we told him they had left without seeing us! The devastation of Cyclone Nargis had at least raised the profile of Burma around the world. Perhaps some good would come out of it in the end.

Next day, I am in the offices of the Federation of Trade Unions Karen (FTUK) to meet up with Ywa Hay, the General Secretary, Dot Lay Mu, the Chairperson and Paw Gay,

96

Secretary of the Karen Health Workers Union. I want to offer some training in trade union organisation and to encourage them to reach out for help across the world, but my task will be difficult as they live in constant fear and harassment. The Thai police have called at their house on several occasions lately, asking questions about who lives there and where they work. The headquarters is a teak house in the village of Mae Pa, a few miles from Mae Sot. It has no sign indicating what it is and has large fences around it for security. The building is owned by the Karen National Union (KNU) - the Karen government in exile. It is registered with the Thai police, so the union leaders have some protection, but the Thai authorities hardly encourage trade union activity among the refugee community, and local factory owners 'discourage' trade union activity in their places of work. FTUK organise workers in the refugee camps and inside Karen State. Federation of Trade Unions Burma (FTUB), I found out later, have secret offices in Mae Sot and organise workers in the factories in and around Mae Sot.

Recently, Dot Lay Mu has been threatened by a gunman at his local church. A man came asking for him, showing other church goers the gun he had beneath his jacket. Since the incident, Dot Lay Mu hadn't left the compound, fearing for his life. Also, Ywa Hay told us one of his officials had been shot dead inside Karen State by an SPDC soldier. I'm setting up training for tomorrow and wonder what security we should put in place!

The afternoon is filled with a visit to one of the hundred or so Burmese migrant schools in Mae Sot and the surrounding areas. This one is about 3 miles outside Mae Sot, on the road to Mae La Refugee Camp. Ywa Hay wants advice on helping the teachers at this school, which we instantly named Chicken School on arrival, on account of the chickens running around the school yard. Six classes are crammed into a farm barn and we have to wade through mud to get in - it is the rainy season, and the heavens open most afternoons. And I know for a fact that none of the children will sleep under mosquito nets, so malaria will be prevalent here.

We enquire about drinking water for the children, as it appears that the container of drinking water normally seen in all schools is not around. The headteacher explains they can't afford bottled water, but that he 'sterilises' all the water before the children drink it. Having done some research on this previously, I wondered whether he used the sunlight and placed water bottles on the tin roof - the heat raising the temperature of the water sufficiently to kill off bacteria if it's done correctly. The headteacher hasn't heard of that. He says they filter all the water directly from the tap. I wonder if he has a reverse osmosis filter, or something similar, but do not ask him to show me. He takes me to the tap, then brings a bucket with a tee shirt stretched out over the top, demonstrating how he filters the water through the tee shirt before giving it to the pupils! I ask what the absentee rate is for the school, and he replies that many students are often off with malaria and diarrhea. We offer to pay for clean drinking water for the school for the next few months and ask Ywa Hay to discuss the situation with the school funders for a long term solution.

Ywa Hay drops us on the edge of Mae Sot, not wanting to come into town as it was the end of the month. Explaining, he says the local police are short of money at the end of the month and will put up roadblocks to check Burmese migrants' work permits. They arrest anyone without proper papers and release them on payment of a 'small fine'. Ywa Hay got caught last month and didn't want to get caught again.

Assistance Association for Political Prisoners (AAPP).

The Assistance Association for Political Prisoners (Burma) is a non-profit human rights organization, founded in 2000 by former political prisoners living in exile on the Thailand-Burma border. AAPP advocates and lobbies for the release of political prisoners, and for the improvement of the lives of political prisoners after their release. The various assistance programs for political prisoners and their family members are aimed at ensuring they have access to education, vocational training, mental health counselling and healthcare.

Khun Saing and Aye Aye Moo ex-political prisoners.

We had a special reason to visit AAPP in 2008. Our friend Khun Saing, a former political prisoner, who we met in Mae Sot in 2004, was now living in Sheffield, England. Khun Saing was in his fifth year training to be a doctor, when he was arrested and put in prison without trial for the crime of helping to document the history of the student uprising from 1988. He spent over seven years in prison, being released once but re-arrested for continuing to peacefully support the student revolution. During his time in prison he helped many prisoners using his medical training. At one time he contracted tuberculosis himself, and would have died in prison if not for his own knowledge and determination. Coughing badly and seeing many inmates with TB, he thought he may have contracted it. With no way of getting a diagnosis in prison he bribed a guard to allow him to go outside for an X-ray. He was escorted to a local doctor who confirmed his worst fears. On returning to prison he received no medicine and was destined to die there, like so many others. Not wishing to leave this earth at such a young age, he contacted his family who bribed the guards to allow them to bring in medicine. After months of bribing guards the symptoms finally receded and he made a full recovery.

On his release, some years later, he decided he should escape Burma altogether and head for sanctuary at AAPP in Thailand. Travelling under cover and at night, he managed to reach Mae Sot where I first met him, and he told me his remarkable story. However, Khun Saing could not forget his fellow prisoners in Insein prison in Rangoon and worked tirelessly for AAPP. One particular friend he mentioned was his cellmate for many years and remained incarcerated. He vowed never to forget him and never give up the cause for democracy in Burma until his cellmate and all political prisoners were released. He often quoted the rallying call 'Not one left behind.'

Before we left for Thailand, Khun Saing had spoken at a fundraising event we had organised in Newcastle upon Tyne. He had married another political prisoner, Aye Aye Moo, while in Mae Sot. Unfortunately, they had to separate when Khun Saing obtained refugee status and came to the UK. AAM was still awaiting assessment - it didn't matter that they were married and she was pregnant! - and so had to stay behind in Thailand. Khun Saing wanted us to pass on some money for his wife and son. His wife had recently given birth, but Khun Saing couldn't visit as travel restrictions on his refugee status prevented him.

On arriving at AAPP we asked for AAM who, thankfully, was still there. Khun Saing had let her know we were to visit. She was grateful for the money but, more importantly, she asked us to carry out a most vital task for her. She had documents which she needed to deliver to the authorities in the UK to assist her in her application for refugee status. We were delighted to be of any assistance we could. She opened an envelope to show us a certificate from the Red Cross who had visited her in prison in Burma. It was proof that she had been a political prisoner. It was the original copy and she feared it getting lost in the post from Thailand, so asked if we would take it to Khun Saing in Sheffield. I had never seen such a document before and didn't know they existed. An awesome request because if we lost it, she could lose her right to refugee status in the UK. I can tell you I looked after that document better than my own passport and wallet! A few weeks later, back in England, I managed to pass the documents on to Khun Saing, along with some photographs of his son.

While Anne and I had been with AAM, Patrick had been talking with a newly arrived political prisoner, CWO, and hearing about his time in solitary confinement in the notorious dog cells. These cells were originally built as kennels for guard dogs by the British, so small it's impossible to stand up, and now used as punishment cells. Patrick needed some light relief and asked if CWO could play chess, as a chess board was set out on the table. Patrick thought he was quite a good chess player, but was easily beaten. To make it a closer contest CWO suggested he played with a blindfold on so he couldn't see the board, but Patrick had to describe his moves to him. I watched with interest but CWO won easily again. Taking his blindfold off, he explained to Patrick how in solitary confinement he used to play chess with an inmate in the next cell. They would imagine a chess board in their heads and call out every move to each other. They were playing virtual chess in their own minds. He said it passed the time and kept their brains active, and now it was a really good party trick!

Karenni Refugee Camps, Mae Hong Son.

Heading north out of Mae Sot, we were hoping to visit some Karen and Karenni friends who had spent a year studying in Newcastle University, but were now back in their refugee camp homes. They had been selected for a one year course and given special visas to study abroad. To get to Mae Hong Son we travel by car along the border road between Thailand and Burma. About 30 miles north of Mae Sot is Mae La Refugee Camp. Security along this road is usually heavy but this time it was particularly bad. The reason: the imminent visit of Laura Bush, wife of USA president George Bush, to Mae Sot and Mae La. USA security was working closely with the Thai authorities and there was a heavy presence of armed guards and checkpoints. Laura Bush had expressed an interest in women's rights and wanted to find out more. She planned to visit Mae Tao Clinic and Mae La Refugee Camp. I heard from my friend in Mae Tao that USA secret agents had visited many times to discuss security. Apparently she can't walk down any path/roadway of less than 5 metres width as it is a security risk.

The route into and around the clinic has been carefully planned. She will fly in on a helicopter and armoured cars will deliver her to her destination. After the visit she will meet up with the president and head for the opening ceremony of the Olympic Games in China.

So having successfully navigated four security checkpoints in 10 miles, we arrived in Mae Sariang, close to Mae Kon Ka Refugee Camp, where our friend, Hla Min (meaning King Moon in Karen), lives. Hla Min travelled thirty miles on a motorbike on an extremely muddy road (if it can be called that), taking about 6 hours from Mae Kon Ka, to meet us. He is determined to renew our friendship from Newcastle and make a request for our help. We met him at the Karen Refugee Office in Mae Sariang. It is great to see this young man in his own environment, having previously only known him in cold Newcastle. He has some video footage he wants us to see, taken on his camera. It shows him and a few friends travelling through Karen State to his village, Ker Kaw Long. They have to pass close by SPDC camps so travel mostly at night. It is very scary. If they get caught they will almost certainly be shot by the soldiers, who would assume they are traitors who have left to fight in the civil war. I am holding my breath just watching the video. He says he and his friends are delivering materials for his village school, which Burmalink UK supports. We gave him the money from our charity, and he has to risk his life to deliver the books and other supplies he has bought in Thailand. That wasn't in the request for funds document that he gave me. I can't believe the lengths some people will go to to help their community.

Hla Min went to Ker Kaw Long School, as did many of his brothers, sisters and cousins. He knows how important education was for him and wants others to get the same opportunity. He has brought us another request to fund the school next year, all neatly typed up. I promise him we will continue funding the school, but beg him to take care and not put his life at risk.

He responds by saying, 'this is the life of a Karen refugee - everyday we put our lives at risk.' Not only does he put his life at risk, he's spent two weeks of his teacher's wages that he gets in the refugee camp to hire a motorbike and get out of the camp. He has a wife and young family in camp, so he needs the money for them. I am astounded at the sacrifice he shows for his family and village. One of thousands of inspirational people on this border.

Hla Min comes to our guest house for breakfast the next day. Over eggs and rice, Hla Min tells me he will meet his uncle at noon at the Refugee Office. He is travelling by bus from Mae La camp. His uncle is blind and has no arms. I have no need to ask how this happened, but Hla Min wants to tell me. At the age of 18 he picked up a landmine in Karen State and it went off. He is lucky to be alive, but he will never see again, and needs to be fed as he has no artificial arms. Every family is touched with tragedy, it seems.

As we leave Mae Sariang, our friend Ywa Hay who has travelled with us from Mae Sot, says goodbye. His family lives in Mae Kon Ka and he is going to see his wife and children. Ywa Hay drops the bombshell news that he has applied to Australia for refugee status and that he is very hopeful he will be leaving Thailand in the next few months with his family.

I'm so happy for him, glad he might soon be a 'free man', but sad that I might not see him again. I shake his hand and promise to meet him and all his family in the free world. The journey to Mae Hong Son through the monsoon rains is very poignant. I dream of Ywa Hay in Australia and of Hla Min back in his village as free men. I know these men will continue to fight for justice and democracy wherever they end up.

Goodbye.
by Maung Maung Tinn.

We must leave the place that we do love.
We must be apart from our native land: our home, our friends and our traditions.
To love and to be attached are so important.
But when life is threatened love and attachment is overshadowed.
We must leave our land.
We are moving away from our village, our farm and our mountains.
Will we return there again?
Maybe, it is the last time we will see these mountains, forest and river.

In Mae Hong Son we meet up with three more special friends: Catholic sisters from the Philippines, who work for the Jesuit Refugee Service in Karenni Camp Number 1. Tragedy has struck here too. Sister Rachel tells us that the young people in the camp wanted to organise a candle lit procession in solidarity with the demonstrations inside Burma, but the camp authorities refused to let them. Some of the younger leaders organised it anyway, but Thai soldiers dispersed it with gunfire. One young man was killed. The incensed refugees attacked the Thai offices in the camp. Relations with the Thai authorities were very tense and we may not get into camp.

Sister Madeleine goes with us to the Thai authority offices in town, to see if Anne and I can have permission to go into camp. We are to deliver trade union training to the Karenni Teachers Union, but we tell the authorities we will be doing sport training only (we intend to do this also, but only after the trade union activity). I show the camp commander my football coaching plans, all printed in colour with lots of drills and set plays. He is keen on football and very impressed. He agrees to our camp passes on one condition - he wants a copy of my football coaching sessions. No problem for me, I hand them over for photocopying. Sister Madeleine is very impressed, she thought we would never get in after the recent events. Had he known we were to do union training, I know we wouldn't have got in. Sister Madeleine is keen that we do the trade union training. She knows the young leaders are very keen on organising but fears that, without proper training, there will be more conflict in camp. She encourages us to deal with it delicately, and asks to come to the sessions so she can then support them when we have left.

Karenni Refugee Camp 1 is about 20 miles away but takes over an hour in a 4x4 truck. As we cross a river in the truck, Sister Rachel explains why all the trucks are now four doors. In the rainy season last year, one of the trucks overturned in the flooded river and two people were trapped in the back of the two door truck. They were rescued by local villagers, but the policy now was that only four door trucks could cross the river. The journey to camp is particularly arduous as there is no road for most of the journey, just jungle dirt track- particularly bad for the back. Sister Madeleine takes us to the hut where we are to do the training. As I enter there is a huge banner hung across the wall welcoming us all to Karenni Teacher Union (KTU) training - I hope the camp commander doesn't call in! Trade unions are not banned in camp, as the UNHCR has overall control, but the Thai authorities are not that enthusiastic, to say the least. Al Khuone is waiting to greet us. We have met a few times in Mae Hong Son. He is the General Secretary of the KTU. A young man, about 30 years old, with a wife and two young children in camp. He is very bright and wants to learn. Shortly after, the teachers begin to arrive, one from each school in the camp. Thankfully, Anne and I have done this in Mae La Refugee Camp and so are well prepared for the 30 delegates.

Training is active, with participants willingly joining in. This is not always the case, especially with refugees. But I think the recent shooting in camp has focused hearts and minds. One major talking point is about repatriation. About half the 20,000 camp residents have applied to leave under a UN scheme to resettle the refugees in the USA, Canada and Australia. They are particularly interested in their rights if/when they arrive in a foreign country. Most are rural people who have farmed the land for many years and know nothing of the West. Many are very intelligent but have not had access to education after primary school. They fear exploitation and poor pay when they arrive. We go through all these issues in detail and explain how important it is to know their rights and get organised.

After training Al Khoune walks me through the camp. We pause at the spot where the young demonstrator was shot dead just a few weeks ago. Al Khoune explains how the soldiers opened fire on a large group of students who were marching towards the Thai authority offices. In dispersing the students with live fire, one was killed. After realising what they had done, the Thai soldiers backed off and left camp. That's when the Thai offices were ransacked. I asked if anyone had been charged with murder. AK didn't know. He said compensation had been paid to the family of the student, as required by Thai law. I explained that this was just a local custom and not international law. They were frightened to ask as they were only refugees. I explained that refugees have rights, just like all human beings have rights.

Back in Mae Hong Son we wanted to go swimming and asked the sisters for a hotel/resort recommendation. The sisters were happy to oblige but cautioned against one in particular. Sister Madeline also liked to swim and had rang a particular hotel asking if non-residents could use the pool. They were told they would be very welcome but a small charge would apply. Delighted, they drove to the hotel and asked at reception for access to the swimming pool, telling them they had rang earlier. The receptionist replied that she was so sorry but the pool was closed for maintenance and maybe they should try again in a few days time. Disappointed, the sisters walked back to their car. Looking into the grounds of the hotel they could see the pool with guests sunbathing and swimming. Back at reception they enquired again about the pool. The reply was different this time.

'Sorry, the pool is only open for residents.' Confused and not wanting to cause a scene, they left. On the way home, after some thought on the matter, Sister Madeline realised what had happened. The sisters have American accents. On the phone, the hotel would have thought they were American tourists but when they turned up, the receptionist saw Asian faces and refused to let them in! They had encountered this racism on several occasions, they told us.

Mae Hong Son was also where we met our dear friend Dave, a retired social worker from England. He lived in Mae Hong Son and was trying to set up a business as a tourist guide to supplement his small pension. We met him in the Salween restaurant owned by Nang, a Burmese Shan lady. Dave would keep an eye on Patrick and Declan when Anne and I went into the refugee camp, teaching them to play cribbage and watching the cricket on the TV with them. One day he asked if they would like to come for a tour of the area, which would include a visit to the Long Neck Village of Ban Nai Soi. Long Neck women are well known for wearing neck rings, brass coils that are placed around the neck, appearing to lengthen it. The boys were keen and went with Dave. Unfortunately, while trying to cross a river, the car got stuck. They all had to jump out and wade to the river bank. Some locals came across their predicament and thankfully helped them out by bringing one of the local working elephants to tow the car out of the river. The boys took great pleasure in retelling the story to anyone who wanted to listen, much to Dave's embarrassment.

On returning to the UK I received an email from Sister Madeline updating me on the training. The Karenni Teachers Union had gone on strike, demanding a pay rise! She was pleased because they had gone about it the way I had discussed. The strike only lasted one day but the teachers had gained a small pay rise. I was really pleased for them.

Gallery

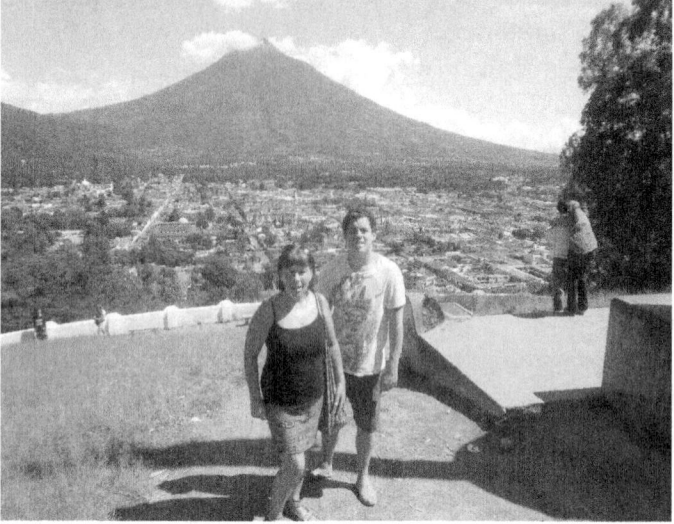

Anne and Patrick in Guatemala

Anne in the bottom of the boat on the Salween river

Anne with Winn Maung on election day 2015

Anne, Edna and Arnold after voting in 2015

Anne, Tony and Declan at JSMK

Archbishop Romero's Chapel

Crossing the Yusana River by raft

Declan at a clinic in Pathein

Declan in Moulmein

Declan with staff at Yardanar Show Hotel

FTUK Daniel, Lay Say, Paw Gay, and Htoo Lwee

Fr Henry, Fr Gregory at Yegyi

Karen children in the jungle

Lay Bu Der school children

Lay Bu Der village school

Lay Say and Paw Gay

Lay Say's father and family

Little Uncle

Monks protesting

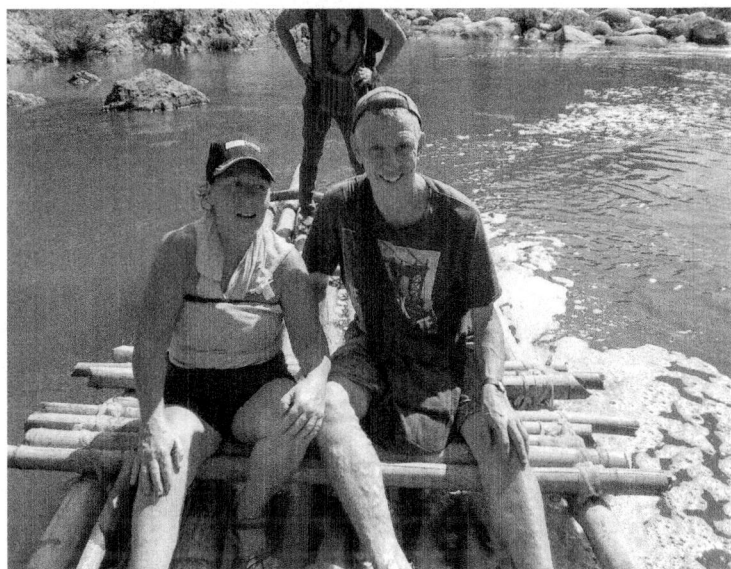

On the raft over the Yusana river

Paw Gay, Anne, and Declan

Propaganda poster in Burma

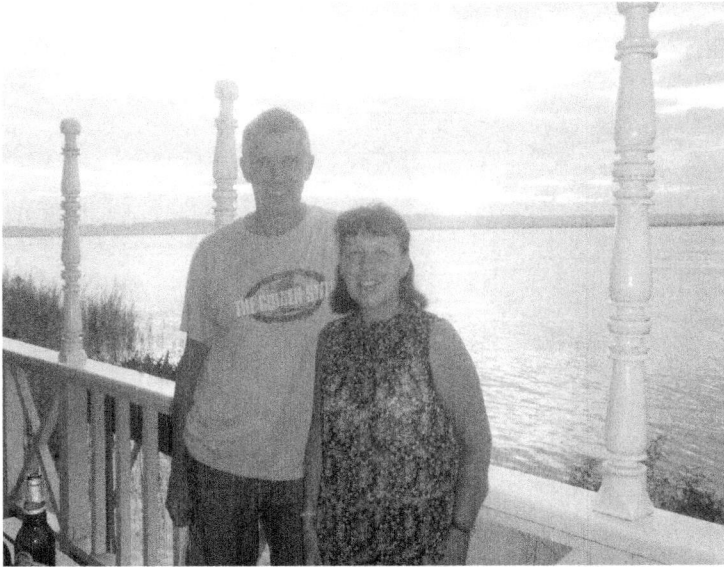

Sunset of the Irrawady River

Tony and Anne with Htoo Lwee and Kyaw Pwa

Tony at JSMK 2016

Truck after falling off the mountain road

Tony and Anne at JSMK

Tony outside NLD office election day 2015

Yusana River and Day Bu Noh in the valley

Water delivery in Burma

Declan at Fr Gregory's school 2004

Garbage tip workers in Mae Sot

Maung Maung Tinn

Meeting Aung San Suu Kyi   22 December 2011

Patrick and Declan at the garbage tip

Patrick, Tony, Declan and Anne in a refugee camp

Sarah, Patrick and Declan in Mae Sot

Ywa Hay, Tony and Dot Lay Mu

Chapter 11.

The Irrawaddy Delta, 2009.

July 2009, and in Mae Sot new hotels and guest houses pop up to meet the demands of a growing population. Mae Sot covers a large area, with huge sugar cane fields surrounding it and new factories springing up along the road to Myawaddy, the Burmese town across the border river Moei. A friend of the family, Lee, a trainee Catholic priest, joins us this year. He is keen to learn more about the world of the underprivileged. There are few better places than Mae Sot once you scratch beneath the surface.

At the DK Hotel there is no one manning reception, so Mya, our friend the head cleaner, greets us. No broken arm this year, but with a mop in one hand, room keys in the other and wellies on her feet, she offers a big welcoming smile and shows us to our rooms upstairs. After dropping off our bags, Lee is keen to explore Mae Sot. We meet up with Anne and Declan, and Declan's friend Philip. They all arrived in Thailand a few weeks earlier and had been into Mae Khon Ka Refugee Camp. Catching up on their adventures, we head for the Night Market for something to eat. Lee is surprised to see the open air restaurants surrounded by corrugated shanty dwellings, with families coming in and out and children playing in the street. I hardly notice, as I am so used to it, but Lee finds it off-putting. With swine flu in the headlines in the UK, Lee thinks he should wash his hands and heads to the communal toilets in the market. I let him go alone and await his response when he returns. The hole in the ground, and the lack of any running water, seems to put him off from eating here! I reassure him that we will only order food that has been cooked in very high temperature oil that will kill all the bacteria, and that we have eaten here lots of times without any bad outcome.

Sterilised by alcohol, we wake the next morning without any ill effects from the food. Lee is pleasantly surprised and keen to eat breakfast in the town. Canadian Dave's is always a good bet; serving both Thai and Western food, it satisfies everyone. Dave is a native of Canada and married to Choo, a local Thai lady. They have a young daughter, Grace. Dave is the oracle of Mae Sot for visiting Westerners. He knows everything that is happening but only reveals it to those who he knows well. He has had his cafe in Mae Sot since 2000 and is now very well established, with an array of delicious foods on offer. Patrick and Declan used this place frequently over the years, with Dave and Choo keeping an eye on them for Anne and I.

After breakfast we head on bicycles to Mae Pa and FTUK's offices. Dot Lay Mu greets us with the news that he has been elected as Assistant General Secretary of the Karen National Union (KNU) - a very prestigious position indeed - second in the Karen government, which sits in exile in this border town.

Paw Gay says a young man wants to see us. He is working in the office and says he remembers us from a few years ago. A small young Karen man arrives some time later and greets us as long lost friends. I don't remember him, but 'memory lady' Anne says she knows him from Fr Gregory's School, in Mae Sot. Paul Poe had grown into a young man since we last saw him in 2004. He remembers our family. He says we gave him his first pair of football boots when we visited his school. He wants to introduce us to a Catholic priest who has just started working in Mae Pa, saying we will really like him. So off we go on our bicycles to another part of Mae Pa. We enter the compound of a large house, take our shoes off and go inside with Paul Poe. The house is quite empty apart from a few chairs and a table. Paul Poe goes upstairs and a few moments later, he comes back down with a man about fifty years old. He looks familiar but I'm not so sure. He introduces himself as Father

Justin and then it all clicks. This is Father Justin, friend of Father Gregory.

We had met him briefly in 2004 when he was staying with Father Gregory. He laughs out loud when he remembers us and his laugh gives him away for certain. I remember him laughing all the time when we last met him. He calls upstairs and two more priests come down. One is Father Henry, who is visiting from Burma. We are planning to visit Rangoon in a few weeks so Henry gives us his number and asks us to call him when we get there. He will show us round, saying we need to be careful. 'The authorities will be watching you - they watch all foreign visitors!'

FTUK training.

Anne and I are invited to Mae La Refugee Camp to do some trade union training with FTUK. 28 people are waiting for us. We are a little late as the roadblocks held us up more than usual, so miss out signing in at security to save some time, and take a shortcut through the barbed wire fence. We shouldn't do this because if we are caught it will be big trouble for Paw Gay, but she seems relaxed about it.

The training starts with introductions, as usual, but today it's more complicated, as we have some delegates who speak only Burmese, and some only Karen, so we have to have a three way translation. Questions are an important part of the training. The Burmese will often sit silently and never join in debate - for some it's because they are traumatised, for others it's just because they've never been asked their opinion.

Most questions are about what the UK and other Western governments are doing about the situation in Burma. Many of these people have recently escaped persecution, they have lost family and friends. They want answers as to why the world does little or nothing. It's very difficult to answer, but I try. Explaining some of the other horrific situations in the world such as Iraq, Afghanistan and Palestine, I try to explain that they shouldn't wait for our help, but need to get organized, for example, in trade unions, and make a difference themselves. Then we go on to discuss how international trade unions can help them with their fight for justice.

Getting survivors to discuss the issues is a real balancing act. It can motivate some and traumatise others. Anne has an important role to play, as she is trained as a mental health nurse.

The afternoon session is about health needs in Karen State and the refugee camps. Anne knows that all-day discussions are not helpful, so she starts her session by playing some games - musical chairs is a favourite. It's great to see former soldiers running around chairs and fighting over who will miss out. They are so competitive - especially the women.

Anne's theme on physical health is soap. She does a presentation on the benefits of handwashing with soap. Everyone is trained and practices hand washing. At first they see no point but Anne has her ultraviolet light and can show them if they have cleaned their hands properly. Convinced about the benefits of handwashing with soap, and armed with the knowledge they have gained, they leave for the day with a plan to request small bars of soap from the refugee camp authorities.

After a successful day in camp we meet back up with Philip, who is heading back to the UK the next day. He has been into several refugee camps over the past few weeks and is completely washed out now. He hardly speaks - clearly showing the effects of meeting so many people, who will have a long lasting and profound effect on him. Philip knows he is going back to a comfortable life, while leaving these friends behind. They have no way of escaping. Seeing it on TV you can switch it off, but living and eating with them is different. Everyone should spend a week or so walking in the shoes of a refugee. The people of Burma have touched his heart and won't let go, and Philip knows it.

Umpiem Refugee Camp.

After Philip departs we head to Umpiem Refugee Camp, about 4 hours by truck along the border road. Dot Lay Mu is coming with us, so he picks us up at our hotel. He stays locked in the truck and sends his driver to tell us he is waiting. As we climb into the truck he apologises for not coming in but is very conscious of his safety since the gunman threatened his life recently. He says there were two men sitting outside the hotel who looked suspicious and he wasn't taking any chances!

Umpiem is very close to the Burmese border and high up in the mountains. On the journey, Dot Lay Mu tells us about the atrocities committed by the SPDC inside Karen State. Land is confiscated without compensation, children are taken as soldiers, forced labour is used to build army camps and entire villages are relocated to internment camps. That's why they flee across the border in the hope of a place of safety. We stay overnight outside of the refugee camp in a very remote village. Declan asks where we will be sleeping. We are shown to a room in a large teak house, with mats on the floor to sleep on. The boys are put off a little, but I say it's just like camping. It's dark and hot and we have no food, so we decide to walk to the centre of the village to see if there is a restaurant or bar. We only have one torch between us so it's tricky, and we must all stay close together. After about 30 minutes searching around the village in the dark, we conclude there is no restaurant or bar and find a shop instead. We buy some Mama noodles, crisps and coke, then head back to our house. After feasting on our noodles we settle down for bed. It's only 8pm but without electricity, there is nothing much to do, and we know we'll be up just before dawn when the local chicken alarm clocks go off.

Next morning, our driver, Big, brings us some boiled eggs for breakfast, but not before we have used the bucket shower in the bathroom. Anne and I have seen it many times, but the boys weren't so sure. Declan goes first; using a plastic pan, he scoops a pan full of cold water from the water barrel and throws water all over himself. I throw him some soap but he's not keen to stay in the shower. It's cold water and quite cool air temperature as we are high in the mountains. Well, at least it saves on electricity, and I contemplate getting one for home!

Two hours later we are all in camp, and the training with the trade unions follows the pattern of the previous day in Mae La. One man tells his story of escaping from Rangoon, where ethnic Karen are persecuted. He tells me of the time he went back to Burma hoping to visit his family. On the way he was arrested by the SPDC, put in chains and forced to work in a chain-gang. After a few weeks he was unchained and told to escape when it got dark. Obviously he feared it was a trap, assuming they would shoot him as he ran away. As dark approached he became more terrified. He and two others made their move shortly after dark. Fearing their imminent death, they prayed hard and set off when the guards weren't looking. They managed to get some distance before they heard the guards calling after them. In absolute panic, the three of them made their way through the jungle, not stopping or looking back. They ran all night and the next day came across a Karen village. They were lucky; the villagers fed them and let them rest, before showing them the way to the border and back to the refugee camp. He was so lucky to escape a second time. His wife and two children remained trapped in Rangoon. He had sent word for them to escape to Umpiem, but they had not arrived yet.

Dot Lay Mu joined us for the last part of the training after he had finished his meetings. Anne asked him to lead some singing as she knew he was an accomplished musician. Dot Lay Mu didn't let us down. He led the group in singing a traditional Karen resistance song about Ba Oo Gyi, the first Karen National Union leader. It was great to hear them belt out their song and humbling to know they were all soldiers, of a sort, in a sixty year war.

Mae Sot.

Every day had something new in Mae Sot in 2009. Anne visited a special needs school with 20 pupils - a most amazing school for Thailand, especially in a refugee community. Special needs children are usually bottom of the pile and don't go to school, hidden away in the homes of their parents. So this is a massive leap forward. Anne is so pleased, she has been campaigning for the rights of special needs children all her life, having had a special needs brother who sadly only lived to the age of eleven. Anne, being his older sister, cared for him at home when her parents were tired and needed respite. A 68 year old lady from the UK is running the school with the help of 4 Burmese girls.

Maung Maung Tinn takes us to the garbage tip the next day. We've all been before and are not keen to go, but Lee would like to see for himself what it is like. Once again, we were up to our ankles in sh*t in no time. Lee sees the acrid black water running off the tip and asks, 'Is this where Cola is made?' What's amazing, is that we discover that the school next to the tip is partially funded by The Body Shop Foundation. I wonder, how many of those beautiful fragrant smells would be required to counter the offensive stench in the school next to the tip?

Rangoon and the Irrawaddy Delta.

Getting up early in Bangkok, Anne, Declan and I head for the Burmese embassy to try to get tourist visas. Fr Henry has said he will meet us in Rangoon and take us to the Irrawaddy Delta if we visit. So we are on a mission, as we've wanted to see rural Burma, which we have heard so much about, for so long, and the possibility of visiting Fr Gregory is an added bonus. The room is packed when we arrive, with lots of people scribbling on forms and everyone looking for advice. The Burmese way is complicated and not easy to follow. One person explains how we can get a same-day visa - of course, it will cost more money, but as we are short of time we decide to pay extra. We hand in our forms and are told to come back at 3pm. The embassy is close to the offices of FTUB, so we head there to wait and catch up with some old friends. Declan goes on the internet and does a search on our family, as he thinks that's what will be happening at the embassy. He instantly comes up with a photo of me with the FTUK and a few articles on my work with FTUB! 'Oh dear', I think and ask Ronnie, assistant secretary of FTUB, what he thinks.

He just laughs and says, 'Wait and see.' I am convinced I will be refused a visa but he says, 'They often give visas to people like you. Their spies will follow you and then pick up anyone you meet with. If you get a visa, be careful who you meet, as you could cause them a lot of trouble.'

Nervously, we return to the embassy. There is a long queue, which we join. Twenty minutes later we arrive at the front and hand over our receipt. The official smiles and goes out the back. Moments later he returns, still smiling, with our visas - no problems. We go outside and give Ronnie a call. He laughs and says he knows many of the officials in the embassy who are very supportive of trade unions, but reminds us to be careful when meeting local people in Rangoon.

Next day, we fly into Rangoon. Looking out of the window of the aeroplane, all we can see are green paddy fields and hundreds of Budhhist stupas, seemingly in every field. There is little or no built environment. Agriculture abounds even close to the capital city. The airport has changed since we were last here in 2006. The new airport is like any other airport in the world, unlike the dilapidated buildings of the previous one. We all sail through security without any problem. There is a queue for normal taxis which we head for, ignoring the many unofficial touts who harrass everyone. We ask for Guest Care Hotel as it's been recommended by a friend in Mae Sot. Thankfully the taxi driver knows the hotel and, of course, speaks good English - many Burmese speak some English, a consequence of colonial days. It's a family run hotel, so no money towards the regime.

After checking in, we go out to find a sim card for our mobile phone so we can ring Fr Henry and tell him we have arrived. The hotel is close to Shwedagon (the famous Buddhist temple) and Coffee Circle (the only real coffee shop in town). We're told that there is a phone shop in the nearby shopping centre so, avoiding the huge gaps in the footpath, we set off in the general direction. The paths are high above the road - at least two feet - to cope with the monsoon rain, but this presents a problem for pedestrians stepping on and off the curb. Being young and fit we can manage this but anyone with a disability couldn't walk these streets. The phone shop is hidden away in the shopping centre - there is little demand for them, as few people can afford mobile phones. Thankfully the guy in the shop speaks English and can sell us an appropriate sim card. Calling Fr Henry, he asks us to meet him at St Mary's Cathedral the next day.

In the evening we head down town and into Chinatown, as recommended by a friend. The tea shops are filthy, they just throw the rubbish in the street and no-one seems to pick any of it up. The locals are very friendly and offer us beer and show us a menu. Anne spots a huge rat running along the road gutter and questions whether we should be eating here. But not seeing any option which is cleaner, we decide to get some deep fried chicken and vegetables, hoping it will sterilise all the germs.

After a good night's sleep we are greeted by three maids at the hotel. They are keen to talk to us privately. One tells us she was involved in the 1988 uprising. She left to work in Malaysia after the demonstrations were violently stopped. After four years she felt it safe to return. She asks to come into our room and closes the door behind her. Very quietly, she whispers that she was once a member of the National League for Democracy (NLD), asking us to tell no one, not even the other maids. She pulls out an old picture of herself and a group of others with ASSK, long before ASSK was put under house arrest. She says she is very frightened that the authorities will put her in prison if they find out she used to be an active member of the NLD.

With this in our thoughts, our plan is to find University Avenue, the home of ASSK, where she is under house arrest. The map we have shows us it is not too far to walk. We pass through a very wealthy district of the city; large detached villas with steel gates and razor wire on high walls to keep everyone out- a big contrast from Chinatown last night. After a mile or so we arrive at University Avenue. It is a few miles long, but we remember it from our last visit. We checked the house numbers and set off towards 54 University Avenue, the home of ASSK. Declan has the video camera on as he wants to get some footage of the house and the soldiers guarding it. We spot the red and white barbed wire clad barriers blocking the road in the distance.

Cars aren't allowed but we should be able to walk past. Suddenly a young man comes running up to us, indicating that Declan should stop filming. Then he turns and shouts something to the roadblock. A policeman comes running from out of the roadblock. We thought the young man was trying to help us but now guess he is the secret police. Within seconds we are surrounded by five or six men in white shirts and green longyis. It's clear they want to see what we have filmed, but none of them speak English. I take the camera, which is still filming, off Declan. I show the police that we are just filming the lake, and are tourists. They become very aggressive and try to take the camera off me. I hang onto it and say they are not getting it. After a standoff for a few minutes, which feels like hours, I show them I am erasing the footage that Declan took. They seem to understand and step back while I press some buttons on the camera. Anne is very anxious, as we all were, so we start walking away, saying we are just tourists looking for the pagoda. We sense they are not happy but off we go with a few of them tailing us. Increasing our pace to close to running, we put as much space between them and us as possible. Ten minutes later or so, we seem to have lost them, and head into a tea shop for a rest. After recovering our composure I show Declan what I did during the encounter. Instead of pressing erase when they surrounded us, I pressed record and got the confrontation on video! Anne says we should erase it in case they arrest us later at the hotel. But I want to keep it and show it to some friends to find out what the police were saying to us. The only real freedom is freedom from fear, are the words I keep repeating in my head. If we had been Burmese we would have been arrested, for sure, and goodness knows what would have become of us.

Later in our trip I showed the footage to a Burmese friend, who was fascinated to see it. He explained that the police were shouting, 'Get someone who can speak English.' He said it looked like they believed that we were just tourists making a video of our holidays, but they were on high alert as the American Yettaw had just been released. He had swam across the lake and gained access to ASSK's home without the authorities knowing.

After a restless night's sleep we decide to explore more of the city, and to visit the Martyrs Mausoleum, where General Aung San, the father of ASSK, is buried. As we walked past Shwedagon we noticed an absence of military personnel or trucks of police, unlike in 2006, when their presence was overwhelming. We were told later that, since the generals had moved the capital to Naypyitaw in the north, the number of police and soldiers had declined rapidly. As we arrive at the mausoleum, we spot a large truck of soldiers entering a police/army compound, reminding us they are still here. We approach the gates of the Mausoleum and ask if we can go in. 'No!' is the terse reply. 'No visitors.'

As we walk away we feel the presence of someone behind us. A plain-clothes policeman is following us. They give themselves away by the white shirt and green longyi they all seem to wear, just like yesterday on University Avenue. He follows a few paces behind as we head back into town. Frustrated by this guy, I stop, turn around and ask what he is doing. His English is poor but he knows I am unhappy with him. Setting off on our way again, he continues to follow. After ten minutes or so I'm sick of it and turn around again. This time Declan comes with me. Like many Burmese, he is quite small and I tower over him. I get very close and tell him we don't need his company. Declan also gets close. I'm not sure we should be doing this but our size seems to intimidate him and he backs off.

We turn and hurriedly walk into a busy market to try and lose him. Looking back he seems to have gone, but maybe he has just been replaced by another. Spotting a taxi, we jump into it, not waiting to haggle over the price of the fare, and ask to go to the shopping centre (I'd read in spy thrillers never to go back to where you're staying!). In the shopping centre my stomach began to churn; we had only been here two days, and had had two confrontations with the authorities already. Big brother was indeed watching us, like Ronnie had said they would.

In the evening we walk to a tea shop near St Mary's Cathedral to meet Fr Henry. Fr Gregory is with him when we turn up. It was great to see him in his own country but something seems wrong. He is very anxious. He knew it was dangerous for us in Rangoon but it turned out he wasn't so much anxious for us, but for himself. He didn't like Rangoon and felt the oppression whenever he was there. The meeting was short, but he told us he was leaving for his village in the Irrawaddy Delta tomorrow, and it would be great if we could join him. He would pick us up at 2pm from our hotel, and off he went. This was very strange, as in Thailand he was Gregory the gregarious, and would laugh and joke with us. It was clear that we needed to use our freedom to promote his freedom.

I decide to push our luck one more time. I really wanted a photograph of ASSK's home, where she is under house arrest, so next morning we hired a taxi to the corner of University Avenue. As we get out we can see the road block a few hundred yards ahead. We pop into a tea shop to discuss what we should do. Deciding not to film, we walk slowly towards the barricade. A hundred or so yards from the road block, plain clothes police come out from the tree lined street and indicate that the road is blocked and we should turn around. After what happened yesterday, Anne insists we turn around and go back to the hotel to await our transport to Pathein. Declan wants to continue further but I agree with Anne, and we turn around and head back to the hotel while we have the chance.

On time, Fathers Henry and Gregory turn up at our hotel in a small minivan. Our guest for the journey is Saint John Vianny-well, a large statue of him. Pope Benedict had announced that 2009-2010 was the 'Year for Priests', and St John Vianny is the patron saint of priests. Getting out of Rangoon is a struggle; the traffic is chaotic, but after an hour or so we clear the city limits and pass over the Irrawaddy river, on the longest bridge in this area. Below, on the river, I can see barges pulling loads of cargo and lots of old boats moored by the riverside. For miles around, all I can see are paddy fields. This was once the rice bowl of Asia, but Cyclone Nargis and poor investment by the government has meant rice yields are down, and now Burma can barely feed its own population. We pass through many small villages on the way, and Father Gregory points out one which was the birth place of Padoh Mahn Sha, the recently assassinated leader of the Karen people. The road is under constant repair and we can't believe what we see with our eyes. Women and children are sitting by the side of the road, breaking stones and filling in potholes by hand as buses and trucks go past at 30-40 miles per hour. This is so dangerous, I can't bear to look. Surely many of these people are killed or injured every year? But there are no statistics on road deaths or accidents, so who knows? Another example of the absolute disregard the government has for its people.

Father Gregory wants to take us to his village and school before we go to Pathein. It is a small diversion off the main road, so we take a fork at a major junction and turn up a dirt road. There are no road markings and few cars, but lots of bicycles and motorbikes. After about ten minutes we are driving through a large village and traffic is busy as the daily market is just finishing. Our driver swerves to avoid a dog running into the road and we collide with a motorbike. The van pulls up and Anne and I jump out to see if we can help. Two young girls are lying on the road by the motorbike. Before we get there the motorbike is scooped up and pushed into the nearby housing. One of the girls gets to her feet, but the other is not moving. Of course, they don't have crash helmets. A man picks the girl up from the floor and carries her away. Within seconds, it's as if the accident had never happened.

Anne follows the man carrying the girl, to see if she can help. By now Father Gregory has caught up with me and looks worried. He has spoken to the locals and they have cleared the crash scene as they don't want the police involved. The girl riding the motorbike is only 14 and too young to ride. The family will be in trouble. He asks where Anne is, and looks concerned, before going to find her. Anne is in a house with the girl and chaos abounds. All the girl's family have arrived. Anne asks to help, as it is clear the girl is seriously injured. One of the crowd is supposed to be the village medic and takes charge in a limited way. He opens the girl's mouth and scoops out five or six shattered teeth. The girl is unconscious and needs a doctor. With the help of Gregory translating, Anne takes over. She suspects a broken jaw and possible head fractures. Gregory is looking very worried as Anne explains she needs to go to hospital. The villagers suggest they take her to Rangoon on the back of a motorbike! There is no ambulance in the village. One would have to come from Pathein or Rangoon to collect her.

Anne speaks to Fr Gregory and explains the girl could die if she doesn't get treatment soon. She is already going into shock. Fr Gregory doesn't know what to do. Anne asks what equipment they have in the village. An intravenous line is available, so Anne gets it and puts her on a drip. She then suggests that we use our minivan to get her to the nearest hospital. Fr Gregory agrees and goes to get the van. By now the father, mother and siblings of the girl are very anxious. They are a Muslim family and all want to go with her to the hospital but the van only has six seats. Gregory, Declan and I can't fit in. Anne carefully supervises her transfer into our van with six family members squashing in. Ironically, Saint John Vianny is there to accompany them on their journey. Declan, Gregory and I wave them off, and then we are taken to one of the houses in the village and told to wait inside. It is a two hour journey to Pathein and Gregory has to try to arrange transport for us.

As darkness falls Gregory returns by torch light with the news that a taxi is on its way to collect us, but will be half an hour. The mosquitos are having a field day on Declan and I. It seems they are very attracted to the new blood. Gregory gets a large cheroot out to smoke. It has several benefits - calming Gregory and keeping the mosquitos at bay. After a while, Gregory explains why he is so anxious. This village and local area are off-bounds for foreigners. We shouldn't be here and if the police find us we will all be in trouble. This explains why the scene was cleaned up so quickly. The villagers didn't want anyone to be arrested or questioned by the police. We would have to stay hidden now, as the police had arrived while Anne was treating the patient. Thankfully they let Anne go to the hospital with the patient when it was explained she was a nurse and they saw she had put a line in to help her.

After what seemed like an eternity, a taxi arrived and we were quickly whisked out of the village and on our way to Pasthein. It was very dark now and, with no road lights, it was very dangerous. After dark every village has a barrier which is lifted after the vehicle is checked out and a small fee is paid. Eventually we arrived at Pathein and were dropped off at a guest house. It was pitch black and deserted. After a while a man came to show us to our room, but no sign of Anne. Gregory said he would go and find her, but we should wait at the guest house until he returned. Declan was very frightened and worried for his mother. I assured him she would be fine as Fr Henry was with her. About an hour later a knock at the door came and Gregory was there, inviting us to dinner. Anne was already at the restaurant and was fine. We both breathed a huge sigh of relief and hurried downstairs.

As Gregory had said, Anne was waiting for us at the restaurant and she explained that the girl was very poorly and she might not make it. The hospital was not really a hospital, just a building with beds in. She had been told she couldn't go in with her patient as she was a foreigner, but asked that she do the hand-over. Security stepped aside when Anne became insistent. She told us the doctors were very young and had little experience. The girl would have to go outside for an X-ray the next day as the hospital didn't have any X-ray facilities! She said she had done her best and all we could do now was pray. At least we had got her to hospital alive and we were all together now. Anne would visit her again tomorrow. Absolutely exhausted, we sleep fitfully that night not knowing if we have been involved in a fatal accident or not.

At 6am there is a knock at the door. Fr Gregory is already up and ready to collect us. He says he visited the girl in hospital and she is doing reasonably well. He has arranged to pay for her X-ray and other treatment, so we shouldn't worry. He takes us to St Peter's Cathedral for breakfast. After breakfast Gregory wants to take us to a few orphanages in the area. After Cyclone Nargis the Catholic church had set up many orphanages to help look after those who had lost their entire family. About 800 orphans are looked after in the Pathein area.

One particular orphan tells Declan his story via translation from Fr Gregory. His name is Richard and it is a story that Declan has never forgotten, one which motivates him to do more. Richard was about 11 years old, he wasn't sure of his birth date, and very small for his age, even by Burmese standards. He survived Cyclone Nargis by climbing a tree and clinging to it for three hours while the winds blew and the water level rose. The rest of his family drowned in the flooding. A very traumatised boy, but in the safety of a home now.

Another remarkable boy living in Pathein is Soloman. He is 17 years old and has no legs, yet he lives as normal a life as possible. We first met him playing football in the courtyard of St Peter's Cathedral with all the other boys. He runs on his hands and kicks with them also. He tackles and shouts just like the rest. A remarkably positive young man who is accepted as normal by his peers.

Anne is keen to check on her patient and returns to the hospital. Again she is not allowed in, but Anne doesn't take no for an answer and goes around the side of the hospital where there is little or no security, and walks in with a group of Burmese visitors. She remembers her route through the hospital corridors and finds the young lady. Her family are staying on the floor near her bed. The floors are filthy and the beds are very rickety, made from wood and bamboo. Thankfully, she is doing much better. She has a broken jaw and will need to see a dentist to check her teeth. Anne is so relieved. She can't stay long as she's not supposed to be there. So saying goodbye, she leaves the hospital while carefully avoiding the security guards, relieved that the girl will live.

Walking around Pathein, we see just how poor the people are. I had seen poverty in other areas of Burma but this was a step down again. People were literally in rags and housing was mostly slums. Even the street dogs were thin as there was so little waste food. Most houses don't even have running water, so it is delivered by traders walking the streets, pushing 45 gallon wooden barrels of water. People bring jugs out of their homes and fill them. The sewers run open by the side of the street and people throw their rubbish directly into the street. Rats run freely around the town. I see people hitting them with brushes, any dead ones being thrown in with the rubbish.

Father Gregory invites us to St Peter's Cathedral for our food. Having tried a local restaurant, and seeing the cleanliness of the streets, we think it is a good idea. The kitchen at the cathedral caters for the priests working there and at the nearby churches, along with a few retired priests. We are so glad we can have some good clean food but feel so sorry for the rest of the community. The cathedral has a small health clinic in its grounds and a queue has formed to see the doctor as we arrive. It is run by two doctors and three nurses. We can see patients being examined in rooms with little or no privacy, but they are just so glad they can see a doctor for free. Small surgical operations are also carried out but, with little evidence of good cleanliness, I hope I don't need an operation. The clinic treats lots of patients with cholera, TB and malaria. Now we see just how vulnerable we are, as this is the best healthcare around. We are five hours from an international hospital and selfishly start to think, maybe we are a little too far away!

At the riverside, the situation is no better. Boys age ten are unloading stones from a boat by hand. They walk back and forth along a wooden gangplank with arms full of stones, throwing them into a waiting truck. It will take hours to empty this huge cargo. In the West it would take a matter of minutes. Houses don't have electricity and people cook on open fires. I had seen this in the jungle and refugee camps but never in a town before. It seems like this place is hundreds of years behind the Western world. The lack of investment and modernity is staggering. And yet we see high tech military planes flying overhead and are told that there is a sophisticated naval base close by. No expense is spared on the military while the people live in rags and slums. A soldier is paid more than a headteacher.

Following Cyclone Nargis, the social services side of the cathedral, headed up by Fr Henry, are running a Disaster Emergency Planning seminar. A Catholic priest from India who is experienced in this is running the course. He explains that people need to prepare by having early warning systems in place, such as listening to the radio for weather warnings, securing vital documents, knowing where vulnerable people live, and having an escape route planned. Good advice, but difficult to implement in such remote and poor areas. He told me that a similar size cyclone to Nargis had hit the USA and killed only 4 people, compared to the 300,000 in Burma. I also chatted to him about security, as a government spy had been following us everywhere and sleeping outside our guest house. He advises us to be careful, as foreigners can be followed for months without interference. The authorities are hoping they will lead them to Burmese people involved in civil rights activities. He also warns us to be careful when using email, as it was monitored and used to check on foreigners and who they were contacting. Big brother once again at large here.

It was with sadness that we had to leave Pathein. The people see so few visitors that they genuinely welcome you. They need all the help they can get to uplift their health and welfare systems, but it will take many years. The rickety bus makes its way slowly along the broken road to Rangoon.

Back at the Guest Care Hotel the chambermaid asks if we would like to visit her home. This is such an honour, so we gladly accept it. She says it must all be done secretly, not even telling the other chambermaids. So we arrange to meet at the corner of the street after she finishes work. As we approach her, she quickly tells us to walk to the bus stop. She will follow and we should get on the same bus as her but not speak to her or stand near her. The streets are packed with buses and people but I manage to keep a close eye on her as she gets on her bus. Squashed at the back, I am much taller than most of the other passengers, so I can see her when she gets off. Such secrecy is a little intimidating but we now understand why she's doing this. The spies will let us get on with our visit and then follow it up with a knock on her door in the night. She can't take the risk.

After getting off the bus we follow her from a distance and spot her entering a tenement building. A few minutes later we climb the narrow unlit stairs of the tenement block. Our friend is waiting on one of the landings. We wait a few minutes to see if we have been followed and then she invites us into her flat. Inside I am so shocked - it is just two concrete rooms. One a bedroom, the other a kitchen/living area. There is no furniture, just a small bed in the corner and a few possessions scattered around the living room. Over tea we start to chat. She would like to offer us food but has nothing in. Now I know why she is so thin and I am embarrassed I've not brought any food with me. I ask if she has eaten tonight.

'Not yet' she replies 'I'll get something from the street stall later.' Like many in Asia, she has no cooking facilities and relies on street stalls for her food. It is unbelievable how little she has, in stark contrast to how much courage she has, inviting us to visit. We chat and she tells us she is not married and lives alone. Her parents died some years ago but she has lots of friends in the neighbourhood. After only a short while, she says we should leave. I think she is a little fearful a neighbour will tell the authorities of our visit. I offer her some money for her evening meal but she refuses it. She is just glad that she can share tea with us. She tells us which bus to get back to our hotel and says she'll see us tomorrow, but please don't tell anyone we've visited. Secretly, I leave some money for her, hoping she can buy a better meal tonight. I was so happy she wanted us to visit but so sad she has to endure this poverty. She is so brave to invite us here.

Burma is very draining on the body and soul. The people thirst for freedom and democracy but are crushed by the military machine. You can almost breathe in the oppression. It seems to fill your lungs and stays there like cancerous tobacco smoke. The rains are falling once again as we head for the airport. I find this country so hard to be in, but can't get enough of the people who are so inspiring. I won't ever forget this experience and know I will be back in Thailand and Burma next year.

Chapter 12.

A 'restless people'
and meeting the Pope, 2010.

I meet up with Declan and Anne in Bangkok this year. They have travelled ahead of me and have already been to Mae Sot and the refugee camps. We have our visas for Burma, so we fly straight into Rangoon to meet up with Fr Henry, who will take us back to Pathein.

Pathein and Karuna Social Services.

In the tropical monsoon rain the children of St Peter's Orphanage continue to play football. I watch from the shelter of the diocesan centre but can hardly see them because the rain is so heavy. Two memories are etched in my mind; firstly the team in black and white Newcastle United shirts, which I gave them. The shirts are from the memorial to Sir Bobby Robson, who died just over a year ago. Thousands of shirts were left at St James' Park, Newcastle upon Tyne, in his memory, which now lives on in Burma. The second is Solomon, a young man I met last year. He has no legs so he runs on his hands and 'kicks' the ball with them too. He holds his own in the very competitive game, but what future does he have? There is an oversupply of deformed and limbless children already on the streets of Pathein, the major town in the Irrawaddy Delta region of Burma. This area was devastated by Cyclone Nargis in 2008, and is only slowly starting to recover.

Father Henry is the project director of Karuna Social Services Pathein (KSSP). The situation in this area is chaotic.

The military dictatorship has plunged a country that used to be the 'rice bowl' of South-East Asia, into one of the most impoverished nations on Earth. Children from St Robert of Newminster and St Mary's schools in the North East of England have been fundraising to sponsor orphans. A donation of £125 will clothe, feed and educate a child for one year. More than 20 orphans have been sponsored in 2010. Father Henry says, 'The people of Burma have been oppressed psychologically for over 50 years. It is difficult for people in rich countries to understand our situation but please, you are welcome to share our experience.'

Declan is visiting for the second time. He recalls his first visit: 'I couldn't believe my eyes when I stepped off the bus in Pathein. I knew I had to turn back the clock 50 years when I arrived in Burma, but in Pathein you are another 50 years behind. Water is delivered to homes in huge wooden barrels which are pushed around the streets. Rats scurry in and out of the rubbish at the side of the road. Electricity is so infrequent it is almost non-existent. It was such a shock. How could people live like this? But the welcome we got when visiting St Peter's Cathedral was so warm and friendly. Everyone wanted to know why we had come to Pathein. 'Nobody ever visits us', they said.'

Most of the orphans lost both parents in Cyclone Nargis. Without the cathedral many would have to fend for themselves on the street. Healthcare is very limited. The clinic run by the cathedral had queues every day, providing free medical care and minor surgery. The staff are very enthusiastic but lack real training; many having only completed distance-learning courses. Anne tries to help where she can, explaining the importance of infection control, and especially of hand washing. A report from a prominent university some years ago stated, 'clean water, hand washing and mosquito nets would save more lives than any other measures in the third world.' Seeing the cases of malaria and diarrhea, I am inclined to believe it. HIV/AIDS was also reaching epidemic proportions but the government was denying its existence, consequently doing little or nothing about it.

Walking into a 'hospital', which is officially forbidden for foreigners, I see the dire conditions of Burma's official healthcare. The wards are just a series of rotten wooden beds, or rather, tables! There are few medicines and no doctors. Patients must arrange for a private doctor to visit them, with any X-rays having to be done privately, by visiting a clinic on the street. Any medicines prescribed have to be purchased at the local pharmacy. But the indomitable spirit of the Burmese continues. Joseph, one of the drivers at the cathedral sums up their positivity by telling us, 'No need for us to worry about anything - we have Jesus.'

As the rain eases, we take the opportunity to try to find Pathein prison. We have been told it is quite large, with a population of several thousand. No photography near the prison is sound advice from Fr Henry. Wandering in the general direction of the prison, we see children sitting on street corners, literally in rags. Young boys are unloading rocks from a boat on the river, trying to earn a few pennies for their family. These are Dickensian conditions - I'm expecting Fagin and Oliver to appear soon. But this is for real.

A bus pulls up, about 50 yards ahead of us, and I see a prison guard step off the bus with a huge rifle over his shoulder, followed by a group of about ten men in black and white striped prison overalls. I can't believe my eyes and hurry to get a closer look, trying to get my camera out of my bag at the same time. As I get closer I see why the men are all huddled together. They are shackled by the ankle and wrists to each other in a chain gang. Another guard jumps off the bus and I can see ordinary passengers sitting on the bus. They are transporting prisoners in shackles on public transport! As they are marched away towards the prison, I discreetly get a photo, but I'm too scared to get closer. Huge gates on a fort like building open as the prisoners approach and more armed guards come into view. Watchtowers stretch along the prison walls every 50 yards or so. Chained gangs of prisoners being marched through the streets, and no one is batting an eyelid. Anne shouts at me to put my camera away and come back, but I'm gobsmacked and just can't stop staring. I've never seen anything like it. It was just like the scenes in Les Miserables, but this is 2010!

'I hope my photograph comes out', I thought, as Anne grabs me and we head back into town.

Later that day we have dinner in a beer station near our guesthouse. The owner is very friendly and welcoming. We order Myanmar beer and look at the menu, which does have a few of the items translated into English. After ordering some food I head for the toilet, passing through the kitchen. 'Oh dear' I think - hygiene standards are not 5 stars, but we need to eat. Thankfully we have ordered food which will be deep fried in very hot oil. Standing at the urinal, I'm joined by a few furry friends. A couple of rats run along the pipe above my head, They stop and stare for a moment, to see who the new visitor is, and then continue on their way. I look around for hand-washing facilities, as Anne's training was fresh in my mind, but, alas, there were none to be had!

The food is surprisingly pleasant. Washing it down with the beer, we start to relax. The restaurant is filling up and people are chatting with each other. A guy of about forty enters with his friend. They both look strong and are well dressed. They notice the foreigners and decide to sit near us. In broken English, one of the men starts up a conversation. The Burmese are generally sociable and like to practice their English, so we encourage him with questions ourselves. One guy is particularly keen to talk, but his English is not good. After a few beers his tongue is looser but it is still very hard to understand him. A young man sitting nearby tries to help with translation. This infuriates the man, who shouts loudly at him in Burmese. The young man drops his head and looks away, clearly chastised. The man then turns to us and shouts, 'I'm the general around here.'

We are frightened now. The owner comes over and tries to pacify the general. He demands another beer and talks aggressively with his friend. The young translator quietly finishes his drink and leaves. The owner has lost her smile and now looks terrified. Other people start leaving and after a few minutes we are the only ones left with the general. 'I'm the boss around here. Where are you staying?' He asks. I think about telling lies, but only knowing the name of our guesthouse, I tell him, 'The Full Moon Hotel.' He asks the room number and this time I do tell him a lie. I'm now very frightened but try not to show it. He insists on buying us another drink and we dare not refuse. The owner brings the beer, then quickly retreats into the kitchen.

We are now experiencing real fear, the type of fear the ordinary Burmese live with every day. Trying to stay polite, we ask a few questions which he finds difficult to understand, but the beer is making him laugh and more relaxed. We change the subject to football and the tension eases. After what seems like an eternity, we finish our beers. We bid the general goodnight and dash across the road to our guest house. Declan is terrified and asks to stay in our room. Collecting the room keys, we quickly run up the stairs to our room. Safely inside, we lock the door and push the wardrobe up against it. It seems a futile gesture but it is the only thing we can do. We await the 'knock in the night' and being asked to come down to the police station for a few questions only to never return!

Sleep eventually comes but every creak or knock wakes me. I can't bear this, even though I know we haven't done anything illegal. But illegal or not, that doesn't matter. The general makes the rules and we must obey. Next morning we're up early, as none of us can sleep, and make our way to the cathedral. We creep past our spy, who sleeps comfortably in his rickshaw outside the guesthouse. He's been there every morning since we arrived and follows us wherever we go. We've surprised him this morning by getting up so early. At the cathedral we tell Fr Henry of our experience and he confides in us that they had had a visitor last night, asking who we were and what we were doing at the cathedral. Fr Henry told us not to worry too much.

'This happens all the time,' he says. He told them we're on a religious pilgrimage. They usually accept this as it is common for Buddhists to go on retreat to the Monastery. Feeling a little better, we enjoy breakfast with a few of the priests but are happy to be leaving today and heading back to Rangoon. We tell Henry we hope we haven't caused them any trouble.

'This is how it is for us. The authorities are always doing this. They rule by fear,' he says ('The only real freedom is freedom from fear', now we know the true meaning of this).

Back in Rangoon the rain still falls. The pollution is appalling, owing to the large numbers of cars and buses that are over 40 years old. Dilapidated diesel engines churn out black acrid smoke, filling the lungs of all who dare venture onto the streets. With few footpaths, and huge gaps in them, it is little wonder the locals are crammed into the buses. Another hazard is that the entrance/exit to the bus is in the middle of the road. The buses are from an era when Burma drove on the left side, but the generals, in their wish to cleanse the colonial past, ordered that they would drive on the right-hand side, thus endangering the safety of their citizens even further. In another spat at the ordinary citizen, motorbikes are banned from Rangoon. In this region of the world, the motorbike is the premier mode of transport of the poor and workers. The generals seem to delight in making it as hard as possible for them.

As the rain continues to fall, I decide to explore People's Park, a great expanse of parkland in the middle of the city, hopefully free of pollution. I'm thinking of Central Park, New York or Hyde Park, London and looking forward to relaxing in a cafe. It's easy to find, with each entrance having a concrete archway painted red and white. The soldier on either side of the archway is armed with a rifle, but they look friendly enough. As I approach the gate, the rifles come off both their shoulders and they move slowly to the centre of the arch. Speaking in Burmese, I don't understand a word of what the soldier says, but the message is clear - People's Park is not for ordinary people. My way is blocked and they indicate that I should turn around and look elsewhere to relax!

Taking shelter from the rain in a tea shop, I notice a young man selling his drugs to another. Yaba (an amphetamine manufactured on a massive scale in the north of Burma) is extremely cheap here and clearly readily available. It brings untold misery but relieves the boredom and emptiness of living in such a poverty-ridden city. A rat scurries off between the small plastic chairs to distract me. I order some sweet tea. A boy, age about eight, is serving, while an older man barks instructions to him. A dirty cloth 'cleans' my table and cakes are offered from the basket he holds. The others in the tea shop throw rubbish on the floor and spit the blood red betel nut spittal into a waste bin. I'm not sure this is good for my health, and wonder if National Socialism is as progressive as the regimes advertises on the huge billboards which are on every major road junction. Leaving the tea shop, I think I might need to check on my medical insurance.

Arnold and Edna.

Next morning, I set off looking for Arnold and Edna's home in an area of town known as Sanchaung. Arnold is the cousin of my friend Colleen, in Newcastle. He is in his seventies and his wife, Edna, is older, early eighties, I think. Colleen has told me they would love to meet up with us. Anne and I have been given a street name but there are few street signs. After asking around in some shops and the barbers, we think we've found the right street. The buildings are tall, narrow tenements, about 8 stories high. We look in one building and see the concrete steps rising up to each floor. It's the middle of the day but the staircase is dark with no lighting. We step outside into the daylight and look up. Each flat has a small balcony but no one is sitting at them. It's too hot, noisy and polluted. I know Arnold and Edna both speak perfect English and so decide to shout at the top of my voice to see if anyone responds.

'Arnold,' I shout, and wait for a response from a balcony. Nothing happens - perhaps they can't hear me above the din of the markets. I ask again in the barber shop if they know of Arnold and Edna. A neighbour says he thinks they live in this block, so I go out again and shout loudly.

After a few moments a man appears on a balcony and peers down at us.

I shout up, 'It is Anne and Tony - Colleen's friends.' He waves at us and gestures for us to come up. Climbing the steep stairs in the dark, we're not sure which floor to stop at. Out of breath, we stop for a rest at the door behind which we think they might live. All the doors are wood, with an outer full-height metal gate which is padlocked. A door opens and a man in a longyi and ironed shirt greets us. He asks us to wait a moment while he goes for the key to the outer metal gate. Opening it a few minutes later, he greets us with a handshake and welcomes us in. Arnold is smartly dressed in his clean pressed shirt. His wife Edna is at work but will be home shortly. Colleen had told us she was in her early eighties but still worked training nurses to supplement a small pension. Arnold keeps himself abreast of Burmese and world affairs by reading extensively, and he likes to go to the tea shops to see a few friends or read a newspaper.

Arnold reminded me of my father in looks, with high cheekbones and tough, light brown skin. He was the son of a Scotsman, who worked on the railways in Burma before the Second World War. When the Japanese invaded, Colleen, her brother Robert and the rest of the family escaped to northern Burma, and then into India and back to the UK by boat. Arnold stayed behind with his family in Sagaing in northern Burma. She missed her cousin so much but over the years has kept in touch with him from the UK. Colleen was in her teens when she left Burma and arrived in Sheffield, before moving on to

Newcastle, but she has never forgotten her childhood and her cousin. At Christmas 2011, it was my great pleasure to meet both Arnold and Colleen in Rangoon for a fantastic family reunion.

After a while a sprightly old lady arrives home. Tiny, but not frail, she knocked on the door and Arnold let her in - he always keeps the door locked. She was not out of breath as I expected from the steep climb, and immediately offered us orange juice and biscuits. Arnold wants to show us around the area. He puts his jacket on and we head off to the nearby shopping centre. Edna declines the offer to come with us.

'I'd like to rest.' she says. Passing through security at the entrance to the shopping mall, we have our bags inspected. Recently there have been a few small bomb explosions in shopping malls so security has been tightened. Arnold takes us to a doughnut shop, thinking it is what people from the West would like. It's very charming and full of young people but not quite where I would choose. But Arnold is so happy to entertain us. Colleen has told him lots about us and he wants to impress. It was fascinating, listening to Arnold tell us 50 years of Burmese history. He has lived through the Japanese bombing of Rangoon and Japanese rule, and has survived more than 50 years of dictatorship. He had told us a lot about the local political situation but he warned us not to talk about it outside - too many spies and too dangerous for him. He clearly feared being taken away and not seen again. Arnold was a great supporter of Aung San Suu Kyi, in the past often walking to her house to hear her speak and show his support for her.

Arnold had lots of relatives in Rangoon, who live in the Insein area of the city. He asked if we would come back tomorrow and he would take us to visit them. Our hotel was close by, so we agreed to call around the next day. Arnold was ready and waiting for us when we arrived. Edna had gone to work so she wouldn't be joining us. In the street, Arnold flags a taxi down and agrees a price to Insein a few miles away. The traffic is chaotic but we are soon out of the city centre and heading to the outskirts. I'm looking forward to hearing about the infamous Insein prison.

As we get closer to our destination Arnold points to the left and says, 'That way is Moscow.'

I'm not sure what he means but in the distance I can see a walled compound. I guessed it must be the prison. Arriving at his relative's house, he says we won't talk politics here. Before we go in, he says, 'The prison is known as Moscow - people don't dare even mention it's name.'

I'd seen a model of it at AAPP in Mae Sot and had talked to political prisoners who had spent years inside. And here I was, so close but everyone was too frightened to go near it or even talk about it. I felt the oppression tighten around me and was beginning to understand what it was like to live in fear ('The only real fear is freedom from fear' - the words of ASSK began to take real meaning again).

We had lunch at a local restaurant where the owner was Karen. Many Karen live in Insein and in 1948, the Karen started an armed rebellion in Rangoon and nearly toppled the government. After ferocious fighting the rebellion was put down by the Burmese army. If it had succeeded, the history of Burma may have been very different. The owner quietly told us she had relatives living in Mae La Refugee Camp but wasn't sure if they were still there, as she had heard that some were leaving. She said most people in Rangoon weren't aware of any refugee camps, as the government banned any news being put in the state controlled New Light of Myanmar newspaper, or on TV news. And no one talked about politics, especially the Karen ethnic minority.

Back at Arnold's we awaited Edna coming back from work. Arnold explains he would love us to stay at his house but he couldn't allow us, as the law states that visitors must stay at registered hotels or guest houses. It is still illegal for a visitor to stay at a friend's home, even today! Arnold tells us his own experiences of the Saffron Revolution in 2007. Monks were demonstrating on the streets nearby and he went out to give them apples. Remarkably, it was days after the demonstrations had been dispersed by soldiers that Arnold and Edna actually found out. There had been a news blackout in Rangoon - nothing on the TV or in the newspaper. He never saw any of the violence the soldiers inflicted on the monks. He told us of empty government buildings being used to house soldiers who had been shipped in from the remote regions and told that the government was under attack, and that law and order must be restored. The soldiers, knowing nothing different, followed orders and shot live rounds into the crowds! He leaves us with a quote from Abraham Lincoln: 'To sin by silence when they should protest makes cowards of men.' I know the people of Burma are not cowards, and reflect on the silent people Arnold is commenting on. And I feel guilty!

Archbishop Charles Bo (now Cardinal).

I first met Charles Bo in 2009 in Rangoon, at St Mary's Cathedral. Anne and I were visiting the cathedral - a beautiful, red-brick building with no glass in the window frames. They had been bombed out during the Second World War and the church couldn't afford to replace them. He was shooting basketballs in the car park and he stopped to say hello when he noticed us. We introduced ourselves and he asked if we played basketball. Keen to have a go, I threw a few balls into the ring. After a few minutes he asked if we would like a drink, so we joined him in an office for some cold orange juice. We chatted about what we were doing in Rangoon and he seemed very interested. We told him of our acquaintance with Fr Henry, who he knew very well, he said, being one of his fellow priests. We had thought he was one of the office staff up to that point. On leaving, we bumped into a few sisters who were very friendly and asked us about our visit. We told them it had been very fruitful as one of the priests had been so friendly. On describing him they told us he was not just one of the priests - he was

Archbishop Charles Bo, the most senior priest in Burma. This was to be one of many meetings with our new friend Charles.

The feast of St Augustine, August 29th 2010.

It was our last day in Rangoon; we were flying back to Bangkok in the evening so a leisurely day was planned. We looked on a street map and noticed a church about a mile and a half away, so after breakfast we set off walking. It was very hot and humid but thankfully there was no rain. After about 40 minutes we spotted the spire of the church. Getting closer, we could see the car park was packed, with crowds of people standing outside the church. We wondered if this was the usual attendance or if something special was going on. Passing through the crowds, we managed to find a standing place at the back of the church. Picking up a mass bulletin we noticed that it was the feast of St Augustine and we were in the parish church of St Augustine, Inya Road, Kamayut. So this was the reason for the large congregation, we thought. The notes of the first hymn came out from the organ and the procession of the altar servers and the clergy followed. The last member of the clergy was our friend, Archbishop Charles Bo. He smiled as he squeezed past us and went down the aisle.

As is custom, the Archbishop gave the sermon. He stood in the pulpit and began what was, for me, the most memorable sermon I have ever heard. It was a 'I have a dream' moment. St Augustine is known for his writings on being restless - 'our heart is restless until it rests in you'. Charles spoke to the packed congregation, but his message was for the generals of Burma and the upcoming elections. Speaking both in Burmese and English, he said:

'A people who can't vote freely will be restless.

A people who live in abject poverty will be restless.

A people who have no freedom to speak out will be restless.

A people who see no future will be restless.

A people who are repressed will be restless.

A people who are restless, can never be free.'

I still remember holding back from clapping. He knew, and I knew, that there would be spies in the congregation. He was taking a great risk. It was unheard of for anyone in a public position to speak out about such things.

After mass we managed to say hello to him as he drank tea with his congregation in the church hall. I was impressed with his ability to sit with his people and be their friend. A man of the people, speaking out on their behalf.

Amazingly, later that day we met him again. Declan, Anne and I were sitting in departures at Rangoon airport when Charles walked past and sat nearby. We all got up to say hello and he tells us he's off to a conference in Bangkok. I tell him how impressed I was with his sermon that morning and how brave he was. He confides in me that he was taking a big risk but smiles broadly, saying 'Perhaps I won't get back in when I return from Bangkok.' I wished him good luck as we headed for the plane, hoping he does get back to continue his work with the people.

Pope Benedict and Declan.

Before I set off for the 2010 trip, I had a phone call from CAFOD in London. Pope Benedict was to visit the UK in September and they would like to invite Declan to speak at an event in Hyde Park, London, which the Pope would be attending. Declan was in Burma with his mother but I would be meeting up with them in Bangkok very soon, and I would ask him. Arriving in Bangkok, I spoke to Anne first about the invitation. CAFOD were planning for a crowd of 80,000 in Hyde Park, with TV coverage all over the world. It would be a great opportunity to speak out on behalf of the people of Burma. We sat Declan down. He was seventeen years old and this would be a very stressful experience, but also a great opportunity. Nervously, he said he would be delighted to do it. He had only three minutes allocated to speak so he would have to be concise. Maung Maung Tinn was especially pleased to hear that Declan wanted to use some of his words from his book, *On the Border*. Fr Henry was another who contributed to preparing Declan for this great opportunity, encouraging him to 'use his freedom to help the people of Burma live free from fear'. Archbishop Charles also gave him words of encouragement to speak on behalf of all the people of Burma.

On returning to the UK in late August, the speech had to be 'checked' by CAFOD, who asked for any political references to be removed. So Declan amended his speech slightly and the final draft was agreed. The event at Hyde Park was set for September 18th. As Declan was under the age of 18, Anne and I were required to accompany him. In London we were offered rooms in the home of a CAFOD employee. By coincidence, the next-door neighbour was Michael Gove, who at that time was Secretary of State for Education in David Cameron's government. When our host told me of this, I jokingly said, 'I'll put his windows through,' as he was making many controversial changes to teachers' work conditions.

Unfortunately, our host didn't understand my sense of humour and in all seriousness he asked, 'Please don't do that!' Holding back my grin, I explained it was just a phrase and, of course, I had no intention of vandalising his home (but I did ask which was his car, so if I got the opportunity I could let his tyres down!).

Declan had to be on stage at Hyde Park on September 17th for the dress rehearsal. Obviously very nervous, he came through it with the help of the other participants of the CAFOD part of the event. Needing a few drinks to help us sleep, we met some friends in a London pub after the rehearsal. Next morning we walked through London towards the park. Security was very tight, with protests expected both for and against the visit of the Pope. We had to get Declan to the event hours before it started as no-one would be allowed backstage three hours prior to the Pope arriving. Declan had to do a sound check as the Park started to fill up. The CAFOD organiser was worried Declan wouldn't be able to do it as he was very quiet and, by a long way, the youngest speaker.

Knowing Declan, I reassured them that this was his normal behaviour - he rarely panics and was not going to let the people of Burma down.

As the time got closer to the start of the event, Declan climbed a sound system to get a look at the crowd. Almost 80,000 stared back at him. I watched him as he climbed down and I asked him how he felt.

'My legs are like jelly and my mouth is dry,' he said.

'Not long to wait now,' I reassured him.

After that I had to leave him. I wanted to see his performance from the crowd, so I headed from backstage into the arena. Anne stayed behind as she had been allocated a seat on the stage. As I took my seat in the crowd I could see a banner with Declan's name on it. His friends from school had come to London to hear him speak. I thought, 'I hope he sees the banner and it calms his nerves.' Moments later, Declan came onto the stage with two other speakers. Declan was on the left-hand side and would speak second. The first speaker was a refugee giving an account of her life escaping from injustice. The third speaker was a former drug-addict who spoke about how a drug rehabilitation centre had saved him from homelessness and addiction. Declan spoke between them. He was calm and clear, and the crowd roared when they heard he was only 17 years old and from Newcastle upon Tyne. He made himself and the people of Burma proud. The speech was being broadcast on the BBC World Service and we knew Maung Muang Tinn and Fr Henry would be listening. They would be even more proud of him.

This is what he said:

My name is Declan Stokle. I'm 17 years old. I live in Newcastle upon Tyne. I'm a year 13 student and I love football. Ten years ago I looked into the eyes of an orphan from Burma, a child who deserved everything that I had, and for the first time I saw the poor and oppressed as human beings.

I've witnessed the devastating human rights violations which Burma's military dictatorship perpetrates on the people. I've lived with Burmese refugee children and shared their meagre food rations. In return they ask that I share their story with the world.

I wondered where Christ was in all the suffering. Then I realised Christ was in me, giving me strength and compassion to help. I've spent the last six summers volunteering in refugee camps in Burma, coaching young Burmese people in football.

I have a dream that one day all the children of Burma - Buddhist, Christian, Muslim, Hindu and those of no religion, will live together in freedom and peace. In the words of a Burmese friend, Maung Maung Tinn: 'We now need others to extend their hands, to help us stand and voice our hopes for peace and security.'

My parents and I have set up a charity, Burmalink UK, to provide healthcare and education to Burmese people. Locally and nationally, I speak in schools and churches to be a voice for the people of Burma.

For me, being a Catholic means speaking up for those suffering injustice - whether on your doorstep or 6000 miles away.

'God has no hands but yours and mine.'

This was how the Guardian newspaper reported Declan's part of the event:

> The Pope's conservative reputation gets a radical young hand tomorrow from Declan Stokle, a teenager from Newcastle-upon-Tyne who has been highlighting human rights abuses in Burma for seven years. Only 17, the sixth-former at St Mary's comprehensive in Gosforth first visited refugee camps on the Thai border with his family when he was 10. The disaster of uncompromising, authoritarian rule will be his message to Benedict, after Catholic Aid for Overseas Development chose him to speak to the Pope, and some 80,000 people due to gather in Hyde Park.

Chapter 13.

A Year in Thailand and Burma, September 2011- August 2012.

Part 1: Life in Mae Sot.

After a year of planning and arranging time off work, Anne, Declan and I set off for Mae Sot in September 2011. Declan had just finished his A levels, and had been accepted into medical school. Patrick had finished his degree in Medicinal Chemistry, but decided to extend it to an MSc and spend another year at university. Sarah would stay at home, working as a newly qualified nurse. With a 'Round the World' ticket, we planned nine months in Thailand / Burma, returning home via Australia, USA, Guatemala and Canada. A trip of a lifetime. It was to prove much more fruitful than we could ever imagine and we all returned with a very different perspective on life.

Arriving in Bangkok, the city was flooding. The rain had started and never stopped. The reservoirs were full to overflowing and water was being released to prevent them from bursting. The river level in Bangkok was at its highest level for years and various parts of the city were underwater. We travelled north by bus to Mae Sot where we planned to work with the FTUK on a project sponsored by Unison, a UK trade union. The fields all along the roadside were flooded. Sandbags lined the road in various places, holding back the water. The road through the mountains was not flooded and thankfully no landslides had been reported. So in the dark, we arrived safely in Mae Sot. Our plan was to stay in the DK hotel for a few weeks while we found somewhere to rent. Thankfully, after two weeks and two viewings, we found a suitable home. A two-bedroomed, newly built house with two bathrooms and an outside kitchen. One bedroom had air conditioning if we needed it. A large gate allowed us to lock it when we were not there.

Wikipedia describes Mae Sot as, 'a district in West Thailand that shares a border with Myanmar to the west. It is notable as a trade hub and for its substantial population of Burmese migrants and refugees. The town is the main gateway between Thailand and Myanmar. As a result, it has gained notoriety for its trade in gems and teak, as well as black market services such as people trafficking and drugs. In recent years the ongoing refugee situation has prompted NGOs and international aid agencies to establish programmes in the town and surrounding area.'

Whenever anyone visited me whilst I was in Mae Sot I always said, 'You must complete the ten things to do in Mae Sot':

1. AAPP.
2. Dr Cynthia's clinic.
3. The garbage tip.
4. The Burmese market.
5. The Migrant schools (BHSOH, Parami and Chicken School).
6. The Friendship Bridge.
7. The sweatshops.
8. Borderline Tea shop.
9. Mae La Refugee Camp.
10. Ex-Pat bar.

To complete most of these tasks, some form of transport is required. There are no local buses in Mae Sot, so people travel by songthaew, a pickup truck adapted with benches in the back. Most of these places are not on a songthaew route so another form of transport is required. Many people use motorbikes as their preferred form of transport but we chose to buy some bicycles for our year out. This proved more difficult than I imagined. Being over six foot tall, Thai bike shops don't stock larger framed bikes, for obvious reasons. We toured some of the many secondhand bike shops in Mae Sot, mostly located in the Muslim quarter. One morning a local policeman offered his help and gave us lifts between the shops in his police truck. Needless to say the local shop owners were a little suspicious of us. Eventually we found one for Anne who is considerably smaller than me, but had to order two new ones for Declan and I. Even then there was a delay of several weeks as the road to Bangkok was now completely flooded and no lorries could head north. But when they did arrive they made getting around Mae Sot so much easier than walking or using small-framed bikes without gears and inadequate brakes.

Still in holiday mode, Father Justin brought us back down to Earth. A few days after arriving, he called, telling us that 16 people, aged 14-23, had been trafficked from Burma and were under arrest by the Thai authorities. He had paid for the release of four girls as he thought they were particularly vulnerable. 'Would you come over and meet the girls?' he asks.

Father Justin.

I first heard Father Justin laughing out loud at Father Gregory's school. It was to be the start of a long friendship, which sadly also ended in tragedy, as most things seem to do in this unforgiving place. He had just returned from inside Burma, where he was working with the displaced communities in Karen State. At first I didn't believe Fr Gregory when he introduced Justin, his friend, as a fellow priest. It was a little like the first time I met Fr Gregory in his camouflage military clothes. It wasn't until he served mass that Sunday in his vestments and knew all the words, that I really believed. What I didn't understand at the time, was this place was not 'normal'. The rules I had been brought up under were out of the window. This was Burma - a country 50 years behind the rest of the world and in the midst of civil war. It was good to see Gregory and Justin get on so well. They were the best of friends and were good for each other.

Justin was posted by his bishop to serve the community of Mae Sot, Mae Pa and surrounding areas. There were hundreds of thousands of Burmese migrants, mostly Buddhist but a small number of Catholics. Anyway, that didn't seem to matter too much to Justin; he was there to serve all the people.

As we found out over numerous visits, Justin always had visitors. The Mae Pa community were always calling in for help and advice. Of the many people we met at Justin's, the most memorable were the four young girls who had been trafficked from Burma to Thailand. He telephoned asking us to visit, as he had some important people he wanted us to meet. We headed out in a tuk-tuk as it was dark. We were greeted in his usual warm manner and then taken straight to meet four young girls, all about 16 years old. They sat, terrified, in the corner of a room. He had just paid the local police for their release from prison. They, and about 12 young men, had been caught at a house in Mae Sot, having entered Thailand illegally. Many Burmese get caught having crossed the border illegally and it is usually simple to release them - pay the police a fine and you are released back into the community, or if you have no money, you are transported to the border a few miles away and handed over to the Burmese police.

'So why was this so different?' we asked. Justin explained that the Thai police had caught the group at a house on the edge of town, known by the police as a holding house for trafficked people. They had raided the house and found them. The traffickers had fled earlier with the money they had taken from the group.

The Thai police were interested in catching the traffickers. They wanted more information, but the Burmese were frightened and not forthcoming. Justin had visited them in prison, taking food, which is normal in this part of the world. He had managed to pay for the release of the girls who he thought very vulnerable, as they were quite innocent young ladies from rural Burma. Prostitution and slavery was all that awaited them if he didn't help. He asked us to speak to the girls and listen to their story - he would translate. Four terrified girls were like rabbits in headlights, even though they were relatively safe now. They told us how they had paid a Burmese couple to transport them from their village to Bangkok where they were assured jobs and accommodation would be available. I have never seen such fear in the eyes of anyone. Justin would contact their families in their villages and they would be able to go home. He would speak more with the police and negotiate a price for the release of the young men. But more frightening was the possible fate of the traffickers. Justin explained that the Karen National Union (KNU) would hunt the traffickers down as it was thought they would return to Karen State. He said if they were found they would be killed. The KNU would not be lenient. They did not approve of trafficking and would set an example. He would plead for mercy with his friends in the KNU but he thought he had little chance of persuading them. I left feeling shocked but knew this sort of thing was happening all over the world. To witness it personally left me traumatised. Justin was dealing with this sort of thing, day in and day out.

We all have many memories of times with Justin, such as when he invited us to a Karen wedding at his house and when, during the Cyclone Nargis disaster, he led the community response to deliver aid to the victims in the Irrawaddy Delta. He made us laugh on many occasions. He was definitely a priest of the people, who stood side by side with the powerless on the battlefields of Burma. I was impressed with this social justice advocate, activist and community builder, who was unafraid to speak the truth.

Thiha Yarzar.

I met so many wonderful people in my year in Mae Sot. One of the first, and very memorable, was Thiha Yarzar. Socialising in

Ex-Pat bar, a trendy (for Mae Sot) place to relax, especially late on a Friday. I was served my drink by a Burmese man who asked if he could sit and chat for a few moments. This wasn't unusual, as many people were visitors in Mae Sot and it was good to get to know a new face before they moved on. Ex-Pat bar was set up by a German man, Marcus, who was spending some time in Thailand on a break from his usual job as a carpenter. He employed ex-political prisoners in the bar/restaurant, trying to give them some work experience.

Thiha Yarzar proved to be a remarkable man. About forty years of age, he had been a student in the 1988 uprising. He was arrested and given the death sentence for his part in organising the demonstrations. He spent nearly 20 years in prison but thankfully the death sentence was never carried out. You can read his own account in his biography *No Easy Road*, written by Paul Pickrem. Clearly he was still struggling with mental health problems following such a long incarceration but, with the help of friends and a new Australian wife, he was putting his life back together.

Aung Lwin and George.

Aung Lwin and George were two more remarkable friends I made in Mae Sot. Both Burmese trying to earn a living in Mae Sot. George was a Catholic and spoke perfect English, Aung Lwin a Buddhist who spoke perfect Burmese (but no English), so George translated for me.

In the summer before I set off for Thailand, I had been reading a book on microfinance in India and how it helps very poor rural communities who don't have access to finance. I wondered if I could trial it in Thailand. Aung Lwin was to be my guinea pig. I met both George and Aung Lwin at Fr Justin's house. I called George my guardian angel as one night, Anne and I were lost after dark in Mae Pa, a township on the edge of Mae Sot where most of the Burmese live. The streets were very dark and it was not a particularly safe place to be after dark.

This night we were trying to find Fr Justin's and had taken a wrong turn. Getting more and more lost, and Anne more and more worried, a motorbike came along the dark road we were on, it's headlamp blinding our vision. It came to a halt right in front of us. Fearing we were about to be robbed, we got off our bikes and prepared to defend ourselves.

'Are you lost?' asked the motorcyclist. I recognised the friendly voice and, as he stepped out of the bright headlamp, I saw it was George. Trying not to show our fear, we told him we were heading to Fr Justin's, and could he point us in the right direction. Turning his bike around he said, 'Follow me.' We were only a few streets away but we might never have found it in the dark, as there were no street lights or names. Bidding us farewell, he cautioned, 'Be careful heading back. Take the main road, not the back one, it's too dangerous. Many people get robbed on that road at night.' Glad to be safe, we took his advice and rarely went to Mae Pa after dark from then on.

Aung Lwin was often at Fr Justin's house. He was an illegal immigrant from Burma, like thousands of others. He lived with his wife and two children on a small patch of land on the outskirts of town, by one of the many sweatshop factories. He was extremely poor and often came to ask for help from Fr Justin, for himself and his community.

I spoke with George about my plan to try to help Aung Lwin and asked if he would take Anne and I to see where Aung Lwin lived. George was sceptical about trying to help, saying Aung Lwin would just take the money and spend it all on his family instead of investing it, but still agreed to take us and translate. Anne and I were shocked by what we found as we parked our bikes by the ditch that Aung Lwin lived alongside. We walked along the mud track and approached his home. A bamboo hut with a straw roof was all he had for his family. No toilet, no washing facilities, no running water. He had a small vegetable patch and a few chickens. This is what I was interested in. Could I help him develop his vegetable patch, so that he could earn a small income and provide a little more for his family?

Aung Lwin was surprised to see us, but delighted we had come to visit him at his home. Probably embarrassed at his poverty, he still invited us into the shade of his hut. There was absolutely nothing in the hut, bar a few mats to sit on. His wife had hold of their baby and the other child, about three years old, came climbing up the steps of the hut. I thought, 'No wonder the refugees don't want to leave the camps - life is so precarious here on the edge.' Aung Lwin had nothing to offer us but Anne had brought some coke and a few sweets for the children, so we shared that while Goerge tried to explain my plan. Aung Lwin was a tiny man, less than 5 foot tall, and very slender. His wife was even smaller but they smiled and were happy to listen. He hadn't heard of microfinance, but I could see he didn't want to offend us. After about half an hour we decided to leave, suggesting Aung Lwin thought about what he could do with a small amount of money and if it would help him earn an extra income.

Feeling ashamed of our wealthy position, Anne and I cycled home, wondering how Aung Lwin managed to feed himself and his family at all. What would Aung Lwin think of me offering him money to develop his small plot of land, which of course he didn't own and could be thrown off at any time? A few days later we returned with George, who now understood our proposal and spoke to Aung Lwin directly. We agreed a 'loan' of about £20 to allow him to buy some seeds and a watering can and a few other simple gardening tools. The plan was for Aung Lwin to pay back a small amount each month once he had grown some vegetables and had sold them at the market. Although I could easily afford to give him the money, the plan was to see if he could earn an income by having a small loan.

We left it with Aung Lwin, hoping it would be useful for him, and agreed with George to let him get on with it for a month or two. George would check he had bought the tools and seeds, so everything was in place. Perhaps we could find a few other people to help; if it worked with Aung Lwin, maybe some of the other families who straddled the road in similar conditions to Aung Lwin?

Tragedy struck a few weeks later. George telephoned to say Aung Lwin was in hospital. He had been attacked and stabbed in the stomach. Shocked, thinking maybe he had been stabbed because of our visit and because he was getting money from us, I was very concerned for him and his family. George called again after visiting Aung Lwin in hospital, telling us he was alive but had a deep stab wound. I asked if we could visit but George cautioned, saying we needed to be careful as the hospital may ask us to pay for his treatment if they see us visiting. George said he would arrange for us to go to a cafe next to the hospital and he would bring Aung Lwin to us.

Next day, George called and told us a time and place to meet him. Arriving early, we sat so we could see everyone coming and going and ordered coffee. After a while George came in, accompanied by Aung Lwin, still in his hospital gown. Clearly very weak, he was pleased to see us and told us, via George, that it had been late at night when he was on his way home. He didn't know his attacker or why he had been attacked. A common occurrence in their world. He lifted his gown to show us the injury - a stapled, vertical scar from his throat to his belly button like a full-length body zip. I almost fainted. George could see we were shocked and explained it was ok. As a scan was expensive and Aung Lwin had no money to pay, it was cheaper for the surgeon to open him up to check if the knife had damaged any internal organs. A usual procedure apparently.

George said we should not stay long, to avoid anyone seeing us. Aung Lwin had a huge bill which he had no way of paying. We suggested we could help but George said not to. The Thai authorities would deal with it somehow. They often had to fix up illegal migrants. Still, we gave George some money and asked him to pass it onto his wife. George suggested that Aung Lwin might have been targeted because people had seen us visiting him and maybe thought he had some money. We'll never know.

Shocked by his stapled chest, and knowing the unhygienic living conditions he would be discharged to, we contacted our friend Doctor Jonathan, a Yorkshireman, who lived in Mae Sot and worked with the Karen hill tribe people and had lots of experience. Meeting him for a drink the next night, he reassured us that Aung Lwin should be ok. He told us it was remarkable how resistant to germs and infections the migrants were. He thought his scar would heal well and he would be able to carry on as before. Reassured, we cycled home, still feeling guilty that we may have added to his problems and worrying how he would pay for his treatment.

Several days passed and George rang again with some good news. Aung Lwin was out of hospital and didn't have to pay any fees! Obviously we were happy, but curious as to why no fees. The hospital told Aung Lwin it was his lucky day. He was being discharged on the King's birthday and as a gift from the nation, he would have his fees waived. Good news indeed and he did deserve a little bit of good luck. Thank goodness for the King of Thailand. George suggested we stay away from Aung Lwin for the time being, and that was the end of my experiment with microfinance. I reflected on my experience and concluded it had to be organised by local people for local people.

Poverty, fear, housing, are always in my life
by Maung Maung Tinn.

I was born in poverty.
I grew up in poverty.
I have children and grandchildren and they are also poor.
In my country, just to earn a regular income to survive is a struggle.
We did not have time to think about why it is like this.
We feel so weak.
We are scared of almost everything.
That's why we left home.

Now I have lived with my family in another country for twenty years.
We still do not have any money to save, even though everybody in the family worked.
None of us has any legal status.
Police can arrest us for this.
Police can come and check anytime.
We cannot sleep well at night.
Before,
we thought: "If we come and work here it will be better than it is in Burma."
In reality,
the situation we face right now is not what we thought.

Federation of Trade Unions Burma (FTUB): Min Lwin and Maung Maung.

We had worked with Federation of Trade Unions Kawthoolei (FTUK) for several years prior to 2011 and had heard of FTUB, but didn't know they had an office in Mae Sot, until Paw Gay mentioned that perhaps we should meet FTUB now we were working with FTUK on their project to grow and develop their union. We had met Ronnie from FTUB in Bangkok, who had mentioned the office in Mae Sot but nothing had come of that. So Paw Gay arranged for us to go to meet Min Lwin, the FTUB co-ordinator in Mae Sot at their secret office. FTUB were a proscribed organisation and subject to frequent attacks, sometimes deadly, by the Burmese Secret Service. Maung Maung was head of FTUB and often came to Mae Sot, however he was on a Burmese government hit list for assasination and had to be very careful about his movements to avoid detection by Burmese spies, who were all over Mae Sot.

On arriving at the house, in an upmarket estate on the outskirts of Mae Sot, we got out of the car and stood by the side of the road while Paw Gay made a phone call. Two minutes later, a solid steel gate slides open on a nearby house and we are invited to come in by a young lady. The gate is firmly closed and locked behind us. Taking our shoes off, we are invited in, and enter a room with a table in the middle with some computers on the outside. A man a little younger than me comes in and introduces himself as Min Lwin.

Min Lwin.

Min Lwin was the FTUB representative for the Mae Sot area. The primary mission of the FTUB, established in 1991, was to build a democratic union movement within Burma while defending rights of Burmese migrant workers in Thailand and India. Min Lwin was also the Principal of Parami Migrant Education Centre. Parami was not only a school for 200 or so children aged 4 - 16 years, it was also an occupational training centre for developing skills such as building work and industrial sewing. After just six or eight weeks training, many are capable of getting jobs in the construction industry and sewing factories around Mae Sot.

Min Lwin tried to organise workers in the local factories and construction sites into the trade union movement. He told us stories of Burmese girls getting their hair caught in knitting machines with no safety guards (Burmese girls are known for their very long and beautiful straight, jet black hair). They were horribly disfigured and dismissed from their jobs without compensation. He wanted so much to protect and help these young girls, many who were only 12 or 13 years old. Health and safety was a major element of his work, as the factories and sites were notorious for flouting Thailand's health and safety laws, not to mention the laws on minimum pay.

About 80,000 work in the textile industry around Mae Sot and many get paid half the Thai minimum wage! This wage is not enough to pay rent, so they sleep in the factory grounds in concrete shelters, without running water or electricity. They share a communal bathing station and use candles for lighting. Many have children with them. FTUB is trying to get the workers organised but it is slow progress with extreme pressure put on anyone who asks for improvements. Entire workforces are known to have been sacked en-mass for asking for a pay rise. There is no shortage of workers coming from Burma. Some factories make clothes for high street chains in Europe and the USA but it's hard to prove as no brand names are added at these factories. They are sent on to other factories for labels to be added. A cunning way to get around inspection by overseas companies.

Min Lwin was to be a good friend of ours throughout our nine months in Mae Sot, helping us with setting up our rented house, showing us where to pay the gas, electricity, water and internet bills. I will never forget the social evenings he invited us to at his school, where we would eat with the teachers and some of the trainees. We would take a few beers and some wine and they provided the music. They loved singing, and we would all have to sing a favourite or traditional song from our home. My sister, Alison, came to one of these events and introduced herself, sang and talked about cultural differences and how she was learning so much from the Burmese. Evenings never to be forgotten, especially hearing the children sing 'Feed the World - Make it a better place'. Coming from orphaned and lonely children, this was especially poignant and memorable.

One of Min Lwin's friends who deserves special mention is Htay Hlaing, a maths teacher at Parami school. About 50 years old, but looking much older, he used to invite me to his home to talk every time I visited Parami. Htay Hlaing told me he had been a labour activist inside Burma, but was arrested and given a 15 year prison sentence. He spent 9 years incarcerated and when he was set free he fled to Mae Sot, where he was helped by AAPP and then Min Lwin. A big character whose wife and family remained in Burma. He was too afraid to go back. His health was not good and if arrested again, he feared he would die in prison, so he used the school as a place of safety. Always wanting to talk politics and discuss the possibility of change in Burma. He told me of the news from inside - a new 'Labour

Law' had been proposed, which would allow the formation of trade unions (the 'crime' he was put in prison for!). Democatic Voice of Burma (DVB) was now permitted to broadcast in Burma. DVB is often a dissenting voice, promoting truth and democracy. Also Youtube had been unblocked, so now young people could view what was happening in the rest of the world. Most importantly for him, 200 political prisoners had been released, including at least one labour activist. He was so pleased to hear and pass on this news. All these changes were being brought in as a part of the 'Peace Process' the government had agreed with the Ethnic groups, and as part of their campaign prior to a general election proposed for 2015.

Maung Maung.

A few days after meeting Min Lwin we were invited back to FTUB office to see how we could link our Unison project with FTUK and FTUB. This would be a great opportunity to help spread the role of trade unions inside Burma, as well as along the Thailand-Burma border. Paw Gay arranged our transport as we didn't know the way to the secret office. Arriving, it was the same process as before to keep the location safe. After the phone call the gate slid open and we were invited in. Waiting to meet us was a stocky man, with a Burmerse longyi on. He greeted us in perfect English saying he was Maung Maung, leader of the FTUB in exile. Not only was Maung Maung General Secretary of the FTUB, he was also General Secretary of the National Council of the Union of Burma (NCUB), and a key leader in the Burmese pro-democracy movement.

In 1988, Maung Maung was the founding member of the Myanmar Gems Mining Union, and then was elected as the President of the All Burma Mining Union (Rangoon). For his involvement in the anti-regime demonstrations in 1988, he was fired from his job with the government. The military intelligence came to arrest him and he left the country, leaving his wife and 3-year-old son behind. In 1991, Maung Maung cofounded the Federation of Trade Unions of Burma (FTUB) from exile in Thailand. Maung Maung is recognised throughout the world as the foremost expert and authority on labour rights in Burma.

Clearly a determined and driven man, Maung Maung was delighted to meet us and showed us around his Mae Sot office, telling us of his personal sacrifices and on the role of trade unions in the fight for democracy in Burma. His colleagues held him in high esteem. He showed us the ladies who followed the news in Burma and tried to keep the international community aware of the situation for workers inside Burma. We were delighted when he asked that some of his staff join us in our training programme with the FTUK.

Over tea Maung Maung told me, 'What we've been doing over the last 18-years is trying to raise the awareness of the people. They have the right to express themselves and stand up to the rulers and say, 'this is not fair'. We've been doing workshops, training programmes within the community, within the workplace and factories. We've talked about how workers should be represented, and it's rightful to ask to have independent trade unions in the workplace. We are also working with the ILO and ITUC, running training programmes on the rights of workers. First we have workshops and training sessions in bordering countries. These are open workshops, they are not advertised. But the members come out from within Burma. They're given basic trade union rights awareness, basic workers' rights issues, international labour standards. Then when these people go back again, they continue the work clandestinely, giving secret programmes and training.'

I asked him if it was risky to attend and he replied, 'We had six young people arrested and sentenced to 28-years because they were trying to hold discussions at the American Centre in Rangoon. Before that, 13 people were arrested because they were trying to organise a workshop. They are risking their lives everyday. People have been tortured. Trade unionists are treated even worse than political prisoners from the NLD or the students. They're separated and treated very harshly by the regime. Their families are threatened. Some of the guys were put in dog cells. Their hands were tied behind their backs so they couldn't eat with their hands. They were forced to eat with their mouths, like dogs. At roll-call they couldn't stand like a man, they had to sit like a dog and bark like a dog.'

Our experiences with Maung Maung were to take a different direction the day after May Day, 2012. A UK delegation, which included the President of a UK teachers union and an Assistant General Secretary, were delighted to have the opportunity to meet Maung Maung, along with the other delegates. Maung Maung gave a presentation of the work of FTUB to our group in their offices and we were invited to question him and discuss current issues. At first his powerpoint presentation didn't work very well and Maung Maung, clearly upset, shouted at one of his young female assistants to 'get it fixed.' The whole delegation of about 20 people were taken aback, but thankfully the young lady sorted the problem and on we went.

Later it took a turn for the worse, when Maung Maung started to criticise FTUK in his presentation for not being more engaged with his organisations. It was a very serious criticism, of an organisation I knew very well and were doing their best under very, very difficult circumstances. The atmosphere in the room was tense.

After the meeting ended many of the UK delegates expressed concern at Maung Maung's attitude to his fellow female workers and the other ethnic trade unions. But as Paw Gay commented after the meeting, 'He has revealed himself.' Paw Gay explained that he had treated her and her union members like this on many occasions, and was one of the reasons she was reluctant to engage fully with FTUB!

More than two decades after a violent military crackdown on pro-democracy demonstrators forced thousands of Burmese activists into prison or exile, Maung Maung returned home. His return was made possible by the government's decision in August 2012 to remove more than 2,000 people from a list of over 6,000 pro-democracy supporters banned from entering the country. He arrived in Rangoon on September 4th 2012.

On arrival, Maung Maung was met by trade union leaders and former political prisoners, and then by six members from the Special Branch police. Afterwards, 'I met my families: my wife and son, whom I had not seen all this time, and the trade union family that had developed over the past twenty years. All was a blur,' he said. His father, now 91, was 'ready to discuss many issues.'

Dr Thein Lwin.

Dr Thein Lwin was the first political prisoner I ever met. I met him in Newcastle in 2000. I was travelling back in a car from a friend's house with Lwin when he casually told me about one of his many arrests and periods of internment.

'The knock came in the night. I answered the door and the security forces were waiting. A bag was put over my head and I was bundled into a truck. They took me to an interrogation centre where I was beaten and forced to tell them about my activities,' he told me. I couldn't believe it. Here I was, listening first-hand to an account of a man's torture, and I had just had a wonderful dinner with him and a group of friends. Lwin was a leading member of the National League for Democracy (NLD) and had to leave Burma or risk further imprisonment for his political work.

When I was first introduced to Lwin he was a visiting lecturer at Newcastle University, where he had gained a doctorate in education. His area of interest was Critical Thinking. He wanted to get the students in Burma to start thinking for themselves, after years/decades of indoctrination by the dictatorship. Over the years I remained in contact with Lwin and on several occasions, taught at his Teacher Training Center for Burmese Teachers (TTBT) based in Chiang Mai, which he founded in 2001. In 2005, he founded the Migrant Learning Centre (MLC) also in Chiang Mai, to train thousands of migrant workers who were flooding into Chiang Mai looking for work in what he told me were the three d jobs- dirty, dangerous and difficult.

In 2012, following the elections in 2011, he was able to return to Rangoon to set up a 'Thinking Classroom Foundation', to train Burmese teachers in thinking skills. Lwin became a member of the NLD's central executive committee. A leading light, and outspoken on the subjects of education and democracy, I was so proud to have known him for so many years. However, in 2015 he fell foul of the NLD hierarchy. A National Education Law, passed in September 2014 amid wide-ranging criticism, was the cause of Lwin's fallout with the NLD. Lwin attended meetings and stood up for students demonstrating against the Law. An NLD central committee member stated that, 'Aung San Suu Kyi personally disapproved of Thein Lwin's participation, on the grounds that he could be construed as a representative of the party.'

For his involvement in democratic reforms in education, he was dismissed from the NLD's central executive committee. Perhaps it was a sign of things to come, with the fledgling NLD and its use of power and it's understanding of democracy and justice.

Part 2: Meeting Aung San Suu Kyi.

Burma's military rulers have repeatedly imprisoned Aung San Suu Kyi, the daughter of Burma's leading independence figure, General Aung San, for her charismatic promotion of democracy and human rights in Burma. Also, for her leadership of the opposition party, the National League for Democracy (NLD), which won an election landslide in 1990 but was never permitted to assume power. The elections were considered relatively free and fair. The NLD took 60 percent of the vote and 80 percent of parliamentary seats. The government ignored the result and remained in power.

Aung San Suu Kyi was first arrested by Burma's military government in 1989 and held under house arrest until 1995. She was placed under house arrest a second time in 2000 and released in 2002. The military junta, the State Peace and Development Council (SPDC), detained her for a third time in 2003 after an attack on her convoy while traveling in the country. Her house arrest order was extended by another year in May 2008, and it was expected to be unlawfully extended again in May 2009.

The military government, however, used the bizarre incident of an American man swimming to her house in May 2009 as an excuse to put her on trial, for the first time ever, during her periods of detention, and extend her house arrest for another 18 months.

On November 7th, 2010, elections in Burma, the first in 20 years, were held. These elections were intended to ensure continued military rule, but with a civilian facade. The NLD was now illegal as it did not register for the elections along with 37 other parties, due to draconian electoral laws that barred parties from having people serving prison terms as members.

On 13th November 2010, Aung San Suu Kyi was released after spending more than 15 years in detention, most of it under house arrest, following an international campaign to get her released.

In June 2011, Aung San Suu Kyi was given the 'Freedom of the City of Newcastle upon Tyne' at Newcastle Civic Centre. Anne and I were fortunate enough to be invited to watch Wai Hnin, from the Burma Campaign UK, collect the honour on behalf of Aung San Suu Kyi . Wai Hnin travelled from London and stayed with us for the weekend. The event took place on a Friday evening and afterwards we headed back to Gosforth for a celebration drink with the scroll secure. In the pub we bumped into our friend and neighbour, Peter, who is a printer. Anne asked him if he would do us a favour and take a copy of the scroll. Next morning he called for the scroll and delivered a wonderful copy for Anne and I later that day. Actually, we couldn't tell the difference, it was so good. Wai Hnin was concerned she didn't have the original when she left for London. I joked with her that I had the original as I waved her off on the train!

On December 11th 2011, we flew to Burma, hoping to present the 'Freedom of the City' scroll to Aung San Suu Kyi. Our friend, Khun Saing, an ex political prisoner living in Sheffield, promised he would contact a few friends in the NLD who we would be able to meet to hand over the scroll to. We arrived in Rangoon in the early evening and took a taxi to the Yardanar Show Hotel. The hotel was owned by the father of a medical student, Mabel, we had met in Newcastle. The taxi driver at the airport had never heard of the hotel but that was not unusual, as many taxi drivers borrowed friend's cars to earn some extra money.

Giving him the street address, we headed into town in his dilapidated car. Getting to the street, he drove along it slowly but we still couldn't find it. He stopped and asked but no-one seemed to know it. But getting out I happened to see a sign for 'Yardanar Show' on the side of a grubby building up a side street. The taxi headed up the lane and turned into a quadrangle with several buildings surrounding it. Two men came to greet us in pristine white shirts and brown longyis, collecting our luggage and showing us to a reception desk – well, a rough table with a bell on it. Neither of the men could speak English so we mentioned Mabel, the name of our friend in Newcastle. This seemed to ring a bell and they indicated for us to sit down.

A few minutes later a man turned up who could speak English. He was very pleased to see us and told us Mabel's father was expecting us and that our rooms were ready. The building we were shown to was a huge, colonial style mansion, with a wide stairway up to our rooms. Anne and I were shown into one, and Declan another. The room looked reasonably clean but there was a strong smell of damp. The beds were incredibly soft and had clean white sheets. We felt like colonial guests as we returned down the stairs to see if we could get an evening meal. Unfortunately the hotel didn't have a restaurant, but they could make us something from the kitchen if we wanted. Ordering a beer, we asked how much it would be as we needed to get some money changed. The manager was again called to explain something to us. Not really understanding, we thought he had told us that the drinks were free - that we would not be charged for anything - we were honoured guests of the owner and would get everything free! After the manager left, the men on reception brought some more beers, indicating we should make the most of the situation. A rather strange situation for us but not totally unexpected, the Burmese often don't allow visitors to pay for anything. A little embarrassed, we had our free beer and enjoyed some simple rice with eggs for dinner.

Later we were to find out that Yardanar Show was a fledgling hotel and we were the first foreign visitors. The manager asked for our passports and said he would bring them back in an hour or two. He had to take them to the local police station and register our visit to the hotel. As the evening unfolded we witnessed the comings and goings of several young couples at reception. It became clear that the rooms could be booked by the hour! The penny dropped - the hotel was being used as a brothel, more than a hotel for tourists. The telephone would ring at reception shortly after a couple arrived and a waiter would deliver a room service order on a silver tray. Normally this was two beers and a pack of condoms! We found this hilarious and the staff at the hotel joined in with our laughter.

The next day we went in search of a sim card for our mobile phone so we could ring a contact at the NLD. Walking out onto the street we turned right, as advised at the hotel. There we would find a main street with internet cafes and a few phone shops. Finding the main street and shops was easy but getting a sim card was not. Yes, they were available, we were told - but each one was £500! We couldn't believe our ears, but the shop owner insisted this was the only price. The government had recently signed a trade agreement with a Chinese firm who had control of the network and all access to it.

Back at the hotel we asked if we could use the hotel telephone. Concerned, as we were ringing the NLD office, we asked if there was a private place to use the phone - we didn't want the hotel to know - these were still dangerous times, with spies everywhere and people disappearing for any sort of political activity.

'No,' came the reply. The only outside line was at the reception desk, but 'Yes' we could use it. Using the number given to us by Khun Saing, we rang the NLD office and managed to speak to U Ohn Kyaing. Explaining the 'Freedom of the City' scroll, he was keen to meet us and said he would come to our hotel the next day at 12 noon. Everything seemed to be going well and we were hopeful of being able to present the scroll to someone at the NLD.

As it happened, our friend Colleen from Newcastle was in Rangoon visiting her family and we had promised to meet up with her. Colleen's brother, Robert, from Sheffield, was also with her. Robert had left Rangoon during the Second World War with Colleen and this was his first return. Robert always recalls his visit to a traditional Burmese tea shop. I persuaded him to take a wander out onto the streets and to meet ordinary Burmese people. Up an alleyway between two tall buildings was an open-air tea shop. It had a tarpaulin stretched between the buildings to shelter its customers from rain and, of course, tiny chairs and tables that everyone sat at. Robert looked shocked but I persuaded him to take a seat. The owner came over and thankfully spoke good English. I explained that Robert had been born in Rangoon and it was his first time back for 60 years, and asked could we sample some of his best Burmese tea and hospitality? As we waited for tea, a rat or two poked their heads out of the sewer which ran beside us. A terrified Robert jumped from his chair and wanted to go but I persuaded him they were friendly rats. The owner served up some delicious tea with condensed milk. Robert commented that it was years since he'd had condensed milk!

'Probably sixty years,' I said. Although an uncomfortable experience, Robert always thanks me whenever I see him for forcing him to experience real Burmese culture. In the evening we all went to a 'real' restaurant near to their hotel and had a wonderful evening with Colleen, Robert and their cousin, Arnold.

Next day, we awaited U Ohn Kyaing at the hotel. The time ticked by slowly but no one arrived. We stood on the street corner to make sure any taxi with him in would see us, but nothing came. Disappointed we rang the NLD offices again but he was not available. Not knowing what to do, we thought we should visit the offices the next day and see if we could arrange something. This would be very risky as we didn't want to be seen near the NLD offices. Next morning at 9am, reception came running to our room: we had a phone call from U Ohn Kyaing, of the NLD. Rushing down to speak to him, he asked why we hadn't come to the office yesterday. He had arranged for us to deliver the 'Freedom scroll' in person to Aung San Suu Kyi and we hadn't turned up. Khun Saing should have told us. Absolutely shocked we had missed such an important meeting, I explained we hadn't received any message.

Fumbling for words, I asked if it could be re-arranged. 'She's a very busy lady,' came the terse reply. I knew that, as many leaders around the world were keen to have an appointment with her. Anne was furious. We had missed a chance to meet Aung San Suu Kyi because we hadn't been informed that we had the appointment. We headed straight back to the internet cafe - there was no internet at the hotel - to see if we had any messages. None from Khun Saing, but one from Mabel asking us not to visit NLD offices as it could be a problem for her father. We hadn't told her, but obviously the staff at the hotel had informed her father that we were receiving phone calls from the NLD. Not only had we missed the appointment but now maybe we had nowhere to stay!

Back at the hotel none of the staff mentioned the NLD so we kept quiet and pretended nothing had happened. That evening we had another important appointment as our friend Fr Henry had arranged for us to have dinner with Archbishop Charles Bo. Hiding our disappointment, we took a taxi to the cathedral and had a wonderful evening with Charles. We explained our problem about missing the important meeting. He was very supportive and suggested we go in person to the NLD offices and try to rearrange. He then told of the night recently when they had a service in the cathedral and Aung San Suu Kyi came along. When Aung San Suu Kyi entered the packed cathedral the entire congregation had warmly applauded her - a very unusual response in a cathedral, but Charles was thrilled at the reception she had got. Many in the military would not have been so warmed by it, he warned us.

Charles and the church had a good relationship with her even though she was Buddhist. Fr Henry had told us that her mother had been baptised a Catholic just before she died, but that she didn't want the people to know, as it might affect the way they portray her. Fr Henry was adamant the baptism story was true and said he knew the priest who had baptised her.

So next morning we set off to NLD central office - a ramshackled wooden building with a few NLD flags outside giving it away. Hesitantly we asked if we could see U Ohn Kyaing, but unfortunately he wasn't there. U Thein Oo, another senior member of the NLD was there and we spoke with him. He promised to try and re-arrange the meeting but, 'the Lady was very busy.' It was now Tuesday 20th December and we had plans to spend Christmas with Fr Henry in the Irrawaddy Delta, but these plans would have to go on hold. Walking back to the hotel we were hopeful something might transpire so we could at least present the scroll to one of the NLD leaders.

Later that night the phone rang at the hotel, and the porter ran over saying quietly it was the NLD on the phone for me. He was smiling broadly and obviously keen for us to speak to the NLD, even if the owner wasn't. Answering, I listened carefully to U Thein Oo. Could we make Thursday 22nd at 12 noon? Aung San Suu Kyi had a 30 minute slot if we were available.

My heart jumped with joy - what an amazing opportunity. She was probably the most famous lady in the world at the moment - and on a par with the likes of Nelson Mandela - and Anne, Declan and I had an invitation to meet her. I rushed back to tell Anne and Declan - they were delighted. We were all hoping nothing would stop us this time.

Next day, Mabel came to see us at the hotel. She explained her father was very concerned about our contacting the NLD but wishing us good luck, she asked us not to discuss it at the hotel or with the staff, and her father had agreed we could stay. Relieved we weren't looking for a place to sleep, we met Colleen and Robert again and told them of our good news. They could hardly believe it - we had an appointment with Aung San Suu Kyi, ahead of British Prime Minister, David Cameron (he visited Aung San Suu Kyi in Burma on April 13th 2012). We were almost famous!

Wednesday 21st December, we went to bed having thought about what we should say and what to wear. Clothing was a problem for me as I didn't have any long trousers with me -

only my tracksuit bottoms. With no time to shop, they would have to do, and my only decent shirt was my Hartlepool United T-shirt. Hardly sleeping - fearing arrest or eviction - I awoke early. Breakfast of rice and eggs, as usual, filled me. We all had to pack as we were heading straight to Pathein on the 5pm bus after our meeting. We booked a taxi and asked him to drop us right outside the NLD offices. Only a few months ago, the taxi would have refused to take us to the door as the government spies would note his number plat,e and later his licence would be revoked; today we dared do it, as we were seeing the 'Lady'. Arriving early, we were met by U Nine Nine, a wonderful elderly NLD politician who told us of his incarceration for 17 years and release in 2009. It would have been enough just to meet him, such an inspirational person, but he told us she was waiting for us upstairs. We climbed the steep wooden stairs and were taken in by her personal assistant. Sitting at her desk, she got up immediately and greeted us warmly. The assistant left us with her. I was surprised that no security check had taken place, but I found out later we had come highly recommended by our friend, Khun Saing, who had shared a prison cell with U Nine Nine.

We all sat down and talked as if we were old friends. I couldn't believe how warm and open she was. Tall and slim and looking very fresh and healthy. She was especially interested in Declan and asked lots of questions about what young people in the West thought of Burma. Asking what Declan was doing with the Karen people in Mae Sot, he told her he was coaching and playing football with them. She told us that football was good for unity and team building, and said she had only ever been to one football match: Chelsea v Fulham, adding she was a Chelsea supporter, having a flat near Stamford Bridge when she lived in London. We told her how helpful the people of Burma were to us.

Interestingly, she replied, 'The people of Burma are more generous to foreigners than they are to themselves.'

We told her that we had met Archbishop Charles Bo recently. She replied saying she was a good friend of his and had met him on several occasions.

She mentioned her visit to the Cathedral a few weeks ago, asking, 'Is it allowed to clap in church?' We assured her it was very polite to clap in church but only used on very special occasions. I asked about her time in prison and under house arrest and how she had coped.

She told us, 'When in Insein prison, the light in the cell was on 24 hours a day and it disturbed me.' Khun Saing had told me a similar story when I visited him at his home in Sheffield. To this day, he still sleeps with the light on at night.

On discussing life in the UK she was concerned about the 'lack of discipline in the UK', adding that the rich must take responsibility for the poor.

She told us, 'Many young people in Burma are just so happy to have a job, and not have to rely on handouts.' With a benefits system non-existent in Burma, she probably struggled greatly with the UK's extensive system. 'Knowing the price of everything and the value of nothing' was how she described many people.

Getting the 'Freedom of the City of Newcastle upon Tyne' scroll out, we asked if we could have a picture and a semi-formal presentation. We told her that Wai Hnin had accepted the 'Freedom' on her behalf.

She said, 'Oh, I know her father, Mya Aye, and have met her mother and her sister.' She was glad Wai Hnin was active in the Burma Campaign UK and said she was encouraging more young people to get involved to change society. 'Some people think politics is 'dirty' and that it excludes 'good' people,' she said. Declan told her he was interested in politics and had spoken out about Burma in front of the Pope in Hyde Park, London, in 2010, with an audience of 80,000 people. She was pleased to hear this and had a long discussion with Declan, ending by turning to Anne and I, saying, 'Politics and religion are both important to develop social justice.'

Asking her assistant to come in, we prepared for the photograph. We all stood in front of her desk and I happened to rest my left hand on the desk. To my complete embarrassment, Aung San Suu Kyi sat back on my hand on the desk. I froze for a second, not wanting to cause a scene. Slowly, I wriggled my hand from underneath her bottom and we got on with the photographs. After a few snaps we finished our conversation with a discussion on Newcastle upon Tyne and what the 'Freedom' meant. I told her she was now allowed to graze her cattle on the Town Moor. Not having any cattle, she thought that wouldn't be too useful.

She finished with, 'The Geordies are strong people. I know from my time in the UK.' It was great to hear her call us Geordies and compliment us all.

It was all over in about twenty five minutes. She apologised for not having more time to spend with us, but her parting words were, 'Hope to see you again.' We headed down the steep stairs and chatted to U Nine Nine on the way out, thanking him for organising the visit. He was only too glad to have assisted. We crossed the road and were taking a photo of the NLD offices when Aung San Suu Kyi came out. A small group of people were waiting for a glimpse of her. Her team of minders kept the crowd at bay as she jumped into a car. The car whisked her away, followed by a truck of minders all in white shirts. A day to remember indeed - certainly one that Declan would not forget, as most of her time was focused on him: the need to involve and inspire the youth of Burma clearly one of her main objectives.

Part 3: Christmas in Labutta, 2011.

Inspired by Aung San Suu Kyi we returned to the hotel. The workers who last week wouldn't mention her name were keen to hear if we had really had a meeting with her. Getting the camera we showed them the photos. With big smiles and thumbs up, they were so happy, hoping for a better future for all the country.

Fr Henry picked us up at 2pm to take us to the station for our bus to Pathein. Driving across the city he was full of questions about Aung San Suu Kyi. He had been in the cathedral when she visited a few weeks before but had never met her. However, we were soon brought back down to earth when we arrived at the bus station. With hundreds milling around we found the ticket office and bought our ticket with the help of Fr Henry. After asking lots of people we eventually got to our bus just before it's 5pm departure. On presenting our tickets the inspector shook his head and said 'No foreigners on this bus.' We protested but he insisted 'No foreigners on this bus. Try tomorrow morning.' Going back to the ticket office, the man in the office replaced our tickets with ones for 9am the next day without explanation but at extra cost. Fr Henry had left, so we were left on our own. A taxi back to the hotel was our only option. Explaining our predicament the hotel staff were all smiles and glad to see their 'famous' guests back. The rooms were still vacant - as I suspect they had been for some years! Rice and eggs were kindly prepared and they wanted to know more about their beloved 'Lady'.

Early the next morning we took a taxi back to the bus station. After negotiating the rush hour traffic we arrived with our tickets, hopeful but nervous - and all we wanted was to get the bus to Pathein - a city we'd been to several times before. Our tickets had doubled in price for this morning's journey so we thought this would allow foreigners on. Presenting our tickets to the inspector he deliberated carefully, checked the price and then let us on. At last we were on our way on the 1950s Japanese bus. Stopping every hour or so at what appeared to be checkpoints we slowly made our way through the Irrawaddy Delta. Six hours later we arrived in Pathein, thankfully at the bus station we knew. Fr Henry had booked us into 'La Pyae Wun' (The Full Moon), the guesthouse we had stayed in before.

After quickly unpacking we walked to the cathedral in the hope they would still be having dinner. Luckily Monsignor Maurice was there preparing the Christmas Nativity in the cathedral courtyard. Seeing us he came over asking about our meeting with 'The Lady'. Word had spread fast. He showed us into their refectory where Fr John was still eating. We joined him and chatted over the usual things. We had met him on previous visits and he would always ask 'How many Catholics are there in England?' Next day Bishop John wanted to see us, 'So could we make a meeting at 10am in the morning?' asked Monsignor Maurice.

Arriving at 9am for breakfast, we were pleased to meet Bishop John at 10am. Coffee was awaiting us and he wanted to speak to us about our 'meeting'. The direction Aung San Suu Kyi would take in politics would greatly affect the Catholic church in Burma and the Bishop wanted to know if we could enlighten him any further. We had met Bishop John previously, a gregarious man aged about 50 with a perfect command of the English language. He told us that Aung San Suu Kyi had sent a letter to all the Bishops asking them to speak out about the situation in Burma. She felt it was their duty to help her to help the people, she couldn't do it on her own. This was a theme, I told the Bishop, that she had talked to us about, that she wanted more people involved, especially 'good' people, and to stop thinking that getting involved in politics was 'dangerous and risky.'

Next day was Christmas Eve and Fr Henry picked us up early for the journey to Labutta. Setting off in the minibus this was to be a Christmas like no other. Labutta is only about 80 miles from Pathein, a journey that would take less than 2 hours on normal roads. The traffic was light but the tarmac road soon became a dirt road and the villages we passed through seemed to become poorer and poorer. Passing through Myaungmya, Fr Henry tells us this is the birthplace of Aung San Suu Kyi. Six hours later we arrived at the fishing port of Labutta. On route we had witnessed workers in the fields watering the rice paddies with watering cans! The gravitational irrigation system had been destroyed in Cyclone Nargis. Fr Henry assured us there was a new 'hotel' which had a 'licence' for foreigners to stay. Sure enough the hotel had the official plague on the wall indicating 'Foreigners are warmly welcome'. The hotel had about 12 rooms all on ground level, but it seemed deserted. Ringing the bell and waiting, eventually a middle aged man arrived in his shirt and longyi. With a big smile he told us the price of $20 per room per night. A little expensive but we had no choice, so we booked in. There were clearly no other guests. Fr Henry wished us good evening saying he would pick us up at 5:30 in the morning. Tomorrow was Christmas Day and by coincidence Karen New Year, so it would be a very special day.

The rooms were bare and simple, but clean. I suspected we were the first foreigners at our hotel. Asking at reception for some food, the owner suggested we walk into town as there were one or two restaurants and bars. Walking along the dirt road it was clear this was a very very poor area. It had been completely devastated by Cyclone Nargis and was trying to get back on its feet. There was no street lighting and no mains electricity to any of the houses. The homes by the side of the road were shacks with straw roofs, with cows and other farm animals sharing the accommodation. I thought I had travelled back in time, 2000 years to Bethlehem. I could think of nothing else as the light faded. The stars started appearing in the night sky and I looked for a bright star above one of the shacks. I was sure that a special child would be born in this place tonight. Born into poverty, but to be a great leader. It was the Nativity scene, just 2000 years later with little seeming to have changed over all those years.

In a complete daze we heard people chatting and could see fire pits. Heading in that direction we thought we might get some food and drink. It was completely dark now and we didn't have torches. Stumbling into the grounds of the 'bar' we sat down on little plastic stools next to one of the fires. A lady came across who greeted us warmly in Burmese. We ordered a beer each and asked about food. She returned with our beers and a menu in Burmese. Looking over to the fire pit next to us we could see people eating what looked like barbecued fish or chicken. Pointing to it, she nodded her head indicating we could have some of that. Sitting uncomfortably on the stools I wondered what Christmas eve in the UK was turning out to be. Was it snowing? Would Santa Claus arrive? There were no Christmas decorations here, but of course this was a Buddhist country and most wouldn't celebrate Christmas at all. After eating some rice and the meat we had one more beer before returning to the hotel, hoping we could find our way in the dark.

Christmas Day arrives as the alarm goes off at 5am. Fr Henry will be here in half an hour. Waking Anne and Declan we exchange gifts. With little option for presents we agreed to one present per person. Declan had the pleasure of buying mine. Although I couldn't tell you what present I received for any other Christmas, I'll never forget the cushion Declan bought for me. I was always complaining about the hard seats at every cafe/restaurant and so he gave me the solution (so long as I remembered to take it with me).

Fr Henry was prompt and we headed for Karen New Year celebrations. There wasn't a cloud in the sky and the sun had just risen. The celebrations would start at 6am in the village of Mwehauk, a short drive from Labutta. Karen flags were prominent on the bullock carts and motorbikes heading to the celebrations. A crowd of about a thousand people of all ages was gathered in a large field. A stage had been prepared and dignitaries were already present on the stage. The sun was warming the day as the first of many speeches started. Fr Henry was sitting beside us and translated for a few minutes and then gave up - the speeches were long and complicated. As is the custom we had two hours of speeches from prominent leaders in the community including Fr Henry. By the end the sun was bright and very hot. I was desperate to get some shade. The finale of the event, after traditional Karen Don dancing, was the giving of presents to everyone. A young girl in full Karen outfit gave me a tin of carnation cream. I hadn't seen one for years and not wanting to seem ungrateful I gladly accepted it. Later I managed to secretly return it to the large box in front of the stage from whence it came. I had no real use for it but I was sure someone in the community would now get it.

Fr Henry then grabbed us and guided us to the other side of the village. Mass was being said at 10am and as it was Christmas Day he didn't want us to miss it. A Christmas tree stood in the corner of the church with a Nativity crib at the front on the altar. I recalled last night and wondered if another saviour had been born in one of the many shacks the people of Labutta call home. It was a wonderful and blessed service with lots of singing and everyone in full Karen outfits. Fr Gilbert was the serving priest and he welcomed us by doing part of the mass in English. The congregation dispersed to be with their families and Fr Henry invited us back to Fr Gilbert's for Christmas dinner. It wasn't traditional turkey and tinsel but as we expected, rice and a little chicken. We were thankful for anything that this poor community could provide. The village of Mwehauk was yet another step down in the poverty ladder. There was no running water and only a few taps. Young men carried water in buckets to the older residents in the village. Fr Gilbert explained that most of the village were Christians and Karen. The town of Labutta was mostly Buddhist and Burman. Mwehauk was like a Karen ghetto set aside for the second class citizens who farmed the poor quality land in the surrounding area. Poorer and poorer I thought - the further into the Irrawaddy Delta one went the poorer the community. It was amazing they survived. No obesity here, little healthcare but lots of malnutrition and disease. Fr Gilbert was very upbeat at first but he was clearly tired and the strain of working with the poorest of the poor was showing. He had lived in this community for many years and could see little light on the horizon. I told him of our meeting with Aung San Suu Kyi and the hope she had for a better future for the whole country. He was sceptical and took himself off to lie down. I could feel his pain but could little or nothing to help him.

At 4pm Fr Henry dropped us back off at the hotel. The owner came to greet Fr Henry and they had an intense conversation for several minutes. Henry came back to explain. The authorities had been to see the owner. They had told him we shouldn't be staying overnight here and he was very concerned they would shut his hotel down. Henry reassured him that if he had his licence he would be fine and anyway we were only staying one more night. Henry told us not to worry and that he would pick us up tomorrow. Declan, oblivious to all this, had plonked himself in front of the only TV in the hotel and was watching 'Home Alone' I noticed he was joined by a furry friend. He jumped when I pointed out the rat in the corner that had just ran under his feet! Anne joined Declan for an evening of 'Home Alone', literally and on TV. She was missing Sarah and Patrick in the UK but we had no way of contacting them in this remote location.

On Boxing Day we returned to Pathein for a few days, spending our time playing basketball and football in the cathedral courtyard with some of the priests and the children from the boarding school. A few days later we took the bus back to Rangoon for our flight to Thailand. On the way we stopped at Nazareth House, a boarding house for children from remote villages who went to the local secondary school. Saya Jonny Mahn (Saya meaning teacher) and his wife Daw Louise

May lived nearby and came to see us. Saya Jonny had been a personal assistant to Aung San Suu Kyi for three years while she was under house arrest and knew her well. He was interested to hear of our visit to see her before Christmas. He was also a senior member of the NLD and had hoped to become an MP in the 2010 election but the NLD boycotted the election as they deemed it would not be free and fair. Fr Gregory came from his village, Kansu, to wish us Happy Christmas. It was great to see our old friend from Mae Sot in his own country. He celebrated mass for us and it was clear the people of this area loved him so much, as we did also. The man in charge of the boarding house was called Raju and his brother John lived with them because he was very sick. Anne was asked to take a look at him by Fr Henry to give Raju some advice. I popped my head into his hut to say hello.

John had extremely swollen legs and was unable to walk, he had not left his house for several months and was very depressed. Anne checked him over and suggested some medicine to Fr Henry. Enquiring what the local doctor had said, they answered 'There was no local healthcare in this area.' They would have to take him to Rangoon but he refused to go. Sadly a few weeks after we left Fr Henry emailed with the news that John had died. In the West a few drugs to get the water off his legs and a little light exercise might have saved his life. People lived on the edge at all times in the Irrawaddy Delta, and I felt Henry's pain at not being able to help more even though he tried not to show it.

We had a few days to spare in Rangoon and wanted to meet up with some relatives of our friend, Daniel from Mae Sot. Daniel worked for FTUK and had two brothers in Rangoon. He had asked us to look them up and gave us a contact called Saw Blessing at the Karen Baptist Theological College. Like undercover spies we set off for the area of Rangoon where the college was located. The college appeared deserted when we got there - it was the Christmas holiday, but there was a man on security. We asked if he knew Saw Blessing who worked there.

He didn't but sent us into the college where a receptionist should be able to help. The receptionist spoke excellent English and knew Saw Blessing. He gave him a call on the phone and explained who we were. 'Saw Blessing would like to see us' he said, but we should go to the tea shop along the road and wait for him there.

Conscious of his safety we did as he asked. About half an hour later a small Karen man entered the tea shop and came straight over. Obviously we were the only Westerners in the tea shop so easy to spot. He knew Daniel very well and had studied with him at the college. We had a cup of tea and some cakes as Saw Blessing told us of his escape from the Tatmadaw in the Karen jungle some years ago. Showing us his hand with a missing finger - 'That was how close I came to death' he said. A bullet from a Burmese soldier had ripped through his finger and he had had to have it amputated in the jungle. He had escaped to Thailand with his wife and three children. They were still in Mae La refugee camp but he had returned to Rangoon to continue his studies and now he was a lecturer at the college. His mother was still in Karen State somewhere. He hadn't heard from her for some years but he would use this holiday to go back and try to find her.

After a while he suggested we go to look for Daniel's brothers. Knowing where they lived, he hoped they would be home. A short walk into the housing near the college and Saw Blessing shouted into a house. A head popped out of the door and a conversation in Karen ensued. Then a young man came out very cautiously. Saw Blessing was much more confident and encouraged him to meet us. He eventually came over and shook our hands. His English was poor but Saw Blessing translated. Soon we were wandering further up the road to find the other brother. Again he came out reluctantly. They didn't want any of their neighbours seeing them talking to foreigners. Realising this was very uncomfortable for them we asked for a photo to take back and show Daniel and then we would be on our way. Both agreed but said it could not include their face! So

Saw Blessing took the photo of them with us showing the two brothers from shoulder down only! It may sound ridiculous but this is what a totalitarian state does to people. Saw Blessing gave us a small package and asks us to give it to his wife if we get the chance to go to Mae La refugee camp. Everywhere we go families are separated from loved ones or they die lonely and isolated. That's what war really looks like I thought as we left Saw Blessing.

Early in January my sister Alison was visiting us when we were back in Mae Sot. We thought it would be a good experience for her to visit Mae La. Paw Gay arranged for us to get in and we took the opportunity straight away to meet up with Saw Blessing's wife. Paw Gay made enquiries and found out she was working as a nurse in one of the hospitals in the camp. She was very surprised to have foreign visitors but Paw Gay eased the path and Anne gave her the present from her husband. It was such an honour to be a bridge between the two who had to live separate lives.

Part 4: Peace in our time.

Karen National Union agree ceasefire, January 2012.

Everyday was bringing news of change in Burma. A Karen Peace delegation travelled to Naypyitaw and a ceasefire was agreed on January 12th with a prisoner release the next day. Dot Lay Mu is very upbeat, hoping this is a turning point. He attended Karen Revolution Day on 31st January inside Karen State and the mood was very optimistic. However, he did point out it was the 63rd anniversary and perhaps it should be renamed Karen Evolution Day!

All the good news and the holding of the ceasefire for two months allowed Paw Gay to suggest Anne, Declan and I to visit Karen State. Previously this would be almost impossible for foreigners, being far too dangerous. She discussed it with Dot Lay Mu who was very supportive. He contacted the KNLA 5th Brigade General and permission was given for us to travel. So on March 6th we set off for our first visit to Karen State along with Dot Lay Mu, Paw Gay and Lay Say. Excited and nervous we jump in the truck and leave Mae Sot heading north for Mae Sariang. Before reaching Mae Sariang the truck heads east to the Salween river and a small riverside village called Mae Sam Lep. Paw Gay takes us into a tea shop while Lay Say tries to arrange transport. The river is wide and fast flowing. Boats hug the river bank waiting for goods or travellers. After ordering coffee and tea leaf salad we wait for Lay Say and enjoy the beautiful view across the river - our first sighting of 'free' Karen State. Lay Say arrives back after 20 minutes and explains that no 'golowahs' ('white men', in Karen language) can leave from here. The Thai authorities are patrolling nearby. Paw Gay and Lay Say have a quick discussion and we jump back into the truck and head to Mae Sariang. We will have to stay overnight there while Lay Say tries to make other arrangements.

Next morning Lay Say picks us up at our guesthouse and says we can go another way but it will cost more money. We agree to pay the extra and head off to the river via the Salween National Park. Our driver now is a friend of Lay Say from the Karen Refugee Committee in Mae Sariang. He is Thai-Karen and will be able to get us through the roadblocks. The truck goes deeper and deeper into the jungle area along the tiniest of dirt roads. With steep drops at the side and rivers to cross it is very scary. Our fate is in the hands of the driver. After what seems like forever the truck stops and we get out grabbing our bags from the back of pick up. Lay Say tells us to sit by the side of the road as the truck heads back. Lay Say scouts ahead, returning after a few minutes indicating we should follow him. We can see the mighty Salween river through the jungle. The drop down to the river is steep but we can see a long boat tethered on the river bank. The deserted river bank is so beautiful and unspoilt. This could be a great tourist resort I thought if some small huts were built. Swimming and fishing in the river and walking in the jungle would be a great adventure. I looked over the other side and saw Kawthoolei close up for the first time. Kawthoolei means 'Land without Evil'. I knew that 'Kawthoolei' was an aspiration for the people of Karen State and not a description.

Can it be healed?
by Maung Maung Tinn

The place where they live is called a "black area"
The government soldiers come to the area and do whatever they
want... rape, kill, leave landmines...
That's why they have run and hidden in the jungle.
During the running their lives are destroyed.

Their children suffer landmine injuries.
Their husbands are shot.
There is no healthcare.
Great loss, which can never be replaced, occurs in the jungle.
The scars from their loss remain in their hearts.

We scramble down the steep river bank and race across the soft sand before jumping into the boat. The boat makes a swift departure and we're on our way. Thailand on one side and Karen State, Burma the other. Along the way the respective flags of each country remind us we are heading along a border. After about an hour Lay Say tells me to lie down in the bottom of the boat and throws some sheets and bags over me. Paw Gay explains that we will soon be passing a Thai checkpoint and they will be monitoring the boats from the river bank with binoculars. They will spot me easily as I am so tall and white. Declan and Anne, being smaller, just have to cover their heads and faces and sit facing the opposite river bank. Hardly being able to breath and with my legs bent uncomfortably, I lie as still as possible and await my fate.

After what seems forever, Lay Say pulls the covers back and says I can sit up now. 'We are passed the danger point,' he laughs. By now my legs are numb and I can hardly move but I'm glad to breathe fresh air and feel the water spray from the boat on my face again. Then I saw Anne laughing. 'Why all the laughing?' I ask. 'This is serious.' Lay Say explains that we had safely passed the army post some time ago and he just thought it would be funny to leave me under for half an hour extra. 'A real experience of what a trafficked person feels like,' he laughed.

After nearly 3 hours we slow and head towards the riverbank. I can see the small port of Mae Tu Tar which is our destination. We jump out of the boat with our bags into knee deep water and Lay Say tells us to hurry up the bank and get into the cover of the trees. There are Thai spotters on the other river bank and we must not get noticed. So up the steep bank we go, our feet slipping on the soft sand before making it to the cover of the trees. Lay Say goes off once again. It is nearly sunset and when he comes back he explains that he wants us to walk through the night as it is unsafe to stay in the village. Thai soldiers may cross the river and arrest us if they have spotted us. Anne, Declan and I don't want to walk through the jungle in the dark and ask if we can stay the night. We fear falling or breaking an ankle in the dark - and there are no hospitals for two days! We agree a compromise, we can stay but will set off at 4am to get out of the village in the dark, doing the first steep climb when it is cool. We must stay hidden in our hut until then.

We are given a hut on the side of the river bank and Paw Gay cooks some rice. We open our tin of sardines we have brought with us and add them to the rice. It gets dark quickly and soon starts to get cold. Paw Gay manages to get a mat and a blanket for each of us. With an early morning start we brush our teeth and try to rest. After about an hour of turning and trying to get comfortable I fall asleep on the undulating bamboo floor but about 2am I am wide awake as it is so cold. I grab another T-shirt from my bag and put it on, but it's still too cold to sleep. That 4am start can't come quick enough for me.

Paw Gay comes in exactly at 4am and we start to collect our belongings together by candle light. Hoping we haven't left anything in the dark we set off up the steep mountain side. Lay Say has a flask of hot water and some biscuits and says 'We'll stop for breakfast at first light.' Introducing us to our guards, he says 'Keep to the path. Don't even go off it for a pee without asking. Land mines could be anywhere. But the path is safe.' The guards are in military uniform and carry rifles, which to me look like relics from the Second World War. The older one leads the way with the younger one bringing up the rear.

Although the climb is steep at least it warms me up. Thankfully I only have a small backpack. My main bag is being carried by a young girl - a 'Muganaw' - an unmarried Karen girl. Lay Say had arranged, for a small fee, for all our bags to go ahead. I thought it was a little like slave labour but Lay Say assured me it was their job and it gave some income for their families. After about 30 minutes, a shout comes from the front and people ahead scramble up the side of the path and into the jungle. Not knowing what was happening I followed. As I hid in the jungle, I wondered where Anne and Declan were. It was too dark to see them. I lay on the jungle floor and all I could hear was my breathing - I wished I didn't breathe so loudly! Then I heard something coming down the track.

'Was it Burmese soldiers?' thinking this could be the end. Then it came into view. A huge grey object slowly pounding the path. It was a huge wild elephant that we had cleared the path for. You don't argue with a 5 tonne beast on its own territory. As it passed by, people appeared back onto the path from the jungle and I spotted both Anne and Declan. I was so relieved and started laughing with Declan. I realised what it must be like for parents with young children fleeing the army. How do you stay together in the dark? How do you stop children crying? I had met so many refugees and now I was tasting a tiny tiny amount of what they have endured for years. Looking back it was funny, but not if Tatmadaw soldiers are chasing you determined to find and kill you.

While hiding in the jungle
by Maung Maung Tinn.

When we heard that the government soldiers were coming to my village,
we left the house immediately.
We did not have time to think about finding important things
to carry rice with us; rice, blankets, mosquito nets, clothes.
Fear dominates us, always.
We cannot eat very well.
We cannot sleep very well.
It is very easy to become sick.

I have a fever from malaria, right now.
I feel so depressed.
In the jungle,
dizziness from malaria and fear of the soldiers come together
with my child's hunger.

We continued up the path and in the darkness I could see flames ahead. I was worried again but Paw Gay reassured me it was fine, it was just the villagers doing 'slash and burn' - a traditional farming technique. As we came closer I could see the flames were close to the path. How would we pass, what happens if it gets out of control? Lay Say seemed unperturbed. We headed on into the fire, with bushes burning either side of the path. The temperature was rising outside and inside me now. Thankfully we soon passed through the burning forest and reached a clearing at the top. Dawn was just breaking so we stopped for breakfast, three-in-one coffee again, made from Lay Say's flask of hot water. Biscuits and boiled eggs were delicious. Food was in short supply in Karen State and I learned that when you are hungry you'll eat anything.

I was grateful I wasn't carrying a backpack as the sun rose and the temperature started to soar. During the heat of the day we continued to walk through the jungle and forests. The benefits of the beautiful unspoilt views were tempered by the searing heat. The sweat was pouring off me and I couldn't rehydrate fast enough. 'Perhaps we should have walked through the night?' I thought. Lay Say bounded ahead greeting his friends in the villages, then came running back to say he had found us a resting place. We stopped at every village so Lay Say and Paw Gay could talk and we could rest. Boiled eggs, coffee and biscuits were brought out each time. Whilst we ate Lay Say disappeared into a hut for a cheroot and some rice whiskey. Our soldier guards joined in with Lay Say. 'I hope we don't have to rely on them to defend us', I thought, 'not after six cups of rice whiskey.'

The villages were truly remarkable, completely unspoilt. No running water, no toilet, no electricity. The children were literally in rags, with holes in their T shirts and no shoes, and often no shorts. A few huts had solar panels and we saw young girls carrying solar panels on their backs up the steep mountains. This was their one compromise with modernity. The fields were ploughed using buffalo with children acting as shepherds to the buffalo in the jungle. Rice and sugarcane were planted, with a little corn and green beans to supplement the diet. There was no obesity here, although a dentist was needed as the children sucked the sugar cane and their teeth were rotten.

As we were leaving one village, a man came running up to us. 'Are you the doctors?' he asked in Karen. Lay Say translated. About four hours walk away was the Jungle School of Medicine (JSMK) in which the villagers knew foreigner doctors worked and often walked in through their village. The man's son had a terrible pain and he wanted us to help. Anne is a nurse so we explained that she might be able to help. The child was about 4 years old but looked nearer two. Like many Karen children he was undernourished. Anne diagnosed what she thought was severe constipation. The boy was in considerable pain. Not joking we recommended Chang beer. We could see empty cans around the hut and suggested a small amount of beer, with careful bowel massage might relieve the pain. Anne also gave him some of our tablets we carried for constipation, asking Lay Say to carefully write the instruction down in Karen - if the pain didn't ease they should walk to JSMK to get more treatment. We left the family behind hoping the boy would recover. It was so hard to see him in so much pain and not be able to adequately help him.

Up and down mountain paths we went taking regular breaks. In one village the villagers were making treacle out of sugar cane. A buffalo walked in a small circle attached to two huge stones that squeezed the sugar cane. The juice was collected and transferred to a fire pit for processing. I'd never seen anything like it before. It looked so medieval but it worked and it gave the children an energy food they desperately needed. Eight hours later we were at the top of our last mountain and Paw Gay pointed out Day Buh Noh, our destination, down in the valley by the beautiful and glisening Yusana river. It looked only a short walk down the mountain but the steep decline was painful on the knees and the sun was beating directly on our faces. Elephants worked the forest, clearing trees for the villagers to use the wood to build houses. Four hours later we entered Day Bu Noh. Bamboo huts and a few wooden houses lined the dirt tracks. Children played in the streams and people were sitting outside houses watching the day go by. Such a simple life with no traffic and associated air pollution, I could feel my lungs enjoying the experience. After 12 hours walking in the heat we had reached our destination. Entering the FTUK compound through a gate and an archway of roses I felt I had been transferred to paradise. The wooden house beyond the flower filled garden looked idyllic. I was in heaven until a group of soldiers came marching past to remind me I was in a conflict zone and many people had lost their lives to maintain this simple way of life.

Our bamboo hut was so beautifully simple. A wooden floor with a mat. A candle in the corner was our light and cooking could be done in the 'kitchen' outside - a wood fire with a pan over the top! People would pay thousands for this paradise. A plastic drum of water with a pan was our shower. You strip down and use the pan to pour water over yourself. It is so refreshing after a long day walking. Getting the dust and sweat of the jungle off is so important to stop skin rashes. Paw Gay introduced us to Kyaw Pwa, a Karen Agricultural Department worker. He looked after this small compound which had a fish pond, about an acre of vegetable plots and a rose garden. He couldn't speak English but became a great friend showing us around the area and guiding us along the paths and through the jungle areas during our stay. Dinner was cooked by one of the FTUK staff. It was banana curry tonight. Unusual, but when you're hungry…Exhausted, Anne and I set up a mosquito net in our room. And even better we had two blankets so we should be warm enough tonight. I slept like a log in my 5 star room! Waking with the cockerals next morning, Paw Gay was already lighting the fire and boiling some water for coffee.

After breakfast of rice and fried eggs we had to go to the village office to report our arrival. This community was still at war, even though there was a ceasefire. As we walked along the path all the men were in full military uniform, many carrying rifles. The full enormity of war hit me then. This was a war zone. I was under military command and we had to report in. The young General in charge was pleased to see us. Dot Lay Mu had spoken to him and assured him we could be trusted. After the usual formalities we were given permission to stay.

It was very hot again, with clear blue skies. Paw Gay suggested we relaxed and go for a swim in the river. From our compound we took a path through the rice paddies that surrounded the entire village to the river. Not only could we swim here but we could also take a bath so we had our soap at the ready. Just as we arrived at the river a loud crack echoed around my head and I instinctively hit the ground wondering 'What the hell was that?' I looked up and saw Paw Gay wondering why I was flat on my face. 'Someone hunting in the forest', she said. 'Don't worry we'd know if the Tatmadaw were nearby.' I'd never heard a gunshot so close. It was so loud. Now I know how it must feel when guns are being fired all around you. So terrifying, especially for children. I've never forgotten that sound.

The swimming was wonderful and we were even joined by some buffalo. Who needs to swim with dolphins in Florida? Suitably refreshed and clean, the day seemed to end before it had begun. The sights, sounds and smells of the jungle were so delicious. They say time flies when you're enjoying yourself. I must have been enjoying myself. Paw Gay had told me many times how beautiful Karen State was and now I could see it with my own eyes and knew why and what they were fighting so hard and long for. I fell in love with these people on that day and my heart is still there in many ways.

Next day, after another wonderful night's sleep, we walked along the river and through the jungle to a village called Lay Bu Der. This was Lay Say's home village and where most of his family lived. Burmalink UK supported the school by paying the teachers' wages and providing some money for books and pencils. We had a meeting with the school committee and a tour of the one classroom school. They were so pleased to see us and thank us for our support. We met Lay Say's mother and father, and his brother and sisters, and all their children. After sharing some rice wine we headed off to New Generation School where we would stay the night. Lay Bu Der had no toilets so Lay Say didn't want us to stay. New Generation school was the home of Kyaw Pwa's family who let us use one of the rooms in their house. Dinner was delicious, rice with chicken. Earlier I had noticed one of the many chickens scratching around the house had an injured leg. I asked Kyaw Pwa about the chicken we had eaten and he confirmed that the poor disabled chicken had been sacrificed for us. Survival of the fittest!

Next day we visited the school and were asked to speak to the students. All of us were only too pleased to oblige. The school was home to 130 secondary school children, many of them boarding as their villages were several days' walk away. It was great to meet the children and the headteacher. A few years later the headteacher was voted in as the civilian administrator for the area and remembered Anne, Declan and I each time we visited for our kind words of encouragement. In the evening we were asked to meet General Kler Doh, 5th Brigade and in charge of this district. Entering his compound with Paw Gay it was very dark. The General was sitting with a small candle on the table. In his vest and longyi and clearly relaxed, he told me the ceasefire was holding but that he didn't trust the Tatmadaw. Over 60 years of war had taught him that. He had been a soldier all his life and lived here with his wife and children. He told me I knew one of his son's who was working with FTUK in Mae

Sot. The son had also vouched for us when Paw Gay had requested permission for us to travel. It was interesting to hear they had checked up on us so much and also that we had so many friends who would guarantee we had 'Karen hearts'. I'd never met a real General before, and certainly not a battle hardened one but we still remain friends and I have met him on several occasions since.

Day Bu Noh health clinic was our next port of call after another good night's sleep. 'It must be the fresh air' I thought. Malaria, diarrhea and malnutrition were the most common ailments the head of the clinic told us. Anne, being a nurse and Declan soon to start his training as a Doctor, spent a long time in discussion with the chief medic while I took a stroll to the local primary school where Lay Say's wife worked. About 30 children were taught by two teachers, just like a rural village school in the UK. The afternoon trip to Day Bu Noh high school was spoilt by a heavy rainstorm. The entire school of about 300 children had packed into the main school hall to listen to us speak when the heavens opened and rain crashed against the metal roof. It was impossible to be heard and so we had to abandon the visit - but at least we tried.

The week went by so quickly. With little food, no TV or radio and no alcohol I couldn't believe I'd had such a magical time. All too early the cockerels woke us for the last time and we headed up the steep mountain at 6am to do the climb before it got too hot. Looking back from high on the mountain I knew I'd be back one day and prayed that the ceasefire and peace would last. Twelve hours later after trekking through an unspoiled jungle we arrived back at the Salween. We had used all our food supplies and there were no shops. Paw Gay managed to get some rice, so she boiled it up. For starters she offered us 'rice soup' - it was the strained starchy water from the rice! I tried to eat it but... Next came the rice with a few leaves from the jungle. Unfortunately (or fortunately) a few ants had invaded the rice. Crushing them in, I thought a little protein won't go a miss. As I said - you'll eat anything when you're hungry.

It is very delicious
by Maung Maung Tinn.

Normally,
I like all the food our mother cooks for us,
but not the bean soup.
Now I am hungry and I am eating bean soup.
I really enjoy the soup.
We have not had any proper meals, rice, fish paste, curry, and
vegetables for a while.
We could get only rice and salt.
When we are hungry, any food, whether we normally like it or
not, is so delicious.
Here, we do not have a choice to complain about the food,
because the place where we are is not our home.... It is the
jungle.
The reason we are here is not for fun.
The reason we are here, is to hide from the government
soldiers.

Next morning we awoke at first light and Paw Gay had managed to get some three-in-one coffee, full of the sugar we needed to sustain us for the day. Three hours in the boat, hiding for half an hour, followed by four hours in a truck and we were back in Mae Sariang. Shattered but hungry we booked into a guesthouse, showered and went out for food. The restaurant that looked so poor a week ago was now first class, and we ate till our bellies ached. I lost about a stone and a half in one week - who needs Slimming World?

The few days I was privileged to spend in Karen State were some of the most amazing days of my life. Talking with army generals late into the night by candlelight trying to understand a people at war. Speaking at schools with teachers and pupils who had known nothing but war and poverty, and yet they were so much like ourselves. They wanted to have a family, travel, live in peace, have basic healthcare, and all the simple things we take for granted. Visiting the village 'hospital' which didn't even have an X-ray machine. Medics travelling miles to visit the sick. Teams of volunteers carrying the sick and injured for days by 'bambulance' - bamboo hammock - to get treatment. They all worked in solidarity to survive. It was a pleasure and a privilege to share some time with these people. I was beginning to understand them.

Part 5: Mae Sot and the trade unions.

Meeting with Zipporah Sein (KNU General Secretary).

A few weeks after returning from Karen State Paw Gay asked if we would like to meet Zipporah Sein, the Genreal Secretary of KNU. Of course we wanted to meet such an important lady, and so early one Sunday morning Paw Gay picked Anne and I up to take us to meet her. The location of her home was not widely known for security reasons. The gate slid open after Paw Gay had made a telephone call and in we drove. Jumping out into the compound we were greeted by Zipporah Sein, a small Karen lady about 55 years old. She shook our hands warmly and invited us in.

Zipporah was General Secretary of the KNU from October 2008 to December 2012, succeeding Padoh Mahn Sha after his assination in Mae Sot. Born in Karen State where she trained as a teacher before fleeing to Thailand in 1995. Prior to becoming General Secretary she was executive secretary of the Karen Women's Organisation (KWO).

Tea was served and we chatted about our recent experience in Karen State and our meeting with Aung San Suu Kyi. She talked about a desire for peace, political engagement and the right kind of economic development. She spoke about the interest of other countries in helping Burma develop, but was concerned they would merely be interested in business and not development. As for the recent elections, she noted little change. The military still ran the country and the constitution limited any real progress, but she would be going for further peace talks with the Burmese government and was willing to engage.

She spoke passionately about the rights of Karen people but understood that perhaps an independent Karen State was improbable. More probable, and what she was aiming to discuss, was a Federal Burma, with independence under the umbrella of the National government. I agreed it was a realistic starting point in negotiations which would need compromise.

On leaving I thought she was a woman not dissimilar to Aung San Suu Kyi in her desire to see change and peace in their country. I hoped they would be able to work together in the future.

Trade Union delegation to Mae Sot, May 2012.

Back in Mae Sot FTUK had invited a delegation of UK trade unionists to visit and celebrate International Workers Day on May 1st. It was a time of great change in Burma, with Peace deals agreed with many of the ethnic groups and by-elections held on April 1st. The NLD was re-registered for these by-elections. They won 43 of the 44 seats they contested (out of 45 available). They did not contest the 2010 elections as they believed the elections would not be free, fair and impartial.

Delegates from Unison, National Association of School Teachers and Union of Women Teachers (NASUWT), Fire Brigades Union (FBU) and University and College Union (UCU) arrived at the end of April. It was a great show of solidarity with FTUK. Dot Lay Mu, Paw Gay, Lay Say and all the other leaders showed the delegation the real life of a migrant/refugee. Visiting the factories around Mae Sot opened their eyes to the scale of the problem. Witnessing the working and living conditions was an education. The visit to the garbage dump was curtailed by about half of the group who couldn't get past the smell of the rotting garbage and had to turn back.

Two highlights of the visit stand out. The first one was an educational social evening. Anne arranged for the showing of a film called 'Moving to Mars' at Ex-Pat bar. It was the dry season and the nights were very warm so we set up the screen outside and sat in the grounds of the bar to be entertained and educated. Moving to Mars is a 2009 documentary following the story of two Burmese families from Mae La refugee camp moving to their new homes in Sheffield. I think our friends in FTUK enjoyed it more seeing how their friends were or were not coping with life in the UK. The UK was certainly not the paradise they imagined. It was great that both groups could see the film and comment on it from different perspectives.

The second highlight of the week-long visit was May 1st International Workers Day. While in Thailand, migrants are allowed to join existing unions but are not allowed to form a union. But with only 4% of the Thai workforce unionised, it is not easy for migrants to join a Thai union, most of which are based in Bangkok. Burmese workers in factories on the borders have tried to organize and take action against the exploitative conditions but they face difficulties because their employers withhold their passports and work permits and so they cannot show their documents to immigration and are sometimes deported.

Min Lwin was instrumental in helping us join in the Mae Sot celebrations. The UK delegates had been asked to bring banners and flags in anticipation of the event. May 1st was very hot with wall to wall sunshine. We gathered at 8am to miss the heat of the day. Many factories had given the workers the day off (but not with pay) and they gathered in the marketplace. Each factory had a banner and the workers from that factory gathered and marched behind their factory name. Trade unions were just about non-existent in the factories so it was much more a celebration of International Workers day rather than a trade union event. Bands led some of the factories and we marched through the streets of Mae Sot with our UK trade union flags. Many of the Thai and Burmese workers were pleased to see the UK workers. After the march around the town, games and competitions took place along with discussions and speeches at various locations. A great day to witness and take part in.

217

Part 6: Travelling the world.

Australia, Guatemala, El Salvador, USA and Canada.

Our nine months in Mae Sot passed so quickly. It was so sad to leave our friends. Declan left on May 20th, returning home to the UK to begin his medical studies. Anne and I left on May 30th heading for Australia. We had decided that our return journey should be the opposite way around. The ticket cost very little more and it was a great opportunity to see some old friends in far off places. So after two leaving parties with our friends at FTUK we left Thailand sad but excited about renewing some old friendships.

Perth and Ywa Hay.

Arriving in Perth, Western Australia it was the middle of their winter and so a little cool. I needed a warm jumper so my first port of call was 'Salvos' - the Salvation Army seconds shop. I found a lovely warm wool jumper and was set for the Australian winter sun.

Ywa Hay, former General Secretary of FTUK, had left Mae La Oon refugee camp with his wife and five children a few years previously and the last time I saw him in Thailand I shook his hand and said one day we would meet in a free and democratic country and he wouldn't have to live as a 'refugee'. I honestly believed that when I waved him goodbye in Mae Sariang, and now I could fulfil that dream.

He arrived at the airport in a car to pick up Anne and I. We didn't have much luggage so it all fitted in easily. He drove us to his detached house in a suburb of Perth. I was so pleased to see him doing well and he was obviously proud of the life he had made for himself in Australia. We were given one of the children's bedrooms, and slippers to boot.

He had trained as a Maths teacher in Karen State as a young man and now had a job as a teaching assistant at the local school, a job he was so proud to do. He told me the children called him 'Mr Hay' which he found amusing.

His eldest son was working as a trainee car mechanic, the three middle children at school and the youngest at home with his wife.

His wife had struggled a little to make the journey from Karen jungle to a modern 'Western' lifestyle. Her English was still poor and they all spoke Karen at home. She preferred her kitchen outside and often cooked in the garden. It was great to see how she adapted 'Western' culture to her jungle upbringing. But most importantly, they were a family and happy together, something they had never known as refugees in Thailand.

Ywa Hay went to work each day but gave us the use of his car so we were able to visit the beach and the attractions around Perth. As I expected Ywa Hay was also greatly involved in the Burmese community in Perth. Many of the refugees couldn't speak English and needed assistance with claiming benefits, doctors appointments, job interviews, etc. Ywa Hay was always on call to give them a helping hand. He was constantly fielding telephone calls and arranging to meet up with people to fill in forms and prepare for interviews. That was the type of guy he was - a real community leader.

When it was time to leave he took us to the airport for our flight to Sydney and we had to say goodbye once again. I wasn't sure when I would see him again so it was hard to say goodbye. But as the Karen only ever say 'goodbye' to the dead he made it very easy with his 'Tee Law Tha La Kee' - 'See you later' as Anne and I headed for departures.

Auntie Pauline, Uncle Bob and Cousin Joanne in Sydney.

Our flight to Sydney was scheduled to take 6 hours so we sat back and looked forward to meeting some of Anne's relatives. Auntie Pauline and Uncle Bob were 'Ten pound Poms' (a colloquial term used in Australia and New Zealand to describe British citizens who migrated after the Second World War). Pauline was Anne's father's cousin, but had been brought up as a sister after Pauline's mother died when she was a young child. Pauline and Bob had left Hartlepool in the 1970's, paying £10 each for their boat trip to begin a new life in Australia. They had two children Joanne and Mark. Anne has a fantastic memory (as many women seem to have!) and remembers her Auntie and Uncle before they left when she was a child. Pauline was much younger than her Dad and she remembers her putting on make-up with her older sister Theresa before a night out on 'the town' in Hartlepool.

However, our flight to Sydney had to make an unscheduled stop. Part way across Australia someone was taken ill on the aeroplane and the Captain had to divert to Melbourne to off load the passenger. After a few hours delay we were on our way again with the Captain apologising over the intercom, and to Anne's delight he told us that he had asked the crew to open all the bottles of champagne on board and for us to 'fill our boots!' Well, Anne needed no second invitation - I think we finished at least two bottles and were quite tipsy when we landed in Sydney in the early evening.

Sydney is quite unusual (or was at the time) because the baggage collection carousels were open to the general public. It had been an internal flight so there was no immigration or customs. As I waited for the luggage on the belt people were coming in and out of the airport building to meet their friends and relatives. Anne had to go to the toilet (I think the champagne had gone to her bladder as well as her head). I was standing looking at the carousel when a voice from behind asked 'Is this the delayed flight from Perth?'

I knew instinctively that it was Uncle Bob. He had such a broad Hartlepool accent. I turned around and looked at the man in front of me and said 'You must be Uncle Bob.' I looked behind him and saw Anne's sister Catherine, but it couldn't be her...I thought 'I've definitely had too much champagne. I'm seeing things.' Then the penny dropped, this was cousin Joanne, there was only a month in age between Catherine and Joanne and boy, did they look alike. All hell broke out as Anne came back from the toilet and saw me talking with these two 'strangers'.

She shouted 'Uncle Bob' and gave him a big hug, and then she saw Joanne and screamed 'Joanne' as she ran over to her. She hadn't seen them for over thirty years and yet she knew them instinctively. When she had calmed down she asked me how I had recognised Uncle Bob.

I said 'I didn't recognise him, but I did recognise his accent. There couldn't be two people waiting for this plane with Hartlepool accents.' Even though he had left Hartlepool over forty years ago, he still hadn't lost his accent. As they say 'You can take the boy out of Hartlepool, but you can't take Hartlepool out of the boy.'

Auntie Pauline was waiting at home for us. Anne said she hadn't changed a bit. We enjoyed a great two weeks staying with Bob and Pauline. One highlight was when we all took a catamaran boat up the river to Sydney harbour ending at the famous bridge. Joanne's children took a day off school to be with us. Another highlight was when Anne and I picked up two of Joanne's children (Katie and Sarah) from school (Christopher being at Secondary school). They were so delighted to see us and asked if we would come in and meet their teachers. They were so happy to introduce their 'Auntie Anne and Uncle Tony' as they had few other relatives in Australia. We enjoyed nights in with Bob and Pauline watching some old movies that reminded them of England, and of course we had the customary barbecue. For me I really enjoyed swimming in the 50 metre outdoor pool on mid-winter's day. The air temperature was still about 20°C and it was bright sunshine, so extremely enjoyable.

Whilst in Sydney we met up with Zaw Tun, an exiled Burmese political activist. He is a former treasurer with FTUB and fell out with Maung Maung in 2010 over accusations that Maung Maung had travelled to Burma on three occasions in 2008 using FTUB finance to buy the air tickets and kept the visits secret. Zaw Tun was now living in exile in Australia with his father. He had resigned from his post in FTUB. We had a great night with him once he relaxed having told us the story about Maung Maung. It is always very difficult to find the truth. I'm sure Zaw Tun's evidence was genuine but maybe Maung Maung had good reason to keep his visits secret. There were lots of stories of spying and espionage in the organisations in exile - part of life living 'underground'. A few months later I heard that Zaw Tun was working again in Burma with the Royhinga for an international NGO. He was on the ground working tirelessly for his people. That's what he did and I remember him fondly for that.

The two weeks in Sydney passed all too quickly and I promised myself that I must go back to see my 'in-laws'. With a few tears in our eyes, Joanne's husband Jason drove us to the airport. We were heading for Los Angeles, USA. I'd never been to the USA so I was very excited. The plan was to use Los Angeles as a hub airport as I wanted to travel to Guatemala to see my friend Lisandro and then Canada to see another friend Billy.

Lisandro and Alison in Guatemala (and Patrick).

Lisandro was born in Quetzaltenango (known as Xela for short). He is a typical Mayan, small in stature, with a moustache and a keen sense of humour. He is a car mechanic who met his wife Alison while she was taking a year out and working in a nursery in Xela. All his family still live in Xela, many of them living in a house he built for his mother. Lisandro's father died some years ago when Lisandro was a teenager. He died of a brain injury caused in a car crash.

Our flight from Los Angeles to Guatemala city was full of returning Guatemalans to their home country. Many hundreds of thousands live and work in the USA. Anne and I picked up our baggage and passed through security and then passport control. The number of heavily armed policemen alerted us to what was to come. Alison and Lisandro had flown from the UK to meet us and were waiting at the airport just outside the security cordone. It was getting dark as we came out of the airport building. A minibus was waiting and they told us to get in quickly. The bus driver drove at speed through the streets of the city until we stopped at the gate to a walled development. A heavily armed security guard came out, looked in the bus and talked to the driver, before opening the gate. The estate consisted of a hundred or so detached houses. One of them was our guest house for the night. 'Are we going out for dinner tonight?' I asked. 'The city is too dangerous after dark,' replied Alison. 'We've ordered take away pizza.' And that was our introduction to Guatemala. We stayed in the guesthouse, ate our pizza with a beer, then went to bed. Next morning we had breakfast of eggs and beans and then left for the airport again. Patrick was due in from the UK and we were picking him up.

Patrick arrived safely and wanted to explore the city. We asked Alison what was the best way. She said we could only go out with the minibus driver and we had all to stay close together. 'Drug lords rule much of Guatemala and the government is corrupt' said Lisandro. 'We need to be very careful here. It's a little safer in Xela.' So a whistle stop tour of the city with the driver ensued. We hardly got out but Lisandro pointed out the main sights. Patrick was most unimpressed but perhaps because he was so tired he accepted it. He had just finished his degree in Chemistry and when he went back would start teacher training in Leeds. 'A fool,' I told him, but I was secretly pleased he was following in my footsteps as a science teacher. At a packed bus station Lisandro negotiated the crowds to get us tickets on the 'chicken bus' as he called it, to Xela. Xela was high up in the mountains and a six hour journey along the bumpy and winding roads. It got cooler and cooler as we climbed and I wished I had more clothes but was grateful for my 'Salvos jumper'.

Xela has a population of about 120 000 and has few foreign tourists. The mountains surround it and the sturdy people farm the steep hills. Most houses are of concrete construction built to withstand earthquakes in this volcanic region. We arrived at Lisandro's home - a two storey concrete house with a flat open top roof on which the washing is hung out to dry. Lisandro's mother was head of the house and welcomed us, with Alison translating as we spoke little Spanish. Our rooms were bare but the bed was comfortable. The shower was perhaps the most intriguing room. An electric shower with the heating element visible in the shower head. Lisandro warned us to use the rubber flip flops whilst in the shower to protect against electrocution! Needless to say I didn't stay long in the shower and more remarkably neither did Patrick!

The days were warm and sunny but the nights and early mornings cold. Lisandro cooked black beans and eggs for breakfast (yes every morning). We ventured out during the day as a group to the city centre to visit the cathedral and have lunch. Lisandro knew many people and it was great to see him in his own environment. He was clearly a popular character. Lisandro particularly enjoyed 'happy hour' in the local bars in the early afternoon where we ordered 10 bottles of the local beer in a bucket of ice. Alison was much more cautious and wanted us to get home well before dark.

We wanted to climb the local volcano Sainte Maria and Lisandro was keen but would only consider it with an armed guard. There had been kidnappings of tourists in the past and he feared for our safety. After much discussion a tour guide persuaded Lisandro that it was safe to climb without an armed guard. So at 4:30am one morning Patrick, Anne and I set off in a minibus with Lisandro, his nephew and a mountain guide. Xela is one of the highest cities in Central America, sitting at around 2300 metres (7,546 feet). Sainte Maria is 3772 metres high (12,375 feet), nearly as high as Everest base camp which is 5200 metres.

Starting the climb at 6am to ensure we are off the mountain before dark, the route was not particularly steep but the climb was extremely arduous because of the high altitude. As Anne, Lisandro and I climbed we had to stop frequently as we were constantly out of breath. Patrick, Lisandro's nephew and the guide had little problem. After about two hours and half way up, Lisandro was completely out of breath and decided he couldn't go on. We didn't want to separate as a group but Lisandro insisted that he would be fine. He was a local and knew his way down the mountain. The rest of us continued upwards getting slower and slower. As we climbed it also became cloudy. This was a huge disappointment as we had been told by the guide that on a clear day we could see directly into the crater of a lower volcano from Sainte Maria. Getting more and more breathless, I noticed Anne's lips were turning blue. We had to stop more and more frequently. It was probably the hardest climb I have ever done. I was beginning to know why mountaineers needed to acclimatise. Eventually we reached the top covered in clouds. We could see very little and the cold drizzle did nothing to elate us.

Stopping only for a short rest at the top and to take photographs to prove we made it we headed back down, Anne's lips recovering their colour as we descended. 'Always leave a reason to come back,' I thought to cover my disappointment of the clouds, as we trudged back to meet Lisandro. We need not have worried about Lisandro, he had found a bar in the village and had not much else to do but drink beer. He was in a 'happy' mood when we found him. We joined him for a celebratory bottle of beer before heading back to Xela.

Next day Lisandro took us to the hot springs in the next village. Jumping on the local bus we rumbled out of Xela. A bumpy ride of about an hour and we were there. The hot volcanic water with all its salts was wonderful to bathe in. Hundreds of locals enjoyed the pleasure in the multitudes of pools. Later in the week I asked if there was a swimming pool in town. Lisandro, always keen to help, took us to the municipal swimming pool. A 30 metre pool with lanes, it looked great. But my swim was not to be. As we tried to pay our entrance fee, we were asked to show our medical certificates to say we didn't have any infectious diseases. This was a first for me. Of course, I didn't have one so I wasn't allowed in. You learn something new every day, so they say.

Before we left Xela I wanted to buy some food for Lisandro's family and asked if he would take us to the meat market. Duly obliging we set off on foot. On entering there were lots of butchers but little meat. Lots of intestine and giblets but little 'chicken breast'. This place was much poorer than I thought. We managed to find a little meat and took it home. Lisandro's Mam was so pleased and cooked us a sumptuous 'last supper'.

Our next stop was Lake Atitlan, a tourist resort, where Alison and Lisandro left us to discover it ourselves. We all travelled on the bus, but they were to stay on an island on the Lake and we decided to be tourists and stay by the side of the Lake. Being lower down the mountain it was a little warmer and had more nightlife and bars, so Patrick was more at home. The place was so beautiful and quiet. A highlight was seeing a hummingbird taking nectar from a flower whilst sitting on the balcony of the guest house one afternoon.

We travelled back to Guatemala city without Alison and Lisandro as they naturally wanted to spend more time with their family. We stayed in a guest house owned by a young Australian couple and they offered a walking tour of the city during the day. They did alert us to not going out after dark as it was too dangerous, so we enjoyed nights watching the Olympic games which they showed on the TV. The day time tour of the city was very interesting. We enjoyed a local lunch and a beer at the market place and were shown the cathedral square which displayed hundreds of red flags with the names of the victims and disappeared from the civil war. The civil war lasted 36 years, starting in 1960 as the poor rebelled against government oppression. It ended in 1996 but the country now has huge problems with drug cartels, like many other countries in Central America.

Archbishop Romero and El Salvador.

I wanted to go to both Niguragua and El Salvador whilst in Central America, both with only a week I chose El Salvador. So we left Guatemala city by bus for San Salvador, the capital of El Salvador. After six hours we were at the central bus station in San Salvador.

In the 1980's El Salvador was deeply polarised along political lines (extreme right government and military versus extreme left communist guerrilla forces) and along economic lines (a very rich minority and a very poor majority). The polarisation had its roots in the country's history, but it was made worse by the Cold War. The Sandinista communist revolution had taken place in Nicaragua in the late 1970's and 1980s. Because of this, and also because of the presence of Cuba to the immediate south of the USA, the US government pumped huge amounts of money into El Salvador. The aim was that the communists would not take hold there. It was a matter of national security for the USA.

In this messy situation, there were some who tried to speak out, to speak reason. Among these were the Jesuits who worked at the University of Central America (UCA) in San Salvador. They wanted equal opportunities for everyone in education and health, and equality before the law. They spoke up for the poor and condemned the illegitimate use of violence by either side.

On November 16th 1989 the leftist guerillas FMLN (Farabundo Marti National Liberation Front) launched a major attack on the capital city. The Salvadoran army was taken by surprise and later that day a rapid-reaction battalion of the Salvadoran army was dispatched to the UCA. Their mission to kill the leaders of the Jesuit community, who they considered the mastermind behind the latest military attack. Salvadoran soldiers dragged six Jesuit priests from their beds and murdered them along with their housekeeper and her teenage daughter. The Salvadoran government tried to blame the killings on left-wing rebels, but their version was contradicted by the evidence of one woman, Lucia Cerna, who was hiding near the site of the murders. The soldiers left a cardboard sign that read 'FMLN executed those who informed on it. Victory or death, FMLN.'

As luck would have it our guest house was opposite the UCA, the scene of the killing of the Jesuit martyrs. So the first morning we took a short walk there. The office and residence of the priests was now a museum in remembrance of them. The pictures in the museum were very vivid, no censorship. Photographs of the bodies of the priests and the housekeeper were on display and the bullets holes in the wall were still visible. The murders attracted international attention and increased international pressure for a cease-fire. It is recognized as a turning point that led toward a negotiated settlement to the war.

Next day we headed into the centre of the city to visit the Metropolitan Cathedral of the Holy Savior where the tomb of Archbishop Oscar Romero is located in the crypt. During the funeral ceremony of the Archbishop held at the cathedral, rifle shots came from surrounding buildings, including the National Palace. In the stampede of people running away from the gunfire, journalists recorded that between 30 and 50 died.

Patrick, Anne and I attended mass in the cathedral at 12 noon. After mass we waited for the crypt to open for visitors in the afternoon. A small gate took us down some steps where the air was cool and the lights dim. There were few visitors this afternoon and we were able to stand quietly by the tomb of Archbishop Romero who was assassinated on March 24th 1980. His tomb is covered by a bronze sculpture, depicting Romero as if he were sleeping while guarded by the four evangelists, with a red jewel representing his heart. It was a wonderfully peaceful place and I felt I was near a man of great principle and courage.

To complete the pilgrimage of El Salvador and Archbishop Romero we visited the hospital chapel (Divine Providence Hospital) where he was assassinated. Setting off from the guesthouse on foot I had a tourist map showing me where it was. Thinking it would be well signposted we started walking in the general direction. Turning off the main road into an estate I thought we were near but there were no signs. Studying the map by the side of the road with Patrick a car driver pulled up. 'Are you looking for Romero's chapel?' he asked in English.

'Yes, it's around here somewhere, isn't it?' I replied hopefully.

'It's not far, just continue along here, then right and up the hill.'

Anne was relieved as the day was getting hot. About five minutes later we passed through the gates of the small hospital and walked up the slight incline to the hospital chapel. A sign on the wall gave details of the assasination. Entering respectfully, the small chapel had been left unaltered since 1980. Óscar Arnulfo Romero y Galdámez (15th August 1917 – 24th March 1980) served as the fourth Archbishop of San Salvador. He spoke out against poverty, social injustice, assassinations, and torture amid a growing war between left-wing and right-wing forces. We stood at the altar where a single gunman shot him as he celebrated mass. His outspoken views had attracted the attention of the death squads. A truth commission in El Salvador concluded that an extreme right wing politician had given the order for him to be assassinated.

Leaving the chapel we walked back down the hill a hundred metres or so to visit the small house the Archbishop lived in within the grounds of the hospital. Nothing had changed in the house since 1980. It was a museum to remember his life. His small car was parked on the drive and his bedroom was as it had always been - a small single bed in a very simple room. A lamp on one bedside table and his bible and rosary beads on the other. His cassock was in a glass cabinet in the hallway and there were pictures of him on the wall with the story of his life. There's also a wonderful 'fable' that his heart was removed from his body and the nuns placed it in a casket and buried it in his garden. The fable continues that some years later the casket was dug up and opened, and the heart had not decomposed but was in its original condition. The place where the casket is buried in the garden is marked by a plaque for all to see.

It was great to see and live modern history and even Patrick was moved by this visit. He thought it would be just another 'church' to walk around but the history of Romero is truly uplifting and the 'pilgrimage' was well worth it for us all.

The City of Angels.

We all flew back to Los Angeles on July 28th and decided to return to the Venice area and 'Muscle Beach'. Anne and I had stayed here for a few days before we went to Guatemala and really enjoyed it. Using AirBnB for the first time was an interesting experiment. We arrived at the airport and took a taxi to our accommodation. It was a double room, which could just fit a double bed in, at the back of a shop. But where was Patrick to stay as we had booked a room for three? We rang the owner who came around and explained there was a door onto the shop and after the shop closed Patrick could sleep on the shop floor!

'No need to worry, there was a mattress and quilt for him!' he said. Not very happy with the situation, it was too late to sort it out as it was nearly dark. So Patrick slept on the floor of an antiques shop, which did close at 5pm but then the owner and his friend used it for smoking 'weed' and generally socialising.

Patrick didn't sleep well and it was very uncomfortable for us too. We had been told we could use the kitchen attached to the shop. Anne was making coffee when the 'real' owner came in and asked us what we were doing. Embarrassed, Anne explained how we had booked this room on AirBnB and it was completely unsatisfactory but the owner was not answering his phone now. The 'real' owner became a little annoyed so Anne came running for me. I explained we were on our 'holidays' and had paid a lot of money for this and we had been conned. Seeming to like our 'English' accent, he calmed down and told us the guy we had rented the room off was his tenant, and that he hadn't paid his rent for several months. So now this guy was subletting to us! He told us to leave it with him for a few hours.

Patrick's first day in 'The City of Angels' was not going well so we headed for the beach in the hope it would all be sorted when we returned. Coming back in the afternoon, the 'real' owner was still chasing his tenant, but we could stay tonight. Next morning 'our landlord' turned up. I was getting angry now, but thought, this is LA - guns and drugs, etc...anyway after a long discussion and telling him the 'real' landlord was after him, he agreed to return our money. We booked into a nearby motel - The Lincoln Inn. It was much more comfortable and a lot safer, for about the same price. I had been put off booking this hotel online as the comments said it was surrounded by 'homeless' people - which it was but I spoke to many of them and they were very friendly and polite. Many had jobs but the recession had meant they couldn't keep up mortgage payments or afford rent so they were sleeping in their cars and using the local take away cafes to eat at. A sad situation but we never felt threatened by them at all.

Patrick enjoyed 'Muscle Beach' and all the goings on. You could sit for hours and see sights like no other place in the world. What a complex and eclectic mix of people. Skateboarders, runners and cyclists used the 31 miles of beach path that stretched the length of the Los Angeles coast. Surfers and swimmers filled the sea every day and 'Baywatch' lifeguards patrolled in their famous red swimsuits from their wooden watchtowers.

Away from the beach we cycled to Malibu and Hollywood. When not cycling the bus service from beach to downtown was just a dollar per person. So getting around LA was very easy and affordable. Downtown LA was surprisingly sparse with people except for the tented city near the cathedral where more homeless lived. The Cathedral of Our Lady of the Angels was completed in 2002 and is well worth a visit. It is a magnificent architectural structure but my first thought was (like many others I believe) 'this must have cost a lot of money'. Some would argue that the church is overly-elaborate and the money could have been better spent on social programmes. Beneath the cathedral there is a mausoleum. We managed to see the crypt of the actor Gregory Peck whilst visiting the mausoleum. Just as interesting is Our Lady Queen of Angels Catholic church which is situated only a few hundred metres from the cathedral. A vibrant place with lots people using the church. I remember the sign displaying the cost of baptism, weddings etc in US dollars, and the one 'requesting' that ladies attending these services should dress appropriately - 'No short skirts or low cut dresses'!

Vancouver and Billy.

Patrick left Los Angeles to return back to the UK on August 4th and Anne and I decided to use the time we had left to visit an old friend in Vancouver, Canada. We had known Billy for many years from Newcastle. He had returned home to his native Canada when his elderly parents needed care and attention.

Arriving at Vancouver airport we had a little difficulty getting through immigration as I didn't have the address of where we were to stay. Immigration all around the world want an address for their records. Explaining Billy was a friend and was picking us up didn't go down well. After a short discussion, and showing him our return ticket to LA, immigration relented.

On collecting our luggage there was no sign of Billy so we waited. About an hour late, he came rushing into the airport apologising, he had been cutting the grass at his father's house and lost track of time. That was Billy. In his 20 year old car with a lawn mower in the back we headed to Vancouver with Billy pointing out all the sights. His home was a four bedroomed timber framed, three story detached building with outside balconies both front and back. We enjoyed breakfast on the rear balcony and evening beers on the front one. In the front opposite was a school with a running track so Anne and I used it to keep fit. Billy also lent us bicycles so we could get around easily.

Cycling around Vancouver was great, especially the harbour area. One day we cycled up to the Lions Gate Bridge and watched the ships entering Vancouver Bay. As it was August the water in the Bay was warm enough (just) to swim in so Anne and I enjoyed a cold water swim. Billy being a long standing socialist took us around a few of the areas where drug addicts frequented. It was amazing to see so many people living on the streets. In the summer they could survive but this city was extremely cold in the winter and I feared for them. Billy explained about the social programmes that helped the drug addicts but that more needed to be done.

Another week that passed so quickly and a city I would love to return to. Leaving on August 15th for Los Angeles to connect with our flight to Heathrow and then on to Newcastle. It had been nearly a year since we left home and although sad to be ending our adventure, Anne and I were looking forward to seeing our friends and family again.

Chapter 14.

The road to Mandalay, 2013.

I was looking forward to a changed Burma when I flew into Bangkok and straight on to Rangoon with Anne. After a year on the border and then a year back at work I felt things must be different. Declan was already in Burma with his friend Colin and we were looking forward to meeting up with them.

Having last visited Rangoon in January 2012 I expected changes after 20 months of 'openness'. With 50 NLD MPs and hundreds of foreign dignitaries, including prime ministers, foreign ministers, and other 'special people' visiting the situation was moving forward, but towards democracy?

The open sewers now had new concrete covers. This made it easier to walk around as the street paths are on top of the sewers. It seems that paint was available now many of the sanctions had been lifted. Buildings that had not seen a coat of paint since before the Second World War were resplendent in new colour. And the taxi from the airport was a 'new' car - well a 6/7 year old Japanese import. But it had windows that closed, windscreen wipers, and other essentials such as brakes. For the first time I felt safe leaving the airport. The taxi driver even had a mobile phone - in 2011 a SIM card cost $500, now they were $10 as companies other than a Chinese firm were supplying them. So lots of obvious changes but no improvement for workers wages, still at $2/3 a day despite hotel room charges starting at $50 a night and up to $300 for a four star hotel, much more expensive than Bangkok. So where is the extra profit going? To the hotel owners, many of whom are Generals or ex-Generals.

We stayed at the Yardanar Show hotel as we did in 2011. This was under considerable renovation. Declan and Colin arrived from a week in the north of Burma and it was great to have a few beers with them. We only stayed one night as our schedule was tight. Fr Henry arranged to pick us up and we set off for a small town called Yegyi, near Pathein. Fr Henry assured us there was a registered guest house we could stay at. So after 3 hours in the minibus we arrived at Zay Yar Guest House. The sign on the wall stating 'Warmly welcome and take care of tourists' indicated that it was a government licenced guest house. We thought our guest house in Rangoon was basic, but this was a major step down. The room was a concrete cell with a mattress on the floor. No windows but they had just added an air conditioning unit. The shower was along the corridor, but unfortunately without any water! So it was a bucket shower from the plastic barrel in the corner. I asked how many foreign visitors they had had since they had been licenced. The owner replied that a few Koreans had visited but we were the first 'Westerners' to stay - and looking at the facilities we might be the last. Obviously they had no restaurant but they did sell beer, so a few beers with crisps and nuts was our dinner for the night.

After a night in the 'cell' we all woke early, 'showered' and headed downstairs for breakfast. Boiled eggs and some toast were available which we were glad to see. Colin was new to this but now understood why we came back from Burma having lost a stone or so in weight. Fr Henry arrived with the minibus and off we went to Nazareth House, the boarding house for about 50 children in a nearby village which our charity Burmalink UK supported. Children from villages several hours walk or boat ride away stay at this boarding house and go to the local secondary school. The children live in two dormitories, one for boys the other for girls. They sleep on the floor with about 20 in each dormitory. They go home during the school holidays to see their families. The good news is that they all look well nourished and happy. Saya Jonny Mann, now an

NLD MP for the area comes to see us with his wife Daw Louise May. It is great to see him again, and especially as he is now one the 50 NLD MPs. He is home from the new parliament in Naypyitaw. I congratulate him on his electoral success and we discuss the political situation. He tells me that work as an MP is very difficult. The rules in parliament and the constitution restrict the NLD from doing much, but he is determined to stick in and make a difference. The next election will be in 2015, so only two years and hopefully lots more NLD MPs.

Fr Justin lives nearby and Fr Henry asks if we would like to visit him. He is very sick and needs lots of care. The last time we saw him he was working in Mae Sot with the poor and marginalised migrants. He has returned to Burma as he needs round the clock care. Fr Justin had told us many times of his village and the fishing ponds the community had built. Fr Henry pointed them out as we neared his home. We go into a room where he is lying on a bed, clearly very weak, but he smiles when he recognises us. None of the infectious laughter he usually greets us with. I am shocked and saddened and realise he doesn't have long to live. Fr Gregory is by his side - friends and comrades until the end. We share stories and good times before we leave. This will be the last time I see my dear friend Justin, but I'm reassured by his faith that he will move on to a better place. I am so proud to have Justin as a friend. A man who has dedicated his life to the poorest of the poor. As I say my goodbyes, he smiles and gives me one of his wonderful laughs. I will always remember the first time I met him, I heard him laughing before I saw him. A remarkable man ahead of his time.

Our friend Colin was very angry that evening after visiting Nazareth house. He can't understand why children have to live in such cramped and poor conditions and why people die without receiving medical help. We understand his anger and try to explain that the children are well looked after. The children were happy to have the chance of secondary education and we were helping them. As for Fr Justin, although he's not received much hospital treatment, the care and support of his community has been second to none. Fr Justin would die surrounded by his friends and that's how he would want it. We do what we can. This is 'life' for many millions of people all over the world. I have not become immune to it, I just have more understanding now. I try to explain to Colin that it is good to be angry - righteous anger - and that what I do is try to channel the anger into action and do something about the situation in Burma and other countries and our own. Although they have no MRI scanners, no radiotherapy, etc... and only enough food to survive, they do have a loving and supportive community and they have a great hope for a better life. We can all help them in their goal for a better life. 'But is 'Western life' that much better?' I ask Colin. I don't think he understands yet, it has taken Anne, Declan and I years to get to this stage of realising we receive more from them than we can give to them. It is sharing friendship and love that we all want. Giving them money is only temporary - love and friendship are forever.

A few weeks later Fr Henry informed us that Justin had passed away peacefully. We all shed a tear for this man of the people who served his community for over 40 years. He will never be forgotten by countless people who loved and deeply respected him. During his lifetime Justin had given them much help and comfort in moments of great need. His life's long energy and work always orientated to create a more just and peaceful Burma and world. Fr Justin was a man of God who in difficult historical circumstances truly lived the values of the Gospel. He died after the first peace agreement was signed in 2011 so he did live to see some of his work bear fruit.

The rain is incessant as we head on to Pathein. More painted buildings and the dirt roads have been resurfaced with concrete in the centre of Pathein, except the road in front of the Mosque - I hope it is only co-incidence but I can't help wondering if this is deliberate? It rains all day and all night so we can't travel far. In between the heavy showers, we show Colin around Pathein. The boats on the river transport goods and food up the river and along to Rangoon. Given their obvious state of disrepair I wouldn't travel on them. We watch young boys unloading a cargo of stones. Each boy has a bamboo basket and carries at least his weight in stones along a precarious gangplank to a waiting lorry. It is back breaking work and very dangerous in the rain.

With nothing much else to do we sit down in a beer station and order some Myanmar beer, watching the world go by we can see the level of water rising by the hour. The wooden huts most people live in are in danger of flooding. Although slightly elevated, I think they might be breached in the next few days. Reading the government paper 'The New Light of Myanmar' we find out that dengue fever is rife in the area - the daytime mosquito is having a field day in the rain. Many will die of this devastating disease. Returning to our hotel we decide that the rains have won and give up on staying in Pathein. The roads are almost impassable with the monsoon rain so we decide to return to Rangoon before we get trapped.

In Rangoon we call on Arnold and Edna. Edna gives us the news that the government has cancelled her pension because she lived in the USA for five years many years ago. 'Little has changed', says Arnold, 'the government is still doing everything they can to oppress us.' On the positive side Edna's salary as a teacher has increased - she'll need it as she has no pension now - and she's 82 years of age! Her new salary is $100 a month (and a beer costs $2. It's a good job she doesn't drink!). Hardly a living wage.

Mandalay, Miektila and Fr Neil.

Colin and Declan fly back to Bangkok and on to the UK while Anne and I fly to Mandalay. Having last visited in 2006 we are hoping to see some significant changes. The last time we were here the road to Mandalay was just a dirt track. Now it has been replaced by an expressway - a concrete dual carriageway linking Mandalay to the new capital Naypyitaw. There is very little traffic on the road and it makes the journey much easier than last time especially as we are in a 'new' taxi.

We arrived at our guesthouse to be told it has no vacancies, even though I had confirmed the booking the day before. They direct us along the street without so much as a 'sorry'. This is hospitality in the new Burma. 'The Nylon Hotel' is fine, a little basic but it will do. Mandalay is very hot, 34C and busy with motorbikes (which are banned on the streets of Rangoon) everywhere and everyone is tooting their horns constantly. What a cacophony.

We have arranged to meet Fr Neil, a missionary priest with the Columbans. He is a friend of Fr Alo who we have known for a long time, who used to work in Burma until the government deported all missionary priests and nuns. We set off for the cathedral on foot hoping to find Bishop Paul, who we know from our previous visit, and will ask him to contact Fr Neil. It's lunchtime and by co-incidence Fr Neil is having lunch with the cathedral staff. He is expecting us as Alo had informed him we were coming. So, as always, the priests invite us to join them for lunch which is a lovely soup with bread, followed by rice with some meat. After lunch is finished Fr Neil asks if we want to visit his school, and as we have nothing else planned we agree.

Fr Neil goes to get the truck and we jump in the back for the short journey to his church, St John's. We arrive to see a large church set back in its grounds. It looks very grand from afar, but close up it lacks maintenance and has no glass in the windows - good for natural air conditioning, but not to keep the monsoon rain out. Next to the church is Fr Neil's school, the Higher Education Centre (HEC). The HEC teaches English, computer skills, human rights and ethics, but most importantly teaches them to 'think' and have opinions. After 60 years of dictatorship many people in Burma have lost the skill of 'thinking for themselves'. There are 90 students aged 19-22 who come from all over Kachin state as well as Mandalay. Those from far away live in dormitories at the back of the school. Fr Neil gathers some of the students together and asks us to spend a few hours with them. As we have done this many times with FTUK and other students in Mae Sot we were only too glad to oblige. I had prepared a short workshop on human rights and had brought some DVDs to leave with them. The students were the best I'd come across. Very motivated, asking lots of questions and discussing progressive ideas. Fr Neil was clearly doing a good job - but I know the authorities would not like him to be producing such erudite future leaders. Fr Neil confided in us that even some of the Burmese priests were a little worried about what he was doing, many of them being quite conservative.

Fr Neil was a big character and coming from Northern Ireland, he knew all about growing up in a troubled country. He had been in Burma for 7 years now but previously worked in Taiwan. Whilst in Taiwan he was arrested and deported for supporting the opposition democracy movement in their push for better human rights - such a dissident! Years later, the opposition came to power and he received a letter from the new president inviting him back, and a free air ticket was enclosed. A criminal with one government - a 'hero' with another. It reminded me of the Brazilian Archbishop Dom Helda Camara who said 'When I feed the poor they call me a saint. When I ask why they are poor they call me a communist'. I promise to send Fr Neil two DVDs - Forrest Gump and Shooting Dogs (about the Rwanda genocide), telling him the students will like them and be able to discuss many of the ethical and political issues the stories touch on.

Mandalay still had its communal bathing stations at the end of most streets as houses are too small for bathrooms. This at first seems shocking but the people know nothing else and it is everyday life for them. From Mandalay we get the bus to Bagan, a UNESCO World Heritage Site. From the 9th to 13th centuries, the city was the capital of the Pagan Kingdom, the first kingdom that unified the regions that would later constitue modern Burma. It is one of the world's greatest archeological sites, a rival to Machu Picchu or Angkor Wat. Some 2,230 of the original 4,450 temples survive, a legacy of the Buddhist belief that to build a temple was to earn merit.

After a long and bumpy bus ride we look for a guest house in the price range we can afford. Since the slight opening up of Burma, this top tourist resort has increased its prices. We find one that is friendly and homely, serving breakfast and not far from the centre of town. As we wander around town we spot the NLD office. With their flags fluttering outside, it can't be missed, so we decide to take a walk inside and offer our support. One young man can speak good English and he tells us how they are recruiting many members now they are no longer 'illegal'. They are already preparing for the elections in 2015. We tell him that on our bus journey we saw the NLD flag outside of a house or office in every village and town, so they are clearly on the rise. Wishing all the workers good luck, we head off to book a bicycle to tour the ancient temples. They have told us where to get the best value bicycle hire.

We spend the full day cycling around the thousands of temples, climbing the ones we are allowed to and taking in the magnificent views. It is an awe inspiring place. I have been to Angkor Wat and it certainly is on a par with it. Today we are lucky that it isn't raining and we sit in a bar and watch the sunset over the mighty Irrawaddy river. We didn't get up early enough to see sunrise over the temples - in the rainy season the sun often rises behind a thick blanket of cloud, so why take the risk of an early rise and such disappointment?

After two days at Bagan we book the bus back to Mandalay. The bus journey takes a different route on the way back through different towns and villages. On entering one town the streets are patrolled by soldiers and I start to think we are not on a bus authorised for tourists. On previous visits to Burma, soldiers on the street were a common sight, but this was the first time on this trip. The situation became clearer as we approached the centre of town. We saw lots of burnt out shops and homes, some in the process of demolition. In the middle of all this destruction stood the Mosque. The penny dropped! This was the town Miektila, the scene of major ethnic violence earlier in the year. A state of emergency has been imposed in Meiktila following three days of communal violence between Buddhists and Muslims. The President, Thein Sein, had said that 'the move would enable the military to help restore order in the riot-hit town.' At least 20 people were reported to have been killed in the violence, but exact figures are unclear. The disturbances had begun when an argument in a gold shop escalated quickly, with mobs setting mainly Muslim buildings alight, including some mosques. Fighting in the streets between men from rival communities later broke out. I had read reports of this on the internet but now I could see the devastation with my own eyes. I was sure we didn't come through here on the way to Bagan. The tourist bus just wouldn't be allowed to see this.

Looking around the bus I noted that Anne and I were the only foreigners. Perhaps we had been let on this bus by mistake. The bus stopped in the town centre to pick up more people and we were allowed off for the toilet and to buy some coffee. We decided to keep a low profile as we assumed we had witnessed something the government didn't want us to see. So two minutes later, relieved and with a coffee we get back on the bus and wait cautiously for it to leave. After what seemed forever, the bus pulled out and we were glad to be on our way. On the outskirts of town we could see temporary shelters by the side of the road built for those who had lost their homes in the riots. A shocking reminder that we were travelling through a country that was still a very dangerous and difficult place to live in.

Back in Mandalay it was August 8th, and 25 years since the 8.8.88 workers' uprising which was so brutally put down by the authorities. In September 1987 the government declared several currency denominations worthless, wiping out the savings of many Burmese. A brief student uprising in response foreshadowed the widespread unrest that broke out in 1988. On 8th August 1988 hundreds of thousands of people joined massive, countrywide general strikes. On August 24th Aung

San Suu Kyi made her first public speech during a rally at Rangoon General Hospital. Two days later she gave a speech in front of an estimated 500,000 people in front of Rangoon's iconic Shwedagon Pagoda. During September demonstrations continued to grow across Burma. Violence escalated on both sides. Crackdowns began. Intelligence forces began rounding up hundreds of demonstrators. Thousands fled to the borders of China and Thailand to join forces with the ethnic armies who were locked in a long-running battle with the Burmese army.

Anne and I attended the anniversary celebration at the Dharma Hall. The Hall and streets outside were packed with democracy activists displaying photography exhibitions and books stalls selling the history of the 'revolution'. We sign a banner expressing our solidarity with the estimated 3000 people who died during the 1988 uprisings. Speeches from inside the hall were relayed on to screens for the crowds outside. A minute of silence is requested to remember the dead and then another minute for all those still incarcerated or who have died in prison. Anne and I are invited into the hall by the people, we are esteemed visitors being the only foreigners and they want us to join in fully with their celebration. We sit cross legged on the floor of the packed hall in the intense heat. It was great to be part of a democracy celebration inside Burma, which would have been banned a little over a year ago.

Arriving back in Chiang Mai from Mandalay, the Green bus takes us to Mae Sot the next day. It is a journey I have done many times and I love stopping at the 'service areas' for my rice or noodles with water served in an aluminium cup. Not the Greggs sandwich and coffee of the UK. In Mae Sot we have an errand to run. We need to go to AAPP to deliver a present. Khun Saing's wife and son still live in Nupo refugee camp, awaiting permission to leave and join him in the UK. We have a remote control car and some medicine to give them. As we are cycling to the office I wonder 'Why do families have to live apart? It must be so hard.' At AAPP we hear that there are now only 121 political prisoners left in jail. Just two years ago there were thousands, but the government has agreed a phased release under the current reforms. But AAPP are still campaigning strongly with the slogan 'Not one left behind'. They also tell us that many former prisoners are harassed in Rangoon by the authorities. Often they are picked up again and warned about the conditions of bail - that they should refrain from political activities. It is certainly not 'Freedom from Fear'.

After lunch we cycle to FTUK office. Paw Gay and Daniel are inside Burma at Martyrs Day celebrations in Karen State. Dot Lay Mu was there to greet us and warmly welcomed us back to 'our office', the one we spent 8 months working in. It felt good to be 'home' and how I missed it. Dot Lay Mu tells us of a school the Karen Agricultural department has been able to set up just over the border with the help of some Japanese investment. He is going there tomorrow and asks us to join him.

So next morning we cycle to FTUK office and meet Dot Lay Mu. He tells us we have to cross the border the 'sneaky way' but not to worry, the ceasefire is now nearly two years old and holding up well. A 30 minute drive in his truck to the Moei river and then a short walk through the corn fields (with the corn six foot high) and we arrive at the river where a boat is waiting. The river is about 30 metres wide and is the border between the two countries. Travelling upstream for about five minutes we arrived at 101 Battalion headquarters of the KNLA.

As there has been no fighting for a few years the soldiers are very relaxed and we watch a group of them playing 'Chin lo', the kick volleyball game played with feet and a bamboo ball. Dot Lay Mu checks us in with the area commander and off we go. Another walk through the corn fields and we find the school. Four wooden buildings surrounded by newly planted vegetables. The 20 or so students are learning about new farming techniques without manufactured fertilizers. The students live in a cramped dormitory but are happy to be learning new skills. They will go back to their communities and implement the new ideas. We do some teaching in the afternoon and stay overnight in one of the huts. They are all hopeful of a better future and we tell them of our meeting with Aung San Suu Kyi and our visits to Rangoon and Mandalay. They are all very sceptical, they have seen it all before. They don't trust the Burmese nor Aung San Suu Kyi.

Before we leave Dot Lay Mu asks us to visit 'Little Uncle' - the jungle surgeon. We walk towards the river and on the edge of the village sits a wooden hut where Gay Kaw Htoo, affectionately known as 'Little Uncle' lives. He is a former KNLA medic who now serves the local villages along with his friend. Inside the hut there is a mat on the floor with a mosquito net over it - the bedroom. In the corner is a large cabinet which Little Uncle opens to show us his supply of medicines. Some paracetamol, bandages and iodine for cleaning wounds is all he has. With Dot Lay Mu translating we ask Little Uncle about his life. He was trained in the army and spent many years on the front line treating soldiers. After a while Anne says she has met him before, with Ywa Hay and we donated some funds for his medical team. He remembers Anne also even though it was about six years ago. He says not many foreigners visited at that time. He tells us his army uniform is in storage now, he looks after the villagers around him. He says that he hopes his uniform is put away forever but...

He gets up and goes to his bedroom and comes back with a six inch bladed folding army knife. He opens it up and tells us that he uses the knife to amputate legs, saying he has used it many times to save the lives of landmine victims. The saw of the army knife is used to cut off a damaged limb with only paracetamol (and maybe rice whiskey) as pain relief. The choice in the jungle during the war was stark - agony or death. He must have been through so much tauma himself and he's only 33 years old. He is married now with a two year old daughter. He asks if we can donate some malaria testing kits which he is running out of. Thankfully, we can donate some money through our charity Burmalink UK. We'll send it via Dot Lay Mu as there are no banks in Karen State. If you want to know more about Little Uncle, Al Jazeera has made a documentary about him. He sent us this letter via Paw Gay about how he used our donation. It needs no comment.

12/08/2014

To,

Anne, Tony, Declan

We thank you very much to support our clinic with some donation. We bought a pair of Solar Cell and Medicine. We used the Solar Cell for our clinic and the health workers. We have got the very good light for the patient especially during the night.

The medicines were very much helpful for the patients who suffer with the malaria and common disease.

We started built the clinic for the community in Nya Li Ah Hta village since May 2014, but because we do not have enough support we cannot build the house for the health workers until now. We still need help to run our clinic further and the needs are as follow.

- A dormitory for health workers
- 3 water containers for waters
- Food cost for (12) people
- A generator for the clinic
- Materials for the training
- A training hall
- Filter machine for water
- Kitchen materials
- 2 bottles of Oxygen
- A pair of solar cell.

My dear friends, these are the really basic needs for our clinic and we submit it to you, your family and friend to find the way for us.

In England I know (4) peoples and they are:-

1. Three people from your family,
2. Ro Ni (Liverpool) the soccer player (who play very good and I always secretly support him).

In solidarity
Saw Gay
Kaw Htoo (Little Medic)

The rain continues as we head back to Mae Sot. Our trip is ending too quickly once again and we have to leave Burma and Thailand and all our friends. We know we'll be back next year as this place and these people are too precious and they are always in our hearts.

Chapter 15.

Hpa An, Moulmein and Vietnam, 2014.

Another year passed in the UK and we heard about incremental changes in Burma as the government prepared for the elections in December 2015. Anne had been in Thailand for a few weeks with Declan before I arrived in late July. I got the bus straight to Mae Sot to meet up with them. The Friendship Bridge between Mae Sot and Myawaddy was now fully open as a border crossing and tourists could travel into Myawaddy and beyond to Hpa An, the capital of Karen State and even further for the first time. Some areas of Karen State were still 'out of bounds' as the fragile ceasefire meant it is officially a 'war zone.'

Declan, Anne and I, and one of Declan's friend's, Joe, took the songthaew to the border and crossed the bridge into Myawaddy. We had arranged for a car to pick us up to take us to Hpa An. We had heard so much about it we were excited to see it after waiting 14 years. The 'taxi' and driver were waiting for us over the bridge and we jumped in. The car was a little cramped but it seemed roadworthy. We looked forward to passing through many of the villages and areas that our friends in Mae Sot had fled from over the past 20 years or so.

Before setting off, the driver asked for our passports. He needed several photo copies of each. We quickly found out why as on the outskirts of town there was a roadblock. We stopped and the driver handed over a copy of each passport. The soldiers looked in the car at us, smiled with that betel nut red grin and let us pass. This was to happen several times on the journey. Each armed group wanted to know who was passing through their territory and charge a small toll. After the checkpoint we pulled in again. By the side of the road was the fuel station - well, two forty five gallon drums and a man with a watering can. A funnel was placed in the petrol tank and the man filled it up manually. Petrol stations just didn't exist in this part of Burma. They had had no need for them in the past and might not in the future!

Saying the condition of the road was 'bad' was an understatement. There was a one way road between Myawaddy and Hpa An, traffic went one way one day and the other way the next. It was too narrow to allow traffic to pass in both directions at once. The concrete soon gave way to a dirt road which in turn gave way to a mud road. Although the road was too narrow for two way traffic it didn't stop cars and vans overtaking slow moving lorries or even fast moving cars. The road started to climb through the Dawna mountain range with steep drops to the side. And still cars were over taking. Unfortunately I was in the front of the car as I was the oldest and had the longest legs. I was terrified and from the back I could hear Anne, her head in her lap, shouting 'Phay phay mon' ('drive slowly' in Burmese). As the road became steeper the traffic slowed which was a small blessing but it didn't last long as our driver had to go past several of the ancient wagons that had got stuck in the mud, with only inches of slippery mud preventing us falling off the steep mountain side. I held my breath and closed my eyes each time. Those wagons that could move would slide backwards every time they had to stop. Their brakes are not good enough on the steep mountain. To stop them sliding too far they used a human hand brake - a young boy jumped off the back of the wagon and threw a wooden 'chock' under the rear wheels. My heart was in my mouth every time I saw this.

Thankfully, after a few hours we made it safely down the mountain but the terrifying journey was not over yet. The driver put his foot down and tried to overtake every vehicle on the flat road. 'Phay phay mon' I tell him and he slows a little.

Checkpoints slow us down and we can see this is disputed territory. Some checkpoints are manned by KNLA forces and others by the Democratic Karen Buddhist Army (DKBA), a rival armed group. Our papers are handed over at each with a small fee. Miraculously after six hours we made it to Hpa An. It was the most dangerous road in the world I have ever been on and I knew I had to return the same way!

Hpa An.

'Soe Brothers Guest House is where all the foreigners stay,' we were told. 'It's the only clean and safe place in town.' The building is an ancient wooden construction which might look good in the sunshine, but it's pouring with rain and we are glad just to get into some shelter. We go in and hope our friend has booked us in. Yes, they have a booking for two rooms. All the rooms are upstairs but there is no traditional staircase. A wooden ladder leads to the rooms, so putting on our back packs we 'climb' the ladder. Along a corridor with six rooms off it and then up another ladder. The corridor on this floor is about two feet wide so one by one we walk along it to our rooms. A bed in the corner with a mosquito net and 'en-suite' but no window again. I call in on Joe and he is lying on his bed staring at the ceiling. He is traumatised by the journey and now can't believe his accomodation. I suggest a shower and then explore the town. Sitting in my room I hear the shower go on and then see the drain water come through the open drain in my room! The place has few windows so it is very dark. We were just about to explore when we were plunged into darkness. This was to be a common occurrence.

In pitch black I 'felt' along the walls, shouting to Declan and Joe we were heading downstairs and to take care in the dark. The ladder to the lower floors had no safety rail so on my hands and knees I edged to where I thought the top of it was. Feeling for it I turned and started to go down, waiting half way for Anne to find her way onto the top of the ladder. With Anne shouting at me 'This is ridiculous! I can't see'. I tell her to get on her hands and knees and shout that to Declan and Joe also. Thinking to myself 'I wonder where I put my torch. Must find it when the lights come back on.' As I get to the bottom of the first ladder, I can see a candlelight. The owner is lighting candles around the guest house. In this timber building, I'm wondering if that's a good idea. Eventually, we all make it to reception. It's still pouring down as the owner explains that in the rainy season the electricity supply is often interrupted. 'The shop on the corner sells torches,' she informs us.

Dashing along the street in the heavy rain we find the bar which has been recommended by the guesthouse. 'It has an English menu,' she tells us. Drenched, we sit down but Joe looks no better, so I order a few beers. I always find a few beers in a new place helps lift your spirits. So four Myanmar beers are ordered along with the menu. It's a Chinese menu and Joe can't find anything he likes, and the place does look a bit grubby, but so does everywhere. Spotting a bar opposite we change locations and do the same. Four more Myanmar beers and the menu. It seems to have fried chicken, so we tentatively order some. The waitress speaks good English and is pleased to serve us - probably because we are the only customers in the bar/restaurant. Some wonderful deep fried chicken arrives and Joe smiles for the first time. Either he approves of the food that has arrived or the beer is having the required effect. With nothing much to do as it's dark now and still raining we drink a few more beers and then return to the guest house. On entering and seeing the ladder to our rooms, I thought perhaps we shouldn't have had that last beer, but at least the lights were on. So after climbing the two sets of ladders and erecting the mosquito net I drift off to sleep.

Next morning there is Burmese tea and sweet cakes for breakfast - just what Joe wanted! Declan tells us Joe hasn't slept at all and wants to go back to Mae Sot. We try to persuade him to stay. 'It will get better, once (if) the rain stops' I tell him. I say the journey back will be tiring but he is insistent. So the guest house owner arranges a taxi to the bus station where Joe can get a minibus back to Myawaddy. He must go today or wait a further two days. By the time Joe gets to Myawaddy the border will be closed but the minibus firm will arrange a guest house for him for the night. Wishing him good luck, he seems happier now he is heading back to Thailand. Hpa An is very poor and very different. Rats are in charge on the streets, water is sold from wooden barrels as most houses don't have running water, the rain is starting to flood the roads, there are frequent power cuts, but other than that it's fine!

Father Paul calls us at the guest house. We know him from Mae Sot, he replaced Fr Justin, and he wants to show us around the area. He congratulates us on surviving 'Death road', laughing as the Burmese often do. He tells us this is Karen State under military rule, not like Day Bu Noh. The people here have to abide by the government rules. It is incredibly poor and difficult for them. Land continues to be confiscated as the government considers land to be owned by the state and not individuals. This makes the farmers very poor as they have to work the land for a basic wage. The Generals take any profit.

Fr Paul has asked Anne to do some health training with the nurses at the local hospital. He is acutely aware of the very poor hygiene in the hospital and would like Anne to focus on hand washing and other very basic practises. We know from visiting other areas of Burma that three things will make the biggest difference. 1. Soap to wash hands regularly, 2. Mosquito nets to prevent the spread of malaria and 3. Clean drinking water. Implementing these three will save more lives than anything else so Anne focuses on them, knowing it can be done even in the poorest communities. On returning Anne tells me of the landmine victims in the hospital, the back street abortions causing untold complications, the shortage of blood, to name a few. I ask her to stop - I can imagine what it's like.

Father Paul serves this community the best way he can. He knows it is difficult for us to stay in this poor country but he is so glad we are visiting. He invites us to mass at his church and then supper. We accept gladly and enjoy sharing mass with the local community. We are then given some simple but nourishing food before Fr Paul asks his driver to take us back to Soe Brothers.

Moulmein (Mawlamyine).

I thought we had reached the bottom in Hpa An but I was to be shocked once again in Moulmein, the old colonial capital. The rickety bus takes about 4 hours on the dirt roads but at least the road is flat and no mountain ranges to traverse. We have a recommended hotel to stay at, so at the bus station we jump in a taxi, asking for 'Cinderela Hotel', but this was to be no 'Fairy tale' experience. The hotel is surprisingly clean and comfortable and it even has a restaurant for breakfast.

After booking in we set off for town to find something to eat. Moulmein is a sea port on the Thanlwin river. 'With a ridge of stupa-capped hills on one side, the Thanlwin River on the other and a centre filled with crumbling colonial-era buildings, churches and mosques, Mawlamyine is a unique combination of landscape, beauty and melancholy. The setting inspired both George Orwell and Rudyard Kipling, two of the English-language writers most associated with Myanmar. Kipling penned his famous poem 'Mandalay' after visiting, while Orwell, whose mother was born here, used Mawlamyine as the backdrop for the stories 'Shooting an Elephant' and 'A Hanging'. Not that much has changed since the days when Orwell and Kipling were around, and if you've ever wondered what life was like during the Raj, Mawlamyine is a pretty good time capsule'. Well that's what the tourist brochures would like you to believe.

Declan, Anne and I headed for the port looking for a bar. That well worn adage 'Have beer and the place will look better' was rattling in my head. It was raining again but we managed to borrow some umbrellas from the hotel. The place was eerily quiet. Nowhere seemed to be open. We spotted some lights by the river and made for them. A few stalls were selling barbecued fish and meat, so we sat at one of the open air tables and ordered a beer before investigating the barbecue. The coals looked hot, and fish and some kind of meat was roasting on sticks. So having few other options we ordered a few pieces asking for it to be well cooked. Although not delicious it filled a void. Children as young as seven or eight were serving and washing dishes. I felt a little queasy when I saw a dish of filthy water being used to clean the plates and cutlery. I was even more disturbed when a stray dog came by and started drinking from the bowl! Asking for the toilet, the waiter pointed to the river, miming that I should 'pee' in the river. I wandered over to the river and could see piles of garbage in the long reeds. 'When in Rome' - I had no choice really. Thinking we might need the hotel facilities soon we started to walk back. Spotting a bar with lights on by the river we went in to see if this was more hospitable. Inside it was very dingy and dark. 'Ladies of the night' sat in the dark fringes but it sold beer and we decided to have 'one for the road' as Anne needed the toilet. On returning from her toilet visit she said the toilet was merely a 'hole in the wooden floor'. It was so dark she couldn't see anything else. We drank our beer quickly and made our way back as Anne was 'passed herself' with fright, thinking we'll either die of food poisoning or be 'mugged'.

As luck would have it we survived the night without 'sickness or diarrhea'. After breakfast we explored in the daylight, heading back to the port. On passing the late night bar, I needed the toilet. It was bright daylight so I could see where the 'waste matters' were going through the hole in the wooden floor - straight into the river. And probably we had eaten fish last night that had been caught in the very same river! Two nights in Moulmein in the monsoon rain is enough for anyone, Anne didn't need any persuasion to return to Hpa An. We looked at a few other guesthouses when we arrived back but they were even worse than Soe Brothers, so we booked in again. Fortunately we had timed it right and we only needed to stay one night as next day the road was open in the Hpa An to Myawaddy direction.

So early next morning we apprehensively stepped into our minibus and headed for Myawaddy on 'the most dangerous road in the world'. The first hour or so on the flat road passed without incident and then we hit a traffic jam to get up the mountain. Wagons were slipping on the muddy road and motorbikes squeezing through the tiniest of gaps, with probable death awaiting down the steep mountain ravines for anyone making a mistake. Traffic soon backed up behind us as we watched wagons spinning their wheels in the deep mud. Our driver took advantage of any gap to undertake or overtake. My stomach was churning - I could hardly look. Ahead I could see four wheel drive pickups full of soldiers moving past stranded wagons and cars. Clearly a frequent user of the road, our driver navigated his way past the stranded vehicles and continued up the mountain side. I wondered how many wagons, motorcycles or cars fall off the side of the mountain every day? The traffic eased a little and we took a wide berth of an obstacle on the side of the road. Looking back I see what we are avoiding. A crumpled and crushed wagon lies below a steep edge. It has clearly slid off the mountain and the cause of the traffic jam. A tarpaulin covers the crushed drivers cab. Our driver tells us he heard on the radio that four people had died when the wagon fell off the side of the mountain. The bodies hadn't been recovered yet. That would have to wait until night when the road is closed and the wagon can be removed. I shut my eyes and say a little prayer for the victims and then one for our driver, that he drives safely.

Eventually we arrived back in Myawaddy and just in time to cross the border before it closed for the night. I can't say how relieved and happy I was to be back at the DK Hotel in Mae Sot. Although not luxurious by any standards I felt clean and safe for the first time in a week. And yet I missed the people of Burma, they were so happy to see us and I hoped their country would open up further. They desperately needed the influence of outside people to develop their nation. A wonderful people so cruelly treated by their own government for so many years. I hoped change would come in the 2015 elections and was pleased we had visited the home villages of many of our friends who had fled. We understood their situation better now. We were all glad we took the time and stayed in Hpa An and Moulmein to walk the life of a Burmese person, even if only for a short while. When we leave a place in Burma that has had a profound impact on our family we often quote the words from the Eagles song Hotel California 'You can check out anytime you like, but you can never leave' - and we never leave our Burmese friends. We may be far from them physically, but they are always in our hearts.

Vietnam, Simon's 40th Birthday.

Simon worked with a Non Governmental Organisation (NGO) in Mae Sot for many years. We spent many nights watching football and drinking beer with him in Mae Sot. Toby is a USA citizen and was a teacher of English in a Mae Sot high school who we met in our year in Thailand. Toby moved to Vietnam to teach and we said we would visit him one year. So Simon was 40 years old in August 2014 and he was going to celebrate his birthday with Toby in Hanoi. Too good an opportunity to miss, so Anne and I flew into Saigon (Ho Chi Min) to join the celebrations.

Walking in the city was particularly dangerous as motorcycles would frequently mount the pavement but Anne and I were determined to see some of the history of the city. We found Independence Palace - the home and workplace of the President of South Vietnam during the Vietnam War. It was the site of the end of the Vietnam War during the Fall of Saigon on 30th April 1975, when a North Vietnamese army tank crashed through its gates.

Perhaps the most interesting visit was to the Cu Chi tunnels. The tunnels are a network of connecting tunnels located in the

Củ Chi District of Ho Chi Minh City, and are part of a much larger network of tunnels that underlie much of the country. The Củ Chi tunnels were the location of several military campaigns during the Vietnam War. The tunnels were used by Viet Cong soldiers as hiding spots during combat, as well as serving as communication and supply routes, hospitals, food and weapon caches and living quarters for numerous North Vietnamese fighters. Actually going into a tunnel is very claustrophobic. There is just enough room to crawl along but no way of turning around. I got into one and started crawling and wished I hadn't. With no way of turning around I was forced to make my way on hands and knees to the next exit/entrance point. I was so relieved to get my head out of the tunnel and breathe some fresh air. It is hard to believe that the Viet Cong lived in these tunnels for weeks and months.

Toby lived in Hanoi in the north so after experiencing the intense pace of Ho Chi Min we were glad to arrive in Hanoi. It was much cooler and less humid, and so much more relaxing. We met Simon and Toby and had a few great nights. Toby introduced us to Beer Hoi and the local delicacy of 'dog'. I enjoyed the Hoi being a freshly brewed local beer but found the 'dog' too tough to eat.

There is one major highlight of Hanoi and not to be missed - The President Ho Chi Minh Mausoleum. The mausoleum is the resting place of Vietnamese Revolutionary leader Ho Chi Minh. It is a large building located in the centre of Ba Dinh Square, where Ho, Chairman of the Workers' Party of Vietnam from 1951 until his death in 1969, read the Declaration of Independence on 2nd September 1945, establishing the Democratic Republic of Vietnam. Anne and I joined the queue to pay our respects. We arrived early as we were told the queue would be shorter. It still took about an hour to reach the mausoleum entrance where we were greeted by soldiers in immaculate white uniforms. All talking was prohibited as we climbed the steps and it was frowned upon to smile or show any emotion. We entered the air conditioned building in pairs and slowly walked alongside and then in front of the body of Ho Chi Min. With his white hair and beard he was perfectly preserved. We continued our way to the exit and emerged back into the bright sunlight. I remember years ago, in 1984, when I was in Moscow seeing the queue at Lenin's mausoleum. It meandered several miles around Red Square and took hours to get inside, so I didn't bother. I was glad this queue was shorter and I took the time. An interesting and unique experience.

Flying back from Hanoi to Bangkok to catch our connection to the UK, I reflected on another fantastic trip. Vietnam was a place I had longed to visit but so had been Hpa An and Moulmein, so in one trip I had experienced them all. I knew next year there would be elections in Burma and wondered if we would see momentous change like Vietnam saw in the 1970's?

Chapter 16.

Elections in Burma, 2015.

Arriving in Mae Sot in October 2015 there was much optimism about the upcoming elections and some departures amongst our friends.

Dot Lay Mu told us he had been accepted on the United Nations repatriation scheme for refugees and would leave for Canada with his wife Naw Pwee. They would live with their daughter. Naw Pwee was so excited as she would be able to get to see her granddaughter every day.

Saw Albert told us of his plan to return to Papun in Karen State next year. This could be very risky as he would be a wanted man. He had spent the last 15 years documenting the atrocities of the Burmese military while working as Field Director for KHRG. However, he was determined not to live in exile and so wanted to go back to his home and be with his extended family again.

Maung Maung Tinn was in Hpa An studying at Art school. He always wanted a formal education - though I told him on many occasions his 'education in life' was so much better. I couldn't think what Art school could teach him, but he was realising a dream.

The Nationwide Ceasefire Agreement, a landmark ceasefire agreement between the government of Burma and representatives of various ethnic insurgent groups had been signed, which meant the KNU was now legal.

Before we left the UK, Anne and I had secured visas to travel into Burma. We wanted to witness the elections and be on the streets of Rangoon when the results came in. We dreamed of wild, all-night celebrations with the streets filled with millions of jubilant people.

We booked our flight from Chiang Mai to Rangoon for November 3rd with Air Bagan, a Burmese airline. Our hotel was booked and we were very excited, although a little apprehensive. On November 1st I got a text from Air Bagan saying the flight had been cancelled. What could we do? We needed to be in Rangoon to witness the election. Anne was furious. We went straight to the Airline office. The flight had been cancelled because of a technical problem with the aircraft, they told us and they couldn't help.

If we couldn't get to Burma, it would spoil all our plans. We hit the internet desperately trying to find another flight at short notice. The only way we could do it was by flying from Chiang Mai to Bangkok and then onto Rangoon. There were no direct flights. So without any other option we booked our flights for the next day. Thankfully, there were no further hiccups and we arrived in Rangoon on November 4th, a few days before the election on Sunday November 8th. Election campaigning was ramping down as we arrived. We managed to get to the end of one NLD rally in Rangoon on Thursday, but that was to be the last rally of the campaign. Election rules meant that all posters, flags, etc had to be removed from public display 48 hours before the election. The NLD had told supporters not to wear any T shirts or badges and to arrive at the polling stations on Sunday anonymously, to avoid any possible intimidation.

Opinion polls indicated that the NLD could win a majority but...Ma Ba Tha (a nationalist Buddhist 'Organisation for the protection of Race and Religion') was lobbying for voters to elect the ruling Union Solidarity and Development Party (USDP) military party. Ethnic political parties were also expected to gain seats in rural areas. Not forgetting the military were guaranteed by the constitution 25% of the parliamentary seats. Also, many seats in conflict areas such Kachin state, Shan state and Karen State would not hold any ballots.

Aung San Suu Kyi is banned by the constitution from the Presidency as she had been married to a foreign national and her two sons are British citizens but she has stated that she will lead the country if the NLD wins a majority in a role other than President.

Burma election, November 8th 2015: 'We are happy in our hearts'.

The election polls opened at 6am on Sunday 8th November and from 5am queues formed. The people of Burma were going to vote for the first time since 1990 - Anne and I had been to church early on this sunny Sunday and prayers had been said for a just and peaceful election. Many tourists had stayed away from Burma fearing violence.

'It's time for change' and 'We are not afraid anymore' were the most common comments from the people as Anne and I visited polling stations in Rangoon. The indelible ink on the left hand little finger proved they had voted. The polling stations were orderly and quiet with just small queues. Many shops and building sites were closed, and there was little traffic on the usually congested roads, people possibly fearing disturbances on the streets. At about 4pm thunder clouds started to gather overhead and then torrential rains came. Was this a symbol of the washing away of the old guard and the bringing in the new?

Late in the afternoon we gathered with thousands of others outside the NLD headquarters waiting for Aung San Suu Kyi to come and speak to us. The crowds were singing and chanting 'We love you, Mother Suu'. We waited until it was almost dark. And then disappointingly it was announced that she would not be speaking that night but maybe the next day when the election result was known. As we were nearby, we called in on Arnold and Edna. They both proudly showed off their ink stained finger. This was the first time in their lives they had voted in 'free and fair' democratic elections. It had taken almost a lifetime, but they were so happy. We shared their enjoyment with a celebratory glass of orange juice kindly poured by Edna.

After a short political chat with Arnold we said goodnight and returned to our hotel switching on the TV to see if we could get any news. Myanmar TV, the state controlled TV station, was showing the count around the country. Literally each ballot was being removed from the box, opened and the result shouted to a man who marked it on a chalkboard. It seemed so peculiar but at least we could see that the NLD were gaining lots of votes. We held off a celebratory drink, wanting to get up early the next day.

Next morning straight after an early breakfast we walked back to the NLD headquarters. Our friend Zaw Tun, who had returned from exile in Australia for the election, excitedly told us it had been a landslide victory for the NLD but nothing had been confirmed by the Union Election Committee so he was holding his breath. People were fearful that the military would 'cheat' and change the result as in 1990. We waited for hours with thousands of supporters, all very excited, hoping for a historic victory. Film crews from around the world were set up at every vantage point. However, we were conscious people were anxious, looking around, fearful the police would come to disperse the crowd. Then suddenly the crowd surged forward into the road and a row of cars pulled up in front of the NLD headquarters. Daw Aung San Suu Kyi, Mother Suu as she is affectionately known, stepped from her car. Photographers flashed wildly as her security team cleared a way for her. The music blasted out on the PA system and people danced and sang, 'We love Mother Suu. We want democracy.' Daw Suu and U Htin Oo (Chairperson of NLD) came out onto a high balcony. Behind them a huge NLD banner. The crowd fell silent as Daw Suu picked up the microphone, wanting to hear from her that the NLD had won the election. The PA system crackled and then Daw Suu spoke. Zaw Tun translated for us she spoke. She thanked all her supporters for delivering an election victory but asked them all to remain calm. It was not yet the time to celebrate. She feared any celebration would be an excuse for the military to crack down and disperse the crowd. There was a lot of negotiation still to do.

Everyone knew the NLD had a landslide victory but would it count? In 1990 the military annulled the vote - would the same happen again? Ever the diplomat, she cautioned the crowd not to do anything that might cause the military to act against them. Celebrations would have to wait, there was still work to do. There would be no street party today.

'We are happy in our hearts' said one wise young man who told us of his years in a refugee camp waiting for this day and how he hoped for a brighter future for himself and his children.

Anne and I had waited for nearly twenty years for this moment - a just and peaceful election in Burma. Our prayers had been answered, but the journey had only just begun. We said goodbye to our friends Zaw Tun and his father Win Maung, both now Australian citizens having been forced to flee persecution under the old regime. We were so happy to be with them and share the momentous occasion.

'We will celebrate in our hearts today. We can celebrate on the streets another day,' said Win Maung.

'We must tame the tiger first' - Cardinal Charles Bo.

After the election in Rangoon, Anne and I decided on a holiday at Chaung Thar beach, about 150 miles away but 8 hours on a bus because of the poor state of the roads. Relaxing in a tea shop one afternoon four men walked in and I immediately recognised one of them as Cardinal Charles Bo. He was on retreat at the beach after an emergency gallbladder removal in Rome a few weeks ago. It was so good to chat with him about the recent election result. He knows it is a landslide victory for the NLD but is fearful that the military will not accept the result just as in 1990. He wisely says that Aung San Suu Kyi needs to 'Tame the Tiger first', meaning she must gain control of the military before she can move forward.

There are 35 Catholic sisters on the retreat at the beach and some pass the tea shop on afternoon strolls. As each few pass the Cardinal calls them into the shop for a milkshake or ice cream. The shop is soon overflowing with sisters from all over Burma. We chat for hours about the situation and the election.

The priests with Charles invite Anne and I to the beach for a game of football (Ballo in Burmese) later in the day when it is cooler. The Cardinal promises he will be on the beach joining in as well. I reminded him of the first time we met when he was playing basketball at the cathedral in Rangoon. He doesn't remember but says he still likes to keep fit.

At the beach, both Anne and I join in playing football with the priests and Charles, but the Cardinal has to stop playing after a few minutes as blood is pouring from his right foot. He has stubbed his toe, of course they all play football in bare feet, and his toe nail is hanging off. Fortunately one of the sisters has a first aid kit and the injury is cleaned and bandaged but the Cardinal has to be substituted! Out of interest I asked had the injury been more serious would he go to the local hospital. He told us that this beach resort with many hotels and guest houses did not have a hospital or clinic. Anyone injured would have to go back to Pathein, a two hour drive through the hills. A few years ago Anne and I had to visit this hospital following a road accident we were in. We know it has precious few facilities, only wooden benches and a few doctors trained by 'distant learning', who have little medical knowledge. The new government has a huge job on their hands as this country has so little of the infrastructure we take for granted.

The Cardinal watches the game of football from a deck chair and hobbles off the beach when we have finished playing. The priests and some sisters go for a swim in the sea to cool off. Charles Bo is certainly a priest who likes to be with his people. While walking he tells us he is going to the Philippines in a few weeks as the Pope's representative. It is a great honour to be asked to go in place of the Pope. He says he is anxious but will pray everything will go well.

One day I hope to be able to boast that I have played basketball and football with the Pope - who knows?

Back in Rangoon, all is quiet on the election front. The NLD has a majority to form a 'government' under the constraints of the constitution but the military are still in charge. Rumours are flying around that the President of the USA, Barack Obama, is coming to Rangoon to congratulate Aung San Suu Kyi in person so there is a lot of excitement. However, nothing comes of this nor many of the other rumours that are flying around. It appears that little will change quickly, and perhaps that is a blessing. Daw Suu is in negotiations with the military and perhaps this will be an evolutionary moment and not the revolution many had hoped for.

Lay Bu Der Village.

Back in Mae Sot we discussed the election with our Karen friends. They are not so excited but do want to hear our eye witness account of the election. They have been waiting for 60 years for change. Waiting a little longer is not a problem for them.

Lay Say was waiting for us in Mae Sot. He knew we were on an extended visit and as it was the dry season he wanted Anne and I to visit the school in his home village that Burmalink UK had been supporting for 10 years. Supporting a primary school in rural Burma is easy. An invitation to visit presents many difficulties.

'Please come and visit us, we want to say thank you,' asks Lay Say. The reason the visit is so difficult is that the village is located in one of the 'black zones' on the Burmese map. These areas are war zones or cease-fire zones where foreigners are not permitted to go. But our Karen friends can guide us past the Thai and Burmese borders guard patrols. We have done this journey before so we know the routine. The first part of the expedition requires two truck journeys totalling 8 hours mostly on dirt roads, to reach the Salween river which separates Burma from Thailand. We stay hidden at the riverside awaiting our boat which duly arrives. Quickly we board and as I am taller than the average Burmese I have to lie in the bottom of the boat. After half an hour we have passed Thai security and it is safe for me to sit up and enjoy the beautiful unspoilt scenery.

No passport control when we arrive at Mae Nu Tar village, Karen State, Burma. We have to stay hidden here and share a bamboo hut with some Karen soldiers who kindly put up mosquito nets for us. Rice is cooked and night falls. We go to bed at 8pm ready for the 5am start at first light. Twelve hours of trekking in 30°C heat through four mountain passes and we arrive - filthy, sweaty, dehydrated, hungry but relieved to reach Lay Bu Der.

The village has no toilet so we use 'jungle toilet' taking care to avoid the pigs. A 'feast' is prepared for us in Lay Say's sisters house. The village committee decided to celebrate by shooting a squirrel to feed us. So rice, squirrel and jungle leaves are cooked. Just to let you know, Anne is vegetarian and squirrels are mostly bones! We eat knowing we should leave plenty as the rest of the family will eat after us.

After having difficulty getting to sleep in the heat and on the hard bamboo floor we are woken at 4am by the sound of 'rice pounding' below our room. All these huts are built on stilts to allow for flooding and to give the pigs and chickens a space. Any waste food is swept through the floor for them to eat.

The village school has 40 children. We know it must be 'outstanding' as the District leader sends his youngest son to this school. The children sing a welcome song and ask lots of questions. Thanks to the donations from Burmalink UK supporters we have been able to support this school for 10 years now. Many children in nearby villages don't go to school because they have to work in the fields or look after younger siblings whilst their parents work. The chair of the school committee gives a speech of thanks, saying how grateful he is for the funding. He tells us he knows how difficult and costly it is for us to visit and how they can offer us nothing but love and prayers. I reckon their love, prayers and friendship massively outweighs our donations.

As we leave for a night at Day Bu Noh, the school committee return to the paddy fields. They will work all night as it is a full moon and the rice needs harvesting. The 12 hour trek back to the Salween tomorrow doesn't seem so bad after all. We will eat eggs and some food we have carried. They will survive on rice, vegetables and a little meat. They have few material possessions but they have community spirit, resilience and above all comradeship.

It has been an emotional journey with its massive ups and downs like the mountain passes we had to climb, but an honour to have such humble friends. On the boat journey back, Paw Gay asks if we would like to meet Dot Lay Mu's brother. I said 'I would love to.' So a short while later the boat pulls over to the riverside and we can see a bamboo hut about a hundred metres into the forest. We clamber out of the boat and climb up the steep sandy river bank. Out of the house, I swear came a younger, thinner version of DLM. It was clearly his brother - they were so alike. He was living a subsistence existence in the jungle. He invites us into his dark hut - no electricity - and makes coffee and tells us that he is a little too old to be a front line soldier so he repairs guns instead and stays loyal to the revolution. 'I will never leave Karen State. I will stay and fight until the end,' he informs us. I was so impressed, a quiet but strong and determined man living in such conditions, serving his people whatever it takes.

I admired his T-shirt and asked him about it. He had a Paulo Freire quote on it "Washing one's hands of the conflict between the powerful and the powerless means to side with the powerful, not to be neutral." Although he didn't know it he was following the advice of his T-shirt, he was siding with the powerless and oppressed. This was one of many life changing moments when I swore never to be neutral, and so never side with the oppressor. I left feeling inspired again. I felt blessed to be able to meet and shake hands with this humble man. I wished I could have brought him home to inspire others but then it wouldn't be the same. The environment, the geography, the house all made it a most inspirational moment for me. The message on his shirt is for me and you.

Often
by Maung Maung Tinn.

I miss my homeland.
I wish to return there one day before my short life ends.
I have been away for a long time.
My youngest son was only 12 years old when we left.
Now he is married with 3 children.....
My homeland is very peaceful,
The mountains are beautiful and the hill at the bottom of the mountains is covered in green grass.
A large rice paddy lies between the village and the hill.
It is full of mud in the rainy season and the people plant rice.
In winter, early mornings are very cold, but people do not worry about that.
People work, talk and laugh....
These sounds echo through the mountains.
Smell of mud,
Beautiful hills and mountains, Sounds of farmers and cow clappers.These are often in my dreams. I miss my homeland.

Chapter 17.

Karen State and JSMK
for the first time, 2016.

Following a great election victory by the NLD, Aung San Suu Kyi was appointed as 'State Counsellor' on 18th November 2015. The President was Win Myint, a close aide to her. Much was expected of Aung San Suu Kyi, but I was doubtful that she could achieve real change under the existing constitution which conferred lots of power in the military. Three important ministries - Home Affairs, Border Affairs and Military Affairs - remain under military control, and the constitution is designed to be impossible to change without the military's buy-in - twenty five percent of seats in parliament are reserved for military officers, while more than seven five percent of Parliament is needed to approve changes to the constitution.

So Anne and I returned to Mae Sot in October 2016 to meet up with our Karen friends and see what had changed for them. Would they be going back to Burma and starting their lives afresh? I knew the answer before I set off from the UK. Nothing much had changed in Mae Sot. The refugee camps along the border were still full to overflowing and millions of Burmese still kept the Thai economy going with plentiful supplies of cheap labour.

Declan had spent July and August inside Karen State working at Jungle School of Medicine (JSMK) as part of his medical studies, and had spoken highly of the clinic and it's main practitioner Dr John. JSMK operates a 14 month training course for healthcare workers in Karen State. The school and hospital/clinic started operations in 2011. The trained medics work in Free Burma Ranger teams providing relief healthcare in Karen State and beyond. Many go on to work in the Karen Department of Health and Welfare clinics. Thirteen villages within one day's walk of JSMK send patients to the school for healthcare. JSMK provides a number of ancillary services including ultrasonography, X-rays and simple laboratory testing (for malaria, HIV, Hepatitis B, etc). Though basic in nature, these services vastly exceed those in other clinics within the area.

Anne and I were keen to visit and asked Paw Gay if she could arrange a visit. Lay Say was unavailable to take us in as he now had a much more senior role in Karen Agricultural Department (KAD), following the departure of Dot Lay Mu to Canada. Paw Gay was looking after her elderly mother who was recovering from a fall but she asked a young Karen man to go with us. Htoo Lwee who worked for FTUK, and was a very capable jungle guide escorted us.

So off we set for Mae Sariang and the Salween river. The truck ride through the Salween national park was just as tough and scary as ever. Htoo Lwee had it all under control. The boat arrived on time at the river side and off we went hidden in the bottom of the boat, Htoo Lwee managed to arrange overnight accommodation in one of the bamboo huts. Our friend Kyaw Pwa arrived early next morning to help us with the 12 hour trek through the jungle to Day Bu Noh. We were much more prepared than previous times and carried food with us - tins of mackerel and tuna, along with noodles.

The FTUK offices at Day Bu Noh were as idyllic as the previous years. The gardens were full of flowers and vegetables. It was like the garden of Eden. Htoo Lwee kindly cooked in the absence of our usual cook, Paw Gay. Supper was rice and tuna before a deep sleep under the clear skies and spectacular Milky Way. The cockerels woke us at 5am and we washed and had breakfast of fried eggs and noodles. Two hours walk along the beautiful Yusana river, then traversing it on a raft, before a two hour climb up a mountain. Arriving at JSMK or Tah U Wah (White Monkey camp) as it is known locally we wandered through the tiny bamboo huts before arriving at a two story wooden house. Dr John was sitting outside carving a piece of wood. He was expecting us but wasn't sure at what time. An American about my age, he was wonderfully calm and welcoming. Ten weeks in the jungle has that effect on a foreigner. With little news from the outside world, life is a 'bubble' of mostly tranquil jungle life, interspersed with medical action when an acute patient arrives. Filtered coffee was prepared - John's little luxury he always brought in. We rested for a while before being shown around the small clinic and observed John on his ward round. A far cry from the NHS. John told us how pleased he was with Declan and hoped he would be able to come back when he was qualified.

The Free Burma Rangers occupied a section of the village higher up the mountain and we were invited to eat dinner there. It was a 'feast' with some fried chicken to add to the rice! Sleeping upstairs on the balcony in the wooden house with the river flowing beside us safely under a mosquito net was so tranquil. At first I thought the river would keep me awake, but it's soothing sound gave me a wonderful night's sleep. Below us slept a elderly man recovering from TB. As he was isolating we kept our distance but did manage to say good morning as we headed for a bath in the river. As it was a fast flowing river we had to choose our bathing spot carefully. Fully refreshed, we were invited for breakfast with FBR. As John was going we felt it courteous to join him.

We only had time to stay for one night as transport had already been organised for our departure out of Karen State and we couldn't change it. It was a great experience and satisfying to know that Declan had contributed to such a fantastic community. A few of Declan's friends came to say hello before we left. Ray Khin and Eh Htaw Bo had looked after Declan and shared their home with him. They asked when he would come back. I said 'I'm sure it won't be long. You know he has a Karen heart.' They laughed loudly in agreement.

We returned to Day Bu Noh along the river, waiting at the river crossing while a bamboo ambulance (Bambulance) took a patient to the clinic. A far cry from our emergency services but nevertheless doing a fantastic job.

I wasn't looking forward to the 12 hour walk from Day Bu Noh to the Salween river but it was the only way out. Setting off just before dawn to climb the first mountain in the cool of the morning we said goodbye to our friends. The journey out was more difficult than the way in. I had lost weight and we had little in the way of provisions. We had eaten all we had carried in. Three-in-one coffee and biscuits for breakfast wasn't enough to sustain me. The Sun was high in the sky and sapping my energy with each footstep I took. My shirt was soaked in sweat and I couldn't replace the lost water from my body. I took my shirt off to cover my calves as they were burning up and extremely red. The direct sunlight was so painful on them. The redness spread up my legs as I walked along, and I felt lightheaded and weary. I needed frequent stops and was struggling. With no other way I continued but I knew my steps were getting smaller and smaller. Anne encouraged me to drink more water.

At last we climbed the final mountain and were in a forest for the downward trek to the river. It took nearly four hours to descend. I could hardly put one leg in front of the other. I knew I had sunstroke but had to make it to the river to get the boat out. The last one hundred yards were agony. I sat down on the edge of the village whilst Htoo Lwee found us a hut. We were told we needed to walk another mile to an available hut. I just couldn't do it. My legs were red from top to bottom. I couldn't walk anymore. I would have to be carried, I said. Further negotiation resulted in the villagers opening a store shed for me. I was relieved not to have to be carried. I struggled fifty yards to the river and sat in the cool water to try to bring my temperature down. I knew I was at my limit now. With little food and such heat I was lucky to get this far.

After an hour in the river I made it back to my hut where I ate rice. We had run out of rations so Htoo Lwee found some protein for me. He collected a lot of insects, boiled them and ground them into the rice. With a few vegetables I greedily ate them. As I said before you can eat anything when you're hungry.

By next morning the redness in my legs was receding and my temperature was back to normal. I had been lucky. We returned on the boat down the river, hiding as we passed the army posts on the way. My third visit to Karen State had been so exhausting. I was starting to understand Lay Say, Paw Gay and all the Karen. They did this journey on regular occasions, in all seasons and with malaria. Now I knew why they were so strong - you have to be to survive.

We knew Declan was in safe hands with the Karen people and found out that they loved him as much as he loved them. Anne and I were so proud that our baby boy had grown his wings and was following his vocation.

The following section was written by Declan following his visit to JSMK and it says more about it than I could ever try to communicate.

An ethical dilemma – deciding who lives and who dies?

I first visited the Thailand Burma border as an 8-year-old child when my parents took voluntary jobs for an NGO helping the Karen people of Burma. I fell in love with the Karen people instantly, their simple way of life living in the jungles of eastern Burma seemed idyllic. However, 60 years of civil war has devastated Karen State.

I didn't see this indigenous tribe as any different from myself. I learnt very quickly that human beings want the same things wherever they are born. To put it simply this is to be healthy and to be happy. A meeting with a Karen boy who had seen his parents murdered by the Burma army confirmed to me that I wanted to dedicate my life to helping the Karen people. In

2010 a fragile ceasefire brought peace to most of Karen State but 60 years of civil war had left a broken people in a broken land.

The effect of war within a land is devastating. In particular war has a catastrophic impact on the healthcare of a nation and Karen State is no different. The proportion of GDP spent on healthcare prior to the ceasefire was 1-2%, ranking continuously amongst one of the lowest in the world. In Karen State latest figures suggest at least 1 in 5 children die before their fifth birthday, 60% of which are from preventable causes and 1 in 12 mothers die during childbirth. More than 45% of children are moderately or severely malnourished.

I have become acutely aware of how important healthcare is as a human right. Watching patients being carried on a bamboo stretcher (or bambulance as they call it) for 3 days into the Jungle School of Medicine Kawthoolei (JSMK) made me even more aware of the shocking effects of neglecting that right. I spent 8 weeks living with the staff, students and patients at JSMK in Karen State and my motivation for this elective is my passion to give a child born in Karen State the same opportunities as a child born in the UK. Sadly, many die before they have even had the chance to live.

'You can't build a peaceful world on empty stomachs and human misery'.

Norman Ernest Borlaug

Ethical Dilemma.

A 2-year-old boy was brought to the outpatient department by his mother as he was severely malnourished. This thin child came in looking like an old man with a bloated belly. He had the classic symptoms of severe malnutrition. He was admitted to the in-patient department due to his condition and after checking his weight and Upper Arm Circumference. He was diagnosed with Acute Severe malnutrition on top of Chronic Malnutrition.

Due to resources our investigations were limited but after getting senior help we gave antibiotics and milk powder with sugar and oil, whilst also doing 1 hourly observations. My supervisor asked that I help take charge of this child's care, with him ultimately making the final decisions. My first task was to talk to the mother and explain that we would require her to feed her son every 2 hours, even during the night. She was initially very pleased to engage, as she recognised her son was very ill.

As part of our assessment of the child we thought it would be necessary to determine why he had ended up in this situation. We found out the family had walked 2 days to our clinic, their nearest available health centre, as they lived in a small farming village. This year had been tough as the monsoon rains had not come as expected, so the ground was not fertile to grow rice and vegetables as usual. They had 7 other children to feed and because of the food shortages this child had only rice for 3 months. We also discovered that mum was still working in the fields, despite being 32 weeks pregnant, leaving their 7-year-old daughter to look after this child at home. This situation is not uncommon in Karen State with the same factors contributing to malnutrition surfacing repeatedly in new patients.

We were extremely pleased that after 2 days the boy had started to put on weight, largely due to the mother's engagement in feeding her child every 2 hours. We started the child on vitamins and minerals, increased the amount of milk powder and informed the parents of our plan. We also discussed family planning, but they were not interested in the vasectomy we offered. They expected some of their children would die due to illness and they needed many children to help in the fields and to look after them when they are old.

Thankfully the child continued to improve, however, his parents needed to get back to their village to look after their other children and to work in the fields. Every morning the mother would find me and ask if they could return home. I explained that it was too soon as their son had only just started to gain weight and could easily deteriorate. Every morning this scenario was played out and every time it was the same response, with my senior believing it was also too soon to discharge the child.

After the patient had been admitted for 10 days we came to a decision that we should discharge the child. The family would not wait any longer, and we wanted to discharge them on good terms so that they would bring the child back if he deteriorated at home. We were not convinced that much had changed at home and were concerned for the child. After many conversations we discovered the next few months would be the hardest for the family because it was the rainy season. They begged us to give them enough milk powder, oil and sugar to feed the child for the next few months.

It wasn't policy to routinely give milk powder to take home as it is a charity run clinic where funding is scarce. Milk powder, oil and sugar are in short supply and the policy is that these items should be kept only for the most acutely malnourished patients and patients should only be discharged once they are tolerating solid foods. Our patient wasn't eating enough solids yet so it was decided to break with policy and give the family enough milk powder, oil and sugar to feed him for a week whilst they increased the amount of solid foods. To give any more would have meant we hadn't enough to give to future patients. We also advised the parents of a feeding station for people in their situation. They explained that it was 2 days walk from their remote village and they couldn't afford to lose 4 days' work.

I worried after we discharged the boy whether we had done the right thing. We could have discharged with 3 months' supply, as the parents had asked for, but patients were turning up daily with malnutrition and we would run out soon if that became the policy. Were the circumstances not extenuating as the family were so poor and feared they could not feed their child? But there are 100s of families in the same situation in the villages around our health clinic. We begged the parents to bring the boy back if they feared he was deteriorating, but what if they didn't?

I was satisfied that we were using the principle of Justice to allocate scarce health resources and we were being fair to the other patients who would arrive at the clinic needing acute treatment for malnutrition. We could not provide 3 months' milk powder for every malnourished child on discharge, so it was not fair to do it for this child. However, one of the most important ethical principles is first do no harm. We couldn't be sure that the child wouldn't come to harm because of the decision we were making and the harm he was at risk of was potentially very severe. We were also neglecting beneficence, as surely the best interest of this child would have been to provide the milk powder treatment as requested. And we were definitely neglecting the parent's autonomy to choose the treatment they deemed best for their son.

We had decided, consciously or not, to put justice above the other ethical principles and I think this was the right decision. We have to look at the bigger picture sometimes and take the decision out of the hands of parents who only want what is best for their child. As practitioners we need to do what is best for every child and the many parents who arrived with their acutely malnourished children, over the next few weeks, were glad we had made that decision.

No child should die because they don't have enough food to eat. Sadly, this is an all too common story in the land they call Kawthoolei – the land of no evil.

Declan Stokle

Chapter 18.

Jungle Doctor, 2019.

'Are you going to be a missionary?' asked Father Louis Antonia, a missionary priest from Columbia as we sat having coffee after mass in Mae Hong Son, northern Thailand in August 2009.

'I don't think I want to be a priest' replied 16 year old Declan Stokle.

'I didn't ask if you wanted to be a priest' said Father Louis, 'I asked if you wanted to be a missionary? My sister is a lawyer in Bogota, Columbia. She works three days a week for herself, and then for two days she offers legal advice, free of charge, to the poor. She's a missionary.' Declan was taken aback by his response. He'd never considered that there were many types of missionaries.

Ten years later in November 2019 Declan is fulfilling a role as a missionary doctor. This is his third time working at Jungle School of Medicine Kawthoolei (JSMK), in Karen State, eastern Burma. However, this is his first time working on his own, being the only doctor in charge of an in-patient unit, and out-patient unit and doing 4 hours training each day with Free Burma Ranger medical trainees. He is literally 'one in a million' - the only doctor in this part of Burma which covers an area about the size of Northumberland and has a population of approximately one million. He has previously worked with Dr John, an American doctor who set up JSMK. Now fully qualified and with experience of working in the jungle, Dr John asked Declan to come on his own so the patients would get the benefit of a doctor for longer. Dr John will come back in March 2020.

Fr Louis had a great impact with just one simple question. I remember from all those years ago Fr Louis saying it was important to live with the poor, spend time with them and walk the life they have - not just donating your spare money or clothes. Fr Louis has moved on now but I'm sure he's still trying to convince people to be missionaries.

I was unable to travel to Thailand or Burma in the years 2017 and 2018 as my mother was very frail and needed lots of support to remain living independently at home. I did not wish to leave her for long periods and wanted to support her as much as I could in her final years. In June 2019 after battling many illnesses she finally passed from this world to the next to join my father in heaven. So after a two year hiatus I was able to return to my journey.

Anne and I had visited JSMK in 2016 after Declan had finished a training spell with Dr John. We were reluctant to go again as it is such a difficult journey, but we couldn't resist seeing our missionary son 'in action'. JSMK is situated in a remote region of 'free' Karen State. The Karen have been involved in a civil war with the Burmese for over 60 years. Since a ceasefire agreement in 2011 it has been possible to help support the development of schools and clinics in this remote area. The area is governed by both military and civilian leaders. The Karen don't trust the Burmese army - who can blame them after what happened to the Rohingya people in West Burma. The KNU, along with other ethnic groups, recently released a statement condemning Aung San Suu Kyi for defending the Burmese military at the International Court of Justice in The Hague.

Leaving Mae Sot in northern Thailand we drove north to Mae Sariang - four hours by road. An overnight stay and then a 5am pick up the next day. After hardly sleeping, thinking we would 'sleep in' we wait outside our guest house. The streets are dark and deserted. Promptly at 5am our truck arrives. We throw our bags in the back and climb inside to be greeted by our friends and guides for the journey, Lay Say and Paw Gay. We have to take a new route this time as the Thai army is patrolling the route we had taken in previous years to stop any foreigners getting into Burma. Three hours through the Salween national park and the dirt road ends. We jump onto the back of waiting motorbikes and off we go through rice paddies and up streams.

Forty five minutes later they stop and the front rider points to the jungle. There is no obvious path so he gets out a machete and starts to clear a path for us. My legs and arms are already cut to bits from going through bushes and long grass on the motorbike. Lay Say leads the way, Anne and I follow with Paw Gay bringing up the rear. The climb is steep and now the sun has risen it's starting to get very hot. Two hours of relentless climbing and we can see the top of the mountain. While resting Lay Say wanders off into the jungle and returns a few minutes later with papaya fruit. This was much needed as we were running low on water. Getting out my pen knife which goes with me everywhere in Thailand and Burma, I start cutting it up and we share the delicious fruit. Refreshed we continue for a further two hours up the mountain and at last we can see the Salween river which is the border between Burma and Thailand. Our boat is waiting by the river bank. We climb down the steep sandy bank and clamber on board.

Uncomfortably on board we sit low in the boat on a very hard wooden bench for the three hour journey. Arriving at Mae Nu Tar on the Burma side we disembark and head up the steep river bank. Thankfully, since the last time we were here, a dirt road has been cut into the mountain side. We hire a truck and head up through the mountains. There are only about a hundred trucks in the area so the road is relatively traffic free. Last time we were here there were only two trucks, both for emergency use only. Elephant being the preferred form of transport then.

An hour and a half later having passed through some of the most unspoilt jungle in the world we arrive at the village of Day

Bu Noh for another overnight stay. A cold bucket shower and some rice and vegetables refreshes us. Tomorrow we must walk three more hours to meet Declan, but before that we put on head torches and set about putting up our mosquito nets which we have carried with us. Malaria is prevalent in this part of the world, though thankfully it is the dry season, so there are fewer mosquitoes. Exhausted but very happy we fall fast asleep at 9pm on the wooden floor in the bamboo hut. Waking during the night for the toilet I head out of the hut and across the compound by torch light. It is pitch black when I switch my torch off to look up at the night sky. The Milky Way is in clear view and I stop and say a little prayer of thanks for my friends for getting me here safely and for all who live in this forgotten paradise, wrecked by 60 years of civil war but undoubtedly a very special place on Earth.

The cockerels wake me at 6am and I crawl out of my mosquito net. Paw Gay is already up preparing the fire for breakfast. Noodles with a fried egg on top are served shortly afterwards. Lay Say arrives back having spent the night with his family about a mile away and so we set off along the Yusana river on foot with plenty of drinking water heading to JSMK. The first two hours are on the flat walking through rice paddies and banana plantations. It is so beautiful and unspoilt. Then we reach the point where we have to cross the fast flowing river. A bamboo raft attached to a rope sits on the river bank. We clamber on board the raft catching our balance so we don't fall in. When we're all aboard, Lay Say starts pulling the rope and we gently traverse the water. A steep climb awaits us but we know it's only an hour or so and we'll see Declan.

Hot and sweaty we see the sign for JSMK and enter the village. Declan is still teaching so we are shown to his hut and wait for him. Second in charge of the clinic, Silver Horn, comes to greet us saying 'Thank you for giving us your son to help us. We are learning so much from each other.' The Karen call Declan 'Day Day Po' which means 'Younger Brother', a fall back from when Declan used to visit with his older brother

Patrick. We sip water and wait for him to finish teaching. Anne is so excited to see him, she gives him a big hug when he appears out of the classroom. Hugging is not the Karen way of greeting, but Declan is only part Karen so he gives his Mam a big hug back. He tells us he is enjoying working with the Karen people so much. He's learning a lot from them - language, culture, cooking, hunting, medical skills...

In the evening he has to do his ward round. They have three patients needing oxygen but only have two oxygen machines. He has to choose between two babies and an old man. It's not an easy decision but with a heavy heart the old man must go without. Declan hopes he'll last the night or that one of the babies recovers enough to come off oxygen to allow the old man to take his turn. With limited resources, Declan says he does his best but sometimes ...

We enjoy a great Saturday and Sunday with him as there is no teaching and no out-patients clinic, only emergencies and in-patients to deal with. With no Catholic church or priest for hundreds of miles we attend a service in the local Baptist church. The congregation are all dressed in traditional Karen clothing, so it's a very colourful service. In the afternoon we go swimming - just an hour walk to a safe swimming area in the river. Buffaloes share the pool with us but it's so refreshing and exhilarating.

Anne and I have to return the same way we came, two days of traveling through the jungle. The director of JSMK, Toh, comes to say goodbye and thanks us for letting Declan stay with them. We're so proud that after ten years of exams and training Declan is serving the Karen community. Declan hugs us both and wishes us a safe journey. He whispers that the old man is fading and that his family will take him home tomorrow to allow him to die in his own village. There is nothing more he can do. His family will carry him by bamboo stretcher (bambulance) through the jungle. But the good news is that both babies are now off oxygen and are much improved. With joyful tears in our eyes we set off down the mountain leaving

Declan to his work. In a few weeks he will leave JSMK - I know that will be with a heavy heart as his love for these people is obvious and genuine. Anne reminds me 'Give them roots and wings.' Declan has flown a long way in those ten years since that conversation with Fr Louis Antonia.

Chapter 19.

Still *On the Border,* 2019.

Maung Maung Tinn is still *on the border* - his book of the same name was published in 2019. Here is a passage from the book.

Have changed in Burma? Excuse me.
by Maung Maung Tinn.

I am over 60.
My mind, my body are too slow and it is totally different from before.
The mouth that used to taste any food, is very picky now.
I more realise why people do not want to be old.
I am different from decades ago, some things from my surroundings are not.
The tap water is not available at my house, as usual.
I bath once a week now, instead of 3 times.
I need to ask for help from others.
To take the water from the well that is only a 5 minute walk.
Of course, I am getting weak.
I cannot even make a charcoal fire for cooking that I used to do easily.
There are so many people coming and going on the road that is in front of my house.
But I feel very isolated.
In the daytime I am alone at home.
But it is busy with fourteen people in the evening.
It is getting crowded in the small place.

Two of my sons' families are back from school and work.
Sharing the experience, arguing about the queue for the toilet,
complaining about so called regular electricity that's never
regular, making noise together with modern music from the
neighbours house.
I love everyone in my family.
They are always warm to me.
They are always happy to help me. They do whatever they can,
but not about money.
Both of my sons are poor. They always struggle to get an
income.
It is never better, even though they have children or
grandchildren right now.
When I see the situation, I am sad.
I cannot support anything to improve their condition.
Some people, like my family, were born just for being poor.
My husband died 20 years ago with severe kidney problems at
the public hospital.
If we had some money at that time, he would not die.
I think, if the patients do not have any money,
the so-called public hospital is just some kind of place to let
them die.
I can't sleep very well, since my husband died.
Before going to bed,
I always think how I would cope, if me or someone from family
gets severely health problems.

There are more refugees and displaced people in the world
today than ever. Millions of Palestinians in Lebanon, Syrians in
Turkey, Afgans in Pakistan and Somalians in Ethiopia to name
a few. The Burmese refugees and migrants in Thailand are the
people I know and it is their story I tell on behalf of all refugees
and displaced people throughout the world. They all long to go
home and dream of a better future but will things have
changed?

Kindness
by Maung Maung Tinn.

It is graceful.
It comes from pure hearts.
It can go to everywhere anytime.
It is for everyone.
It is flexible with every religion, every nationality, every skin colour.
There is no boundary for kindness.

Printed in Great Britain
by Amazon